Marcel Michello

Daddy, Where Are You?

Daddy, Where Are You?

The Moving Story of a Daughter's Search
for Her GI Father

Shirley McGlade

with Mary McCormack

SMITH GRYPHON

PUBLISHERS

First published in Great Britain in 1992 by
SMITH GRYPHON LIMITED
Swallow House, 11–21 Northdown Street
London N1 9BN

ISBN 1 85685 012 9

A CIP catalogue record for this book
is available from the British Library

Typeset by Computerset, Harmondsworth, Middx.

Printed in Great Britain by
Butler & Tanner Ltd, Frome

Contents

Acknowledgements   vii

Foreword by Jack C. Crowley   xi

1   Together At Last   1

2   Love and War   4

3   Overpaid, Oversexed and Over Here?   19

4   'Yank's Leftovers'   31

5   Not the Only One   52

6   Starting to Search   64

7   War Babes   74

8   'I Think I'm Your Daughter'   85

9   Friends in America   103

10   Gains and Losses   118

11   'Remember You're Half American'   133

12   Reunions I: Sons' Tales   146

13   Reunions II: Daughters' Tales   159

14   Finding a Family   175

15   War Babes versus the American Government   188

Postscript   206

If You Want to Find Your Father . . .   208

ACKNOWLEDGEMENTS

Grateful thanks to Joan Meier, to the war babes and the fathers for sharing their stories, to my husband Barry, for his unstinting emotional, practical and moral support and to my father who provided a happy ending.

This book tells the story of Shirley McGlade and some of the 'war babes' she has met through her *War Babes* organization. The names of all persons have been changed to protect their identities and keep confidential their personal situations, with the exception of the author herself, her father Jack Crowley, her immediate relatives, and the public figures who are referred to. However, their stories appear here as they themselves have told them to the author.

FOREWORD

When I was asked to write a few words as an introduction to my daughter's book I really didn't have any idea of what to say or how to say it. But, if you are starting at the beginning, looking for someone you have never known, or someone you once knew, you should understand and acknowledge that 'inner drive', which some call 'curiosity', others the 'need to know'.

Whatever it is called, don't give up!

Everyone has the right to know where they are from, how they came to be on this earth and their origins.

Searchers for their past will sometimes feel that a deliberate effort has been made to conceal evidence of events, names, dates, just to prevent them from ever compiling a chain of facts leading to finding out who they are. Don't give up!

If on your own you feel you have come to a dead end that leads nowhere, find an organization that consists of people just like you. As a group, the shared experiences, failures and successes can help you overcome any obstacles you are likely to encounter. With some luck, perseverance, and help, one day you may be able to say, 'I've been searching for you, and at last, here I am, because I didn't give up! You are someone I wanted to know and needed to find.'

One day, some years ago, I heard a shaky, little voice on the phone say, 'I think I'm your daughter.' My mind went through amazement, disbelief, shock, wonder, curiosity, guilt, apprehension, you name it, I felt it. Oddly enough, denial never occurred to me, and since then I've often wondered why. Phone calls, letters, and photographs followed, and finally an actual visit. I had a daughter! That mysterious bond of affection between a father and a daughter was born.

It hasn't been easy. Forty years is a long time and we each had our own lives and our own families. Some people have expressed interest in how we know we are father and daughter. That's one of the easiest questions to answer: besides some very obvious physical characteristics and personal traits, there is a definite mutual bond of affection that just occurred naturally. We both knew when Shirley said, 'Hi, Dad' and I said, 'Hello daughter.'

JACK C. CROWLEY, SHIRLEY'S DAD
30 MAY 1991

1
Together At Last

Friday, 22 May 1987, around midday West Coast time, cruising at 30,000 feet under a clear blue California sky. The television interview is over, the camera crew have their pictures and I can get a bit of peace at last. Nearly there; I still can't believe that I am almost at the end of the journey – two journeys, in fact: the fourteen-hour long-haul flight from Gatwick to Sacramento; and the journey of self-discovery that's lasted most of my forty-one years, the quest to find out who exactly is Shirley McGlade.

Down there is the State of California, once just a name on a map to me or an item on the television news. What did it mean before? Sunshine and smog . . . Reagan and raisins, hippies and Hollywood. Yes, somewhere down there is Tinsel City where they turned out the movies that found their way to a scruffy little cinema in the back streets of Birmingham. There, as a child, on a Sunday afternoon I'd forget about my hated stepfather and the taunts of small-minded neighbours and lose myself in the latest screen epic. And I'd eagerly watch the handsome hero with his strange American accent and wonder – did he look like that? Is that how he spoke?

When you entered the cinema you were in a different world, and up here in the air if it's not another world at least it's a very different country from the one I know. The passengers chat to each other and generally treat air travel as casually as I'd treat a trip into town on the number 29 bus. Two men even ran to catch the plane as I might have done the bus in the days before my joints turned stiff and disobedient.

Both passengers and crew are friendly, uninhibited and incredibly nosey: I've been asked personal questions by total strangers, beseeched to speak in my 'cute' accent and wished no end of good luck from all sides. I suppose boarding the plane in Forth Worth, Texas, for the second leg of the journey, with a television crew in tow was bound to attract attention: Still, I can't help wondering how people would react if the same thing happened on, say, a Birmingham to London flight. Would the other passengers come down to ask me who I was and what was going on? Definitely not: more likely they'd avert

1

their eyes and act as if a middle-aged housewife with a reporter and a cameraman dogging her footsteps was an everyday event, and certainly none of their business.

They are two different breeds – the English and the Americans – and suddenly at the thought of this the butterflies in my stomach wake up and go into their clog-dancing routine. I feel nervous, weepy, happy and sad; the emotions, like the questions, chasing round and round in my head. Will we get on? Will we find anything to talk about? How will his family react? What if he's disappointed in me? Will he even recognize me? I'd told him I was plain and overweight, exaggerating on the grounds that I didn't want him to expect too much. Did I overdo it? Is he now expecting a 25-stone monster to stagger off the plane? Maybe he couldn't face it and stayed home.

I feel disorientated, hot and generally crumpled – and I desperately wanted to look like Joan Collins when I walked out to meet him. There are some clothes to change into in my hand luggage, but somehow with the interview and the two men in front chatting me up to hear my quaint accent, there hasn't been time. And then there is the other problem – my rheumatoid arthritis, the bane of my life. It makes walking difficult at the best of times, and the very idea of trekking down the aisle to the toilet and struggling in and out of clothes in a confined space has me reaching for the pain-killers. But no, I've had more than the prescribed dose of those already. Now it's got to be mind over matter as far as the pain is concerned.

I reach down and try to smooth out the creases in my skirt. When my husband Barry and son Martin saw me off on the first leg of the journey in the morning gloom of Gatwick Airport, the skirt was bandbox neat. I wish, not for the first time, that Barry could have come with me, but he has a job to hold down and, besides, he hates flying. I never underestimate the effort he's put into understanding and supporting me over the years. It can't be easy living with a woman who is obsessed with another man. He was reluctant to say goodbye in the departure lounge. He said I looked so scared and vulnerable he wanted to take me straight back home and persuade me to forget the whole idea. Yet last night, when I almost lost my nerve and chickened out, it was he who calmed me down. I was – and still am – so afraid I'd come all this way only to be rejected and I couldn't cope with that. Better to have an unfulfilled dream than a real-life story with an unhappy ending.

It was Barry who insisted that it wouldn't be like that, that I'd be welcomed and appreciated – and if this other fellow didn't treat me well, he'd have him to answer to! Because the idea of trying to get to sleep early seemed so laughable we drove out to a country pub, where I resisted the temptation to get blind drunk in the hope of blotting out the terrible anxiety. A couple of drinks relaxed me and at some point during the night I dozed off. My internal alarm went off well before the clock though, leaving me wide awake to face the most important day of my life.

In the end it happens so quickly. A smooth landing, yet more warm wishes from the stewardess, a short walk across the concrete and through a doorway into the airport building. And then it's as if I've stepped on to a brilliantly lit stage. There seems to be an audience, people craning their necks to see someone, but I am almost blinded by the lights. My first thought is that there is a celebrity on the plane and that I have inadvertently stepped into their limelight.

Then I see him, centre stage – a tall, white-haired figure, standing very still, so still it's like looking at a blow-up of the last photograph he sent me. An optical illusion, I think, jet lag. Amazingly he moves towards me. I want to run to him but my feet seem rooted to the ground. I have also lost my power of speech. How many times have I imagined this meeting? I had the words of greeting all worked out in my head. I would tell him how good it was to see him, how I'd longed for this moment for so many years. I open my mouth to speak but all that comes out is a strange little squeak like a strangled hamster. But suddenly we are together with our arms around each other, hugging, and I am oblivious to the television lights and people staring and the fact that we are the celebrities.

He is warm and real after all, far better than any of those celluloid heroes – Jack Crowley, the man I spent the first half of my life day-dreaming about and the second half searching for, my father. For this meeting I have spent months in dusty libraries and hours on the telephone. I have given countless interviews, dragging family skeletons out of the cupboard over and over again. I have set up an organization that takes up every moment of my spare time (and quite a lot I don't have to spare), runs us into debt, and has taken on the might of the American government.

But this story goes back a long way . . . right back to the good-old/bad-old days of the Second World War and another meeting, this time between Jack Crowley and a Birmingham girl called Lily Ross.

2
Love and War

On a Saturday night in November 1944, in the bedroom of a little two-up, two-down terraced house in Long Street, Birmingham, Lily Ross was getting ready to go dancing. It was a work of art and ingenuity. First the legs. The war had put paid to stockings, unless you had upwards of five shillings a pair to spend on the black market, but it was amazing what you could achieve with a handful of sand, rubbed in till your legs tingled and turned a delicate tan. All the best dressing tables contained a little pot of sand pinched from the sandbags in the street. And of course the best stockings had to have a black seam up the back, so, teeth clenched in concentration, pencil in hand, Lily tilted her body backwards to draw two black lines from heel to thigh. Practice made perfectly straight, eventually.

In the subdued light of the dance hall, the sand and pencil stood in well for stockings, and if it didn't convince all of the people all of the time, so what? All the girls used the same trick, except for a few who, it was rumoured, got their precious nylons from big-spending American GIs based at camps around the city.

Next it was time to put on her skirt and blouse, before she froze to death in the unheated room with its bare walls and linoleum floor. Lily loved pretty clothes and with her wavy auburn hair and reed-slim figure, they looked good on her. Not that a factory girl's wages or clothing coupons stretched to anything fancy, but she had a talented and obliging friend who could run up a neat little number on her sewing machine if Lily could find the material. Lily herself was a dab hand with the sequins, sewing them on, one by one, to add a bit of evening glitz to a plain little blouse. A dab of lipstick on her lips and another on the cheeks, a smear of vaseline on the eyelashes, a final pat to the Rita Hayworth curls, into the peep-toe shoes – and she was ready for a good night out.

It's hard to think of your mother as a pretty young woman, brimming with life and energy. The mental picture most of us carry around is one formed as adults when our parents are middle-aged or elderly. And, yes, I remember my mother, Lily Ross, as an elderly widow, troubled by agoraphobia and poor health. But my memory goes back a long, long way. I can also remember her very clearly as that young woman of the sequin-sewing, sand-on-the-legs routine, which still went on when I was a small child. Even if I hadn't prised such details out of her, I'd have had no difficulty at all in imagining how she looked on that fateful night when she set out to enjoy nothing more dramatic than a few hours dancing, and ended up meeting the man who was to change her life.

If I have difficulty understanding anything, it's how the woman I knew came to conceive me in the first place, and find herself in the shocking position of being an unmarried mother. She was, by all accounts, 24 going on 17, naïve and more innocent than any woman of that age had a right to be, even in those unliberated times. Years later I used to joke with her that the last time something like that happened, three wise men had come out of the East! To her dying day, my mother retained a sort of innocence about all sexual matters. She couldn't talk about anything to do with sexuality or reproduction and was liable to get up and leave the room if a love scene came on the television. For this my Nan, her mother, should probably take the blame – or the praise, if you prefer to see it that way.

After Grandad died when Mum was little, Nan had grown fiercely protective of her only child. They were unquestionably working class and never far off the breadline, but that didn't mean you weren't respectable or didn't know how to conduct yourself, especially with men. Though my Mum had her share of admirers, by the age of 24 she had only had one serious boyfriend. And Nan soon nipped that little romance in the bud on the grounds that the young Irish lad in question was 'too religious'. She was not a woman easily impressed by men.

Naturally Nan had warned Lily about the American GIs based in camps around Birmingham, with their flashy gifts of nylons, cigarettes and chocolate – not available for love, money or ration coupons in England at the time – their big talk, casual chat-up lines and seemingly fatal attraction for British girls. It was an assessment based on rumour, gossip and observing the worst elements, but from what she'd seen of the Americans, Lily was inclined to agree with it. That night, like a dutiful daughter, she was avoiding the city-centre haunts of the GIs where the jitterbugging had replaced the waltz and foxtrot, in favour of a local dance hall a short walk from home.

The Masque Ballroom, just off the main Birmingham to Stratford-upon-Avon road, was a popular spot. Before the war it had been a great meeting place for local boys and girls but now the boys, like everything else in heavily rationed

Britain, were in short supply. Most were otherwise engaged on the battlefields of France and Belgium.

Lily wasn't looking for a boyfriend, just a dancing partner. Dancing was her passion. She only had to think of Joe Loss and Geraldo for her feet to start tapping. By the time her friend Violet arrived, anticipation of an evening twirling around the Masque's sprung floor had given her that glow that turns an averagely pretty woman into a beauty.

The funny thing, my mother was fond of saying later, was that she almost didn't go to the Masque that night. She'd originally planned a night at the pictures with Eva, her friend who was later to be my godmother, but then Violet, always a lively spark, suggested dancing – and my mother, feeling rather guilty, cancelled the first arrangement. Fate seemed to be taking a hand in the proceedings. And it did so again when Violet's boyfriend, who was in the Air Force, turned up unexpectedly at the dance. Violet's gain was Lily's loss. While the couple waltzed the evening away, she was left sitting rather self-consciously at a table between sparse dances. When there was a shortage of men – as there was tonight – at least the girls could dance together. Now she didn't even have that option.

It was while she was praying for Fred Astaire to materialize that she saw him – an American serviceman, newly arrived, in that smart, sand-coloured uniform that made our poor British soldiers' outfits look as if they were tailored from old sacks. The stranger was on his own, which was unusual as GIs never seemed to go anywhere without a clutch of buddies. Her first thought was, 'How did he get here, way off the beaten track?' Her second was something on the lines of 'Wow!'

There was just time to take in the sleek dark hair, the tall, slim frame, the rather solemn air – before she realized he was returning her gaze. Flustered, she cast her eyes downwards, then as the band swung into a quickstep she heard a soft deep, American voice enquiring with unexpected politeness, 'May I have the pleasure of this dance?'

My mother couldn't believe her luck. She stood up and glided into the arms of the GI with the Hollywood looks, ready to float around the room to the intoxicating beat. She was a good dancer, everyone said so, but it takes two to tango – or quickstep – and her idol had feet of clay. Well, it felt more like feet of cement really, and both of them left, the way they kept landing on her vulnerable peeping toes. This man couldn't dance to save his life.

They struggled on until the number ended and then, to her relief, he suggested they sit the next one out. He introduced himself as Jack Crowley. If fate had taken a hand in guiding my mother to that spot on that particular night, it had played an even bigger role in directing Jack Crowley's steps. A sergeant in the 35th Infantry Division, he was serving in France when a landmine exploded nearby. He suffered a concussion blast, with two broken eardrums and was, for a time, nearly deaf. He was deeply disturbed by his period in the thick of battle, witnessing his comrades dying around him and to this day he finds it hard to talk about. He blotted out a lot of the war years from his mind, including, I discovered many years later, the period with my mother that she remembered so well.

At the time they met, Jack Crowley was stationed at a Rest and Transit Camp at Pheasey Farm on the north side of Birmingham, a long way from my mother's home on the south side. What he was doing alone in Sparkbrook on that Saturday night, or why he went into the Masque Ballroom remains a mystery. Sadly he cannot recollect the night at all.

He was something of a loner and often took off by himself for places of interest around Birmingham, like Stratford-upon-Avon and Oxford. I suspect he was on his way back into the city centre by bus after one of these trips when he spotted the bright lights of the ballroom and decided to stop off for a drink. And then he saw my mother and his plans changed. But it's guesswork. We'll never be able to put that piece of the jigsaw in place.

My mother didn't question what brought him there. She was too busy enjoying his company. He was a gentle, handsome man, with a voice so quiet she had to lean forward – even when there wasn't a band playing – to hear him. Later she had the same problem with me and spent a great deal of time telling me to speak up and stop whispering like my father! All in all he was a million miles from the loud boastful Yanks of public prejudice.

He certainly didn't tell her he came from Hollywood and was a big buddy of all the stars, as the girls in the factory joked that all the GIs did. Nevertheless he told her a few whoppers for obscure reasons; that his name was spelled 'Jacques' in the French way and that he was a lumberjack, when in fact he'd never been closer to a tree than your average Brummie! To be fair he had worked for a timber company. The only contact my father claimed with Hollywood was that he grew up in the same town in Idaho as the blonde glamour girl of the time, Lana Turner. That little snippet of information, absolutely true, was to lead me up a blind alley and set me back years when I tried to trace him.

Mum agreed to let him walk her home. He was shocked by the smallness of the houses and the narrowness of the back streets – not in a snobbish way but with genuine amazement that people could live happily, packed so claus-trophobically tight, when he'd taken for granted the wide open spaces of a massive country. He liked the people of Britain, but my mother always knew he could never have lived on our small island.

They said goodbye at the top of the road. She certainly couldn't invite him in. She could just imagine the look on Nan's face if she turned up with an American, however charming. He intimated that he would like to see her again, maybe tomorrow night, but she passed it off as part of the politeness that came so naturally to him, certain their paths would not cross again. He probably had half a dozen girls on a string. The GIs came and went, posted overseas without warning, leaving behind girls with broken hearts – and worse. She knew that from the tears of the girls at the factory who'd been going out with one, only to have him vanish off the face of the earth between one date and the next. This was not for Lily. It had been a lovely evening; better leave it at that.

He asked her which bus to catch into town and if she'd help him sort out the money he needed for the fare. Laughing, she counted out the exact sum in pennies and threepenny bits into his hand, like for a child. He never mastered the British pounds, shillings and pence and without my mother to help, offered shop-keepers and bus conductors a handful of change with the invitation to pick out the coins they needed. They said goodnight and she hurried off down the street to her own 'entry'.

Entering the house where my mother and my Nan – and later myself – lived was like passing through a time warp. It was the sort of poor Victorian house that you can now pay to see in the working museums of the Midlands and the North of England, with its grime-blackened bricks, its picturesque black-leaded grate with the kettle above to provide endless cups of tea, and the frequently flooded cellar that housed mice, cockroaches and spiders among the coal.

I often wonder what my father must have made of it. A group of these houses, each with its tiny garden in front, clustered around a courtyard. This communal space housed toilets, dustbins (or miskins as my Nan called them) and the wash house where the women of the yard gathered to do their laundry. This arrangement made it impossible to avoid close contact with the neighbours, which, as I discovered when I was a child, could occasionally be a disadvantage. But mostly it made for camaraderie, especially among the women. During the war years, the ladies of the yard, most of them middle-aged or elderly, with husbands at war or dead, would regularly take themselves around to the local, the Belgrave, for a well-deserved glass of stout. My mother sometimes went with them, and on the Sunday evening, after her meeting with Jack Crowley, that's where she was to be found.

The evening was taking on a mellow glow when the door to the snug swung open and there he was again – just like the tall dark stranger making an entrance in one of the cowboy films that were doing the rounds. My mother couldn't believe her eyes, but she knew the stout wasn't that strong! How had he found her, she wondered. No problem, he told her. He'd stood and watched which entry she'd gone up last night, and he could always find his way around Birmingham if he had a very good reason. He'd knocked on one wrong door before being directed to my Nan, who was too astounded to do anything but give him directions to the pub where my mother was enjoying her evening out.

Had it crossed Mum's mind that he would turn up on the doorstep – which it hadn't – she would have expected Nan to chase him away with a few choice Anglo-Saxon expletives, but instead she had responded to his politeness and charm. The ladies in the Belgrave did likewise. He bought them all drinks and settled down to join in the chat.

From then on Jack was always welcome in Long Street. He got to know friends and relations and the inside of all the local pubs as well as the many country beauty spots, then just a bus ride from Birmingham city centre. Nan would put the tea caddy to one side and make him a special cup of coffee because she knew that was what Americans drank. And Jack, polite as ever, forced a smile as he downed cup after cup of a beverage that he told my mother bore no resemblance to any American coffee he'd ever tasted. The local kids loved him, as much for his friendly, open attitude as for the chewing gum he gave them. My Mum never, sadly, gained access to the supply of nylons rumour had it the Americans carried around to impress the girls, but she didn't go short of American cigarettes, which the British regarded much as the Americans regard our coffee.

He bought her a ring from a local jewellers. She treasured it until she realized he had gone for good. Then she took it off and gave it away, wishing she could discard the painful memories so easily. Did he tell her there was a wife back home from whom he'd received a 'Dear John' letter asking for a divorce? My mother thought so, but wasn't sure. She also thought she recalled him mentioning that he was separated. I suspect she really didn't want to know too much. Reality might intrude and spoil the magic.

At one point – she never could remember when or what prompted it – he gave her his service number. It was, he said, in case she ever needed to contact him. She lost it or threw it away, not being able to envisage any circumstances in which she might need it. After all, even if he had to leave the area in a hurry, he knew where she lived. There is no doubt that my mother was deeply in love with my father and that she was optimistic and trusting enough to believe in happy ever after and love finding a way. But what about my father? I find it so frustrating and sad that his mind has played such a mean trick in blanking out this time in his life. My mother believed he loved her and, knowing him as I do now, I believe that he is – and was – a warm, sincere, decent man who would not mislead anyone about his true feelings.

Theirs was a love story, but a love story set in unusual times. It was played out against a background of threatened separation, danger and death, when the usual rules did not apply. Lonely women who in peacetime wouldn't have dreamed of embarking on a love affair threw themselves into relationships with men who by normal standards were virtual strangers. Men who had promised to be true found other women taking the place of distant girlfriends or wives in their thoughts. There wasn't time for the etiquette of courtship. A man could be here today and dead tomorrow. Many chose to live for the day they could rely on.

This particular little romance, one of thousands similar, ended abruptly one Thursday night in May 1945, when Jack Crowley failed to turn up for a date. He'd never missed a date before and my mother knew there had to be a good reason. At first she thought he might be ill. Then the other awful possibility struck her – he'd probably been shipped out. The movement of troops was swift and secret. He could have been sent to Europe to fight, or back to America. She'd soon find out, she thought; he'd write as soon as he could.

The days passed and no letter arrived, and in addition to her loneliness and anxiety, a new fear was taking shape in my mother's mind. She went to the doctor and came out in a state of shock. He had told her that she was five months pregnant. I found it strange that it had taken her so long to realize, but my mother explained that like many girls, disturbed by the war, working long hours in unfamiliar factories on war work and often undernourished on meagre rations, her menstrual periods were irregular. And if there were other clues, perhaps she was too scared to acknowledge them, even to herself. For though the war had temporarily shaken up social attitudes, having an illegitimate baby in 1945 was still about the biggest disgrace a woman could bring on herself and her family.

She believed absolutely that if my father knew – no, when he knew – everything would somehow be sorted out. But how could she get a message to him? Who could she ask for help? She went to my Auntie Slim – my Nan's sister, always referred to like this, by her surname. She became the chosen confidante partly because my mother could not, at that stage, bear to face her own mother, and partly because her aunt was a tough character who could be relied upon to take over in an emergency.

True to her reputation she marched my Mum up to the American base at Pheasey Farm – only to find it was being disbanded. All but a handful of men had gone and those left behind insisted they were not at liberty to say where. Auntie Slim's next step was to take my mother to the American Red Cross in Birmingham. She was determined that my father should know about the pregnancy and do 'the decent thing'. Mum, by this stage, had changed her mind. She couldn't face the embarrassment and shame of having her condition broadcast and in a desperate effort to get out of going in, she pretended to faint on the steps. Aunt simply left her there and went inside to demand a welfare visitor be sent out to see my mother at home. By this time Nan too knew the score. A welfare worker duly arrived and told Mum, Nan and Aunt, quite bluntly, that it was not their policy to trace and inform fathers. 'There are thousands of girls in the same position,' she said. 'Have your baby, come back afterwards and we will find it a good home.' It sounded, my mother said, as if it was a puppy under discussion.

If there had been any doubt in any of their minds, this woman's attitude dispelled it. Nan gave Mum a hug and said that adoption was out of the question. Auntie Slim agreed. The family would rally round. They would manage somehow to bring up the baby. My mother breathed a sigh of relief. 'I'd decided I was going to keep you whatever anyone said but I badly wanted and needed their support. I loved you already and I loved your father too much to consider parting with you. What if he got in touch (and I was still sure he would)? I could hardly tell him I'd given his baby away.'

She went on hoping for a long time, but gradually the hope died. 'I couldn't believe he'd just forgotten me. The only reason I could accept for him failing to get in touch was that he was dead, that he'd been killed in battle.' I suppose that seemed slightly less painful than believing the other alternative.

On 17 September 1945 I was born in the little house in Long Street, Birmingham. I was registered in my mother's name. It would be over forty years before I found my father and asked his permission to add the appendix 'Father's name – Jack Crowley' to my birth certificate.

·

The story of my parents' meeting and parting is just one of thousands similar, though it took me a long time to realize that they – and I – were not unique. Between 1942, when the GIs arrived bringing a touch of vitality to these blitzed-out, war-weary isles, and 1945 there appears to have been a mass surrender of British womanhood: 70,000 of them became GI brides and, for a variety of reasons, thousands of others failed to tie the knot and were left holding the baby. I think all of us who have tried to find our fathers have dwelled long and hard on our parents' relationship. We want to know how they met and why they parted.

It's desperately important to believe that our mothers and fathers loved each other and that we were not the result of a one-night stand or a casual affair – but on the other hand we don't want to be palmed off with a pat on the head and a fairy tale.

At first, of course, the only person you have contact with who knows the whole story is your mother – and it's a story some mothers are reluctant to tell. Even when they are willing to establish the basic facts, they don't welcome questions that threaten to reopen old wounds. They fear hurting and embarrassing relatives, often for the second time, and the shame of their 'past' still clings even in today's enlightened atmosphere. My own mother was horrified when I did my first interview with a local newspaper. She couldn't believe that I was going to expose what she still saw, forty years on, as the stigma of my illegitimate birth. Here we were, living in a nice neighbourhood, where nobody knew our history and I was about to start washing the dirty linen in public!

Though it took a long time to drag the truth out of her, I was relatively lucky. Many other war babes are given scant information with which to try and build up a picture of their background. The stories of those wartime liaisons, when they do emerge, are often touching, and a few are tinged with a certain black humour in retrospect. Often it seems that everyone and everything was conspiring to part the lovers – public opinion, the hierarchy in the American forces, parents on both sides of the Atlantic, and even enemy propaganda, which purported to tell British troops in graphic detail what their wives and girlfriends were getting up to back home with the Americans.

It would be unrealistic indeed to deny that many of the GIs had an eye for a pretty face and a golden opportunity, or that some British girls, missing their menfolk and worn down by the deprivations of war, didn't jump at the opportunity of some fun. But listening to the war babes' accounts of their parents' relationship, it's hard to find many promiscuous male opportunists or goodtime girls. Like Lily Ross and Jack Crowley, they were just ordinary people living through extraordinary times.

Take Paula's mother Helen and her GI father Ben, for instance. Helen grew up in a Yorkshire mining village, but early in the war, when women were conscripted to replace the men in factories, she moved to Sheffield to work. At a dance, she met and fell in love with Ben, a young, Jewish military policeman from Baltimore. Their relationship was a serious one spanning three years. When in 1944 Helen became pregnant, it didn't seem a major disaster. After all they were planning to spend the rest of their lives together. Ben was sent to France and Helen went home to have her baby. When Paula was three months old, he got leave and came back to see her.

Why he didn't come back for Helen and his daughter when the war ended has remained a mystery, despite the fact that Paula has met her father. 'I was so thrilled to find him that I didn't want to hassle him for explanations,' she said. 'I hoped it would come out naturally in the course of the relationship, but it never did, and then, sadly he died. We'd only actually met once.'

I do know that after the war American servicemen were actively discouraged from continuing relationships formed with British girls. This seems indisputable. Some of the war babes have reported in affidavits that their mothers were offered £100 if they consented to sign an agreement promising not to try to contact or make demands on the father of their child. There was also negative pressure from Helen's parents to forget Ben. Paula explained: 'My grandparents liked Ben at first, but when he didn't return after the war, my grandmother, a lovely lady but very strong-willed, was determined that my mother was not going to waste her life pining for him. She sent her away to relatives, destroyed my father's letters and wrote telling him to forget my mother and me. It took my mother a long time to get over him. I was 10 years old before she married, and it seems my father was heartbroken too. Some of his family remained in touch with my mother for a while after the war and there is a letter from his sister Frances, in which she writes: "Ben's been here tonight and he was crying. He loves you both so much but he doesn't know how to get back to you."'

There are lots of cases of parents conspiring to nip these romances in the bud, whether from genuine concern that their daughter was making a mistake or from understandable selfishness. No mum or dad wanted to see their daughter, and the grandchild they probably adored, setting sail for some unknown destination several thousand miles away.

Nor was it only British parents who interfered. Marilyn, the first war babe I met, has a letter from her father to her mother which proves that his mother did everything she could to end the relationship. 'When my father, Glenn, went home after the war, he must have confided in his mother that he had a child here and a woman he planned to marry when she got a divorce. His mother obviously didn't see this as the ideal set-up for her son and was determined he was going to settle down with a nice American girl instead. It seems she began intercepting letters from my mother and from my Uncle Joe. It's not clear if she got rid of certain letters or passed them on to my father after reading them, but at some stage she wrote a hostile letter to Uncle Joe, Mum's brother, about the relationship, which must have caused a lot of upset.'

On 30 October 1947, after he moved out of the family home and was working in a steel mill in Ashtabula, Ohio, Glenn wrote to Lillian, Marilyn's mother. It is the only letter that remains from a three-year correspondence. The following are extracts from it.

All I can do is ask your forgiveness for any anguish I or my mother may have caused. Believe me, Lil, I never knew she had written to your brother . . . I had a hunch she was reading my letters. I accused her of it once but she denied it . . . I'm terribly sorry she's hurt you and want to start over again. I want you here with me more than anything in the world . . . nothing could ever make me forget you.

Darling how is our Cookie [his pet name for Marilyn] coming along? I hope she's healthy and being a good girl for you. I wish I knew how she looks now. If you have a snap please send it to me. All my love always.

And he closes with two lines of kisses.

Reading the letter after her mother's death was an emotional experience for Marilyn, who was only told of her origins shortly before her mother died. 'My mother was married when she met Glenn and to be honest, I'd been ashamed that she went with another man while her husband was in the army. It seemed sordid. But when I read my father's letter the emphasis shifted from something dirty to a love story. He sounded a caring man and in the photograph of him which was with the letter he looks it too. He wasn't an immature young lad but a man of about 30 or so, I'd guess from the picture, old enough to know his own mind.'

Marilyn's parents met when Glenn was stationed in Bromsgrove, Worcestershire. He became friends with Lillian's brother Joe first. 'Both my uncle and my mother and my little half-brother were living at my parents' house at the time,' Marilyn explained. 'Joe brought his new friend home and that's how he got to know my mother. He seems to have become one of the family. He stayed at the house for around eight months after I was born.

'I think he returned to American convinced that my mother was going to divorce my stepfather. There's a reference in the letter to her seeing a solicitor. I don't know why exactly my mother changed her mind and got back with my stepdad. She only ever spoke to me once about the matter and I haven't been lucky enough to find my father. Maybe it seemed too much of a risk going that far away with two children, to a family of in-laws who certainly weren't going to welcome you with open arms. And maybe the pressure from his family finally got to him too.'

Sue's mother, Nancy, was married but separated from her husband when she met James, Sue's father, at a village dance. She was also the mother of two young children: Maureen who lived with her grandmother in Derbyshire and

Tony who was with her in Sussex. Nancy, who now lives with Sue and her family, is one mother who is happy to talk about her romance with the man she calls Jimmy and admits was the love of her life.

She remembers clearly the moment she first set eyes on him. 'He was so tall, 6' 3" and I'm only 5 foot. He looked wonderful, but I didn't think he'd be the slightest bit interested in me. I was with a friend, a tall vibrant girl whom I thought much more his type, so when he came towards us I assumed he was going to ask her to dance, but it was me he asked.'

James, at 24, thought she looked like a 'high-school girl' and was astonished to find that Nancy was seven years his senior and mother of two, but it didn't stop his asking to walk her home, pushing his bicycle along the country lanes. 'He couldn't dance,' Nancy remembers with a laugh. 'All the Americans could do was the jitterbug, which was a bit of a drawback. But I liked him straight away. He was charming and not a bit brash, as a lot of them were. We started going out together. We'd go for long walks. We used to laugh and talk and even sing to each other. He had this lovely sense of humour and he got on so well with Tony, my little boy.

'At first we were just friends. I didn't want to start a love affair. I was unhappily married. I'd been hurt and I certainly wasn't looking for another man. When Sue found her father, he told her, "I went out with your mother for months before she let me touch her," and that's absolutely true.

'There was another complication. Jimmy already had a wife in America and a child he had never seen. He never lied to me. In a situation like that everything is tinged with sadness. Whatever you do someone is going to get hurt. I don't think either of us planned to fall in love – but that's what happened.

'It was a difficult time when I was pregnant, but I kept it from my family. It's not something you broadcast. We were living in such an isolated spot that there weren't many people to see, but those who knew were very kind. They took me to their hearts. Jimmy had to leave England twelve days before Sue was born. We were both heart-broken. We'd been together for eighteen months. I knew he always meant for us to join him. He planned to set up his own dry-cleaning business and send for us when he got established. But things don't always work out the way you plan, do they? He was travelling about. We were corresponding through box numbers and sometimes he didn't get my letters. Sue says at that time you might as well have been trying to keep in touch with someone on the moon as in America!

'I had a terrible time when Sue was a baby, trying to work as a home help and look after two children. I could get Sue into a day nursery but then there was nowhere for Tony and he had to go to a residential nursery. It proved impossible in the end. My husband offered to have us back, but under certain conditions, which I would not comply with. Then he demanded custody of his two and I was deemed the guilty one and he got the children. I wouldn't wish what I went through on my worst enemy.

'When Sue first started to search for her father, I was against the idea. Her birth had caused plenty of problems on this side of the water, I didn't want to cause more on the other side at this late stage. But she wouldn't have it, and fortunately it's worked out wonderfully well.'

When James came over to England three years ago, he and Nancy met again. 'It was lovely to see him,' she says. 'He'd changed a bit in looks and put on a lot of weight, but in other ways he was just the same. It wasn't a case of being reminded why I'd fallen in love with him. I've never forgotten that. He was very, very special and I know he felt the same about me.

'We went to look at the place we met and at all our haunts, holding hands like a pair of youngsters. It was funny the different things we remembered. I remembered his wonderful sense of humour and the things he'd said that made me laugh. It was he who remembered the romantic things, like the way I looked on a particular occasion or how I wore my hair.

'You can't recapture the past or start again after forty years. I regret the different paths our lives took but there's no bitterness. I've never blamed him for anything. One day he said to me, "I love Sue."

"I know you do," I said, "she's yours."

"No, Nancy," he said, "she's ours."'

You can't always pin the blame for a lost love on the American army, parents or superfluous spouses. Some relationships just seemed doomed from the start. The attempts of Kay's parents to get married is a case in point. Kay is the child of Anne, who was in the Women's Army Territorial Services, and Ronald, a sergeant in the 16th Infantry of the United States Army (Catering), based in Somerset. Ronald was from Dallas, Texas, where he'd lived on a small farm on the outskirts of the city. Anne came from Scotland. They met at a dance in Yeovil Barracks in 1943, were together for eighteen months and planned to marry. Before they could do so, and while Anne was pregnant, Ronald was sent to France, where he was badly wounded. When he returned it was to a hospital in Southampton. Meanwhile Anne had returned to her native Scotland, where Kay was born in a home for unmarried mothers in Perth in October 1944.

The couple were as keen as ever to get married, so the Chaplain of Ronald's regiment went up to Scotland to take Anne and her baby down to Southampton where they could be married by special licence. The matron of the home, however, didn't approve of a very new mother and baby being shunted around and persuaded Anne to stay put and let Ronald come up as soon as he was able for a wedding there. This was agreed and once more plans were made. A wedding dress was bought, a church arranged, friends invited. Then two days before the wedding, Ronald was shipped back to America. With that catalogue of disasters behind them Anne and Ronald must have bowed to fate and decided the match was not to be. They corresponded for a while before losing touch completely.

But even marrying your GI was no guarantee of living happily ever after or indeed of living together at all. Lesley's parents – her mother Beatrice was a Land Army girl and her father, Don, stationed at a US army base near King's Newton – met at a railway station. But this was no brief encounter. They married, but when Lesley was 4 months old her father had to go back to the United States. The plan was for Beatrice and Lesley to join him, but it never happened.

'I suspect my maternal grandmother had a lot to do with it,' Lesley says. 'My mother had been pregnant when she got married – a great disgrace. The general feeling seems to have been that the whole unpleasant episode should be swept under the carpet and my mother should start again. I'm not very close to my mother and she doesn't talk about that period of her life. I know they kept in touch for four years, but then my mother divorced my father and remarried, changing her name and address, so it would have been difficult for him to find her if he tried.'

Lesley's American grandmother, however, saw the relationship in a better light than her English family. For the first few years of Lesley's life, until her grandmother died, she sent her little presents, and it was the sender's address on the wrapping paper, lovingly kept for forty years, that led us to Don in the end – only to find that he had been searching for his daughter for years too.

There are many sad and touching stories, but I think that Heather, who has become a good friend as well as a name on the War Babes file, would be the first to agree that her parents' story has a touch of black humour too. Heather's father was a handsome Mexican-born GI. He told Heather's mother, Dolly, that his home was in San Diego and that the picture he carried around in his wallet was of his sister Anna. (It was in fact of his wife, but that need not bother us at this stage of the story!) Dolly was introduced to Richard by her sister-in-law, Nancy. Nancy was going out with an American serviceman named Brad and his pal, Richard, would sometimes tag along. Dolly went out with him to make up a round foursome – and fell for Richard. One thing she omitted to tell him though was that she was married with a child and that her husband, Arthur, was not away, but living at home and working as a bus driver. Heather takes up the story.

'It's hard to understand why my stepfather wasn't suspicious with this going on under his nose, but Mom said he worked long hours and wasn't home a lot. They weren't getting on well anyway. She once told me she only married him to get out of the WAAFs, and she wasn't sleeping with him at the time I was conceived, which left no doubt I was Richard's child even before they saw my colouring.

'In my Mom's defence I think she really was besotted with Richard. She told me he was gorgeous-looking, not very tall but with black hair and lovely dark eyes. She said when he turned up in his white suit she'd never seen anyone like him in her life. And that from a woman who's been married and divorced three times.'

The romance came to an abrupt end in a Leicester pub. Dolly was having a drink with Richard when Arthur walked in. She hurried over to her husband, presumably to try and find an explanation which would satisfy him. While they were talking, Richard, very much the jealous lover, marched over and warned Arthur to 'stop pestering my girl' – only to be told by Arthur that this was no girl, this was his wife! Heather has heard the story both from her mother and her stepfather, with whom she has always got on well.

'There was a fight and Arthur came out of it the loser – at least physically. But my Mom felt so sorry for him, lying on the floor, that she told Richard to clear out. She said she didn't want to see him again, and she didn't get a chance to take back the remark because he was posted abroad very soon afterwards.

'There was a great deal of family pressure on my mother to have me adopted, but Mom never gave in and Arthur stood by her. Brad hadn't been sent overseas and he lost touch with Richard. But when he saw me he said he'd tell Richard, if he ever saw him again, that he very definitely had a daughter. Even as a baby I was the image of my father. Brad also gave my Mom a picture of Richard to show me when I was older, but my stepdad threw it at the back of the fire. He didn't want to be reminded.'

3
Overpaid, Oversexed, Over Here?

'S uddenly the GIs were here . . . if they'd dropped from Mars we couldn't have been more surprised,' Norman Longmate quotes a woman from Derby as saying in his book, *The GIs: The Americans in Britain 1942–45*.

So who were these 'Martians' and what were they doing here? The historical facts are straightforward. The first GIs to set foot on British soil landed in Northern Ireland on 26 January 1942. From then on they arrived on the mainland in steadily increasing numbers, reaching a peak in 1944. Many were just passing through or returning from the battle fronts of Europe. Others were stationed here permanently to build and run camps and bases or to service the combat troops. The American Air Force flew their daredevil missions from British bases, many of them not returning. The Navy worked out of ports from Scotland to Cornwall. Altogether two million American servicemen spent some time in Britain during the latter half of the war.

They came to fight alongside our own men and though resented by some, they were desperately needed. Since the outbreak of war in 1939, there had been speculation and hope that the Americans would join in the fray. But though they offered support, the lease-loan of vital equipment and even food parcels, the American people were, understandably, resistant to the idea of politicians sending their young men off to fight distant battles on foreign shores. They were not, after all, directly involved.

All that changed on 7 December 1941, when the Japanese Air Force attacked the American base at Pearl Harbor in the South Pacific. Four days later Germany and Italy also declared war on the United States; and the Americans were mobilized and on their way to Britain. They crowded into every nook and cranny of the British Isles, astounded at the smallness, the quaint customs, the poverty – and the weather! They came in a hurry and were based in anything from tents (temporarily) to Nissen huts to stately homes requisitioned for the war effort. Some were billeted on British families who happened to have a spare room.

When staying with families, one GI father recalled, they were told neither to pay extra rent nor to bring back food from the base because this would reflect badly on the British soldier who might be billeted there next and would be in no position to do the same. If they wanted to help the family, they were advised to eat out sometimes and spare the meagre rations.

The Americans' horror at how little and how limited was the British diet drove many of them to disobey the order. Families who put up GIs, or became friendly with them, report being supplied with gifts of food (from their own generous rations or smuggled out of the well-supplied camp kitchens), cigarettes, chocolate, chewing gum and every girl's dream, nylons. Their generosity was appreciated but, apart from that, the natives who had to learn to live cheek by jowl with these newcomers were not, always, sure what to make of them. Martians they weren't but they were certainly foreigners even if they did speak the same language – and that was sometimes in doubt. They knew nothing about the customs or even the size of this island – smaller than many American States – and what we knew of Americans was filtered through the unreliable world of Hollywood.

Spotting the problem early on, the United States War and Navy departments produced a handbook for new arrivals. Among other things it advised them to be friendly but not intrusive, and to avoid showing off or bragging. It warned against making fun of British accents, 'sounding off' about lukewarm beer, cold boiled potatoes and English cigarettes. And if the British looked dowdy, it was because clothes, like everything else, were rationed. Above all, the book insisted, they were not to make wisecracks about British military defeats and never, ever criticize the King and Queen.

The author was correct in his assessment of what would irritate the British public. It was loudness, boastfulness, uninhibited behaviour and jovial criticism of our way of life that got up British noses. But most of all it was the young servicemen's tendency to chat up every woman from 14 to 40, and to lavish presents and compliments on them in a way foreign to British manhood that had fathers locking up their daughters. Husbands and boyfriends didn't even have that option. Far away, with a war to fight, they could only add this anxiety to their numerous others, their fears fuelled by enemy propaganda about what the Americans were getting up to with the girls they left behind.

British womanhood didn't quite capitulate *en masse*. Some regarded the GIs as a bit of a joke. There was a feeling in many quarters that 'nice' girls didn't go out with Yanks. I've heard it put more strongly too – that the girls who did were no better than prostitutes. It's an attitude you get from older men, talking from bitter memory.

Cruel jokes thinly veiling the antagonism abounded, as in 'I hear she wears American knickers. One Yank and they're down.' The birth rate tended to rise near American camps and in acknowledgement this sign is said to have appeared at a busy junction close to one: 'GIs please drive carefully – that child may be yours.' But you can talk to many a respectable, grey-haired granny who was a teenager in the war years and come up with a very different picture . . . of the sheer fun and excitement of being with one of these amusing characters who called you 'Babe' and 'Honey'. They tell of innocent dates filled with laughter that ended with a respectful goodnight kiss and boys whose old-fashioned manners swept mothers off their feet.

'I think they – a lot of them anyway – had a way with women,' said Elsie, who was 16 when she dated her GI from Wyoming. 'They made you forget you were wearing a horrible Utility skirt and a cardigan your mother had darned half a dozen times. It was hard to remember that this was something like a holiday romance to them and that they'd probably forget your name as soon as they left England.' Even more off-putting was the thought that they might have also forgotten, accidentally on purpose, the name and existence of a wife back home – a fairly common occurrence.

A great deal has been said about the American men, but who were these British women, reputedly toppling like ninepins for them? Certainly they were a different breed from the females inhabiting this country only a few years previously. British womanhood had been undergoing a compulsory and not always pleasant learning experience since the outbreak of war, and it's hard to imagine the end products of this being a pushover for anybody.

They'd learned to turn their hand to anything – to patch, turn and trim clothes that even the poorest would have previously thrown out; to grow their own vegetables and make meatless stews and eggless puddings (incidentally previewing a healthy diet that would be all the rage forty years later). They'd learned to live without their men around, to enjoy meaningful lives neverthe-less, and to step into the men's work shoes in factories and fields alike, while they were away. The old boundaries between men's work and women's work all but disappeared for a while. Somebody had to perform the tasks that kept a country running, not to mention the vital and often dangerous war work in places, like the munitions factories, that were prime targets for German bombers.

There were still women in service, in nursing and in canteens, but suddenly they were also delivering the post, driving buses and working as railway porters too. If you looked really hard you could fine female steeplejacks, bricklayers, brewery workers – or anything else you care to mention. They even fought for equal pay, to the amazement of many men who didn't understand why women should grumble about getting a third of their rate for the same job.

So essential were women workers that the government introduced conscription for unmarried women between 20 and 30 (eventually the age limit was raised to 50). Among the choices of occupation offered conscriptees were the women's services, the land army and other vital work such as the munitions, aircraft, tank and radio industries. Factories desperately needed recruits and were fairly unpopular due to the monotony of the work and straight-through shifts as long as twelve hours. Since factories have a tendency to be in big, industrial cities, farms in the country, and the women's services a definite living-in job, it meant that young women often had to leave home for the first time. So they'd learned independence and how to make friends with people from all walks of life, who they'd never have met in normal circumstances.

British women had learned about fear and bereavement and hardship; about the loss, temporary or permanent, of people (husbands, boyfriends, brothers to the war, children to the evacuation programme); and the loss of possessions and even homes when the bombs rained down. They'd learned about camaraderie and how to distil pleasure from the most miserable or mundane events. How to live for today.

The war brought pain to the women of Britain but it also brought many of them a sort of freedom. And not only single women. Married women, including those with children, were often working and earning good money. For the first time in their lives perhaps, they were learning the pleasure of being in charge of how that money was spent, and of taking the family decisions themselves. Far from being sad creatures, floundering helplessly without their menfolk, it seems that they had never been so liberated, and wouldn't be again, once the war ended, until the 1960s. I wonder if this was what gave some of them the confidence to take charge of their lives and embark on relationships they wouldn't have considered at another time?

Unlike the women's libbers of the 1960s though, sexual freedom ended abruptly in the maternity ward. The pill was decades off, family planning was a minority activity in Britain and abortion was a dangerous backstreet affair, and even then only for the streetwise. The wages of sin were pregnancy, and with this highly visible sign of wrongdoing, the old feelings of guilt and shame came back. The only mystery about the American's high illegitimate birth rate is what the GIs were doing with the condoms, which were given out routinely to them, and which one Wren, quoted in Norman Longmate's book, recalls the American sailors used to carry around in their hats!

Talking to war babes you quickly get to know that it wasn't only the unattached and fancy-free who had affairs with GIs. That married women strayed during the war, with men from this country or elsewhere, is obvious from the divorce figures which rose from 10,000 in 1938 to 25,000 in 1945. Most proceedings were brought by men, on grounds of adultery. There are no statistics to indicate what proportion of them had returned home to find a tiny war babe in the house.

One way of assessing women's lives and worries at any time in recent history is by reading the problem pages of women's magazines. A chapter in *Women in Wartime* by Jane Waller and Michael Vaughan-Rees suggests that World War II agony aunts received a regular supply of letters from readers who were pregnant and desperate for help and advice. It was the married women who were most desperate, and the stock answer was to tell their husband the truth and ask his forgiveness. There didn't seem to have been any way of avoiding truthfulness in the situation as adoption could not be arranged without the permission of the husband, even when he was not the child's father. But as Leonora Eyles, the agony aunt of *Woman's Own*, points out, rather chillingly, children's homes would take the baby providing you could show that your marriage had not broken down.

It's fascinating to read such letters and their replies and to speculate on the atmosphere in which our mothers led their love lives and gave birth to us. Ms Eyles, for instance, was criticized occasionally for being too lenient with men who committed adultery. 'Tolerance and understanding are the only way to save the situation,' she briskly advises one wronged wife. 'I would forgive him and never mention it again.'

On the other hand a woman, married for five years and childless, who had met someone else while her husband was away, was treated to a stern lecture on the dangers and deprivations faced by soldiers like her husband 'so that all of us can live in safety and comfort. Do you think you are worth it?' she goes on. 'Can you believe that you and others like you who have no idea of remaining loyal to their marriage vows, who talk lightly of "being in love" with another man, are worth the lives of all our gallant men?' Agony aunts tend to reflect public opinion, not create moral codes, and it would be a strong woman indeed – or a besotted one – who would go ahead with an affair in the face of such criticism. The surprising thing is that so many women did.

It wasn't just young women with romance on their minds who warmed to the Americans though. When they took the trouble to look behind the brash exterior of the noisy minority, British people of all ages discovered the obvious; that they were not a gang of clones but as varied as any other group of people anywhere. Many were homesick young men who missed their families. Through no fault of their own, they were about to face danger and death on foreign soil and they were frightened and lonely. Mothers looked at them and saw their own sons, and wanted to take care of them.

Various schemes were introduced whereby British families would have one or more men to their homes for Sunday tea and, particularly, for Christmas dinner. People who got to know the GIs socially or through work issued such invitations spontaneously. Friendships which were long to outlast the war were made, with American families writing and sending food parcels to the British families who had 'adopted' their sons. But inter-country relations were not all sweetness and light. One large group never took to the GIs – the British servicemen.

The British soldiers' hostility to the Americans was, I'm sure, based mainly on envy. The GIs earned five times as much as their opposite numbers in the British army. They lived in better conditions, had more equal relationships with their superiors and in contrast to the British soldiers' rough, heavy battledress, wore smart uniforms. The British men also resented what they saw as the Americans' brash boast that they were here to win the war for them because the British weren't up to it themselves. George, one of the GI fathers, however, denies he or any of his friends ever thought like this. 'We had great admiration for the staying power of the British troops. The war had been on for three years when we arrived. They were still in there battling away and would continue for another three years. Goodness knows what state their morale must have been in by 1942, when we came bouncing in fresh from home comforts, but we never doubted their courage.'

'The hardest thing to bear,' one old British soldier recalls, 'was not them thinking they won the war but the fact that they probably did! Maybe that's an exaggeration but we certainly couldn't have done it without them. We were at a very low ebb when America came in and we needed them. But we didn't have to like them.'

Most of all, the British male resented the Americans' legendary success with women. The taunt, which eventually became a sort of macho compliment, that the GIs were 'overpaid, oversexed and over here' sums up the attitude even today. What is less well known is the standard American retaliation that the British were 'underpaid, undersexed and under Eisenhower'. It all seems petty and sad in retrospect remembering that there was a deadly common enemy to fight and that both countries needed each other. Nevertheless there were regular skirmishes between the two groups when they met, and feelings ran so high that, certainly for some of the old British soldiers I've met, they have not cooled down to this day.

One thing that the British in general found hard to understand was the segregation of the black GIs from their white fellow soldiers. The two groups didn't mix socially or professionally. There were separate 'black' units and the men in these performed the most menial tasks. Colour prejudice, which was rife in the USA, had barely raised its ugly head in Britain. There were few people from ethnic minority groups here and the black GIs were something of a novelty and a source of curiosity. They were accepted on equal footing with their white comrades initially. If anything, they were preferred for their politeness, impeccable manners and lack of arrogance. Walter from Mississippi, who was based near Birmingham, confirms this: 'I don't think I ever encountered colour prejudice during my time in England. I made many good friends among white people. As long as you knew how to behave, people accepted you. Your colour didn't make a darn bit of difference, which was a lot different from back home.'

This state of affairs was too much for some white GIs who were openly horrified at the mixed-race fraternizing. Their antagonism boiled over into aggression towards the blacks, with brawls becoming commonplace. There was a great deal of violence and even a few murders, and eventually the places of entertainment which had admitted black and white freely felt compelled to impose their own segregation. Pubs and dance halls, particularly in small towns, began to hold black nights and white nights. Girls who were seen to dance with a black man would be boycotted by the white GIs.

But British girls still met and fell in love with black GIs, and for those who gave birth to mixed-race baby there was a double stigma. There would be no hope of passing the child off as their husband's if they got married later to a white man – or if they were already married at the time of the affair. Nor was there much chance of marrying their baby's father. These star-crossed love affairs were doomed to failure by the attitude to mixed-marriages in the Unites States. Marriages in general between British women and US soldiers were discouraged by the military establishment, but when the prospective bridegroom was black into the bargain, it was simply out of the question.

Joe from St Austell, Cornwall, heard from his grandmother about the problems his mother and father, Joseph, faced when they tried to tie the knot. His mother was only 16 when she met his father, who was in the navy. When she became pregnant, Joseph applied to his commanding officer for permission to marry. The request was turned down as was his second application.

'There were two military hearings,' Joe explained, 'during which it was made plain to the couple that they could not be permitted to marry under any circumstances because of the colour difference. At the second hearing my father was warned that if he did not stop seeing my mother he would be charged with unlawful sexual intercourse. The fact that my mother was a willing partner and very much wanted to marry him, and that her family were behind them, made no difference. Nor did the fact that she was a young girl about to bear his child. He was black, therefore I had to be born illegitimate and perhaps be placed in a home – they didn't know.'

In fact Joe was luckier than many. His mother had the support of her family and she managed to keep him. He was looked after for the first few years of life by his grandmother and aunts and later joined his mother and her new husband, a not altogether happy arrangement for him.

Most unmarried mothers of mixed-race GI babies were persuaded or bullied by family and friends to place the baby in care and get on with their life. If her family refused point-blank to help, there wasn't much a young woman could do in those days of limited welfare benefits except go along with their decisions. John C's mother was one who gave in to her family and she told the grown-up John how she sat up with him all night, holding his hand and weeping before handing him over to the children's home in the morning. He was 6 weeks old and she didn't see him again for twenty years. As if family pressure wasn't enough, there was at least one council in England which compulsorily took mixed-race babies into care at birth.

Janet's mother, Laura, managed to hold on to her daughter, thanks to an understanding husband who obviously didn't fear gossip. Janet was the result of an affair her mother had with a handsome, 22-year-old black GI, Walter. When Walter found out that Laura, who was already married, was expecting his child, he wanted to take the baby back to his family in Mississippi. But Janet's stepfather returned from the war and adopted her, so she grew up instead in Birmingham, in a white family.

Janet recently found her father and during his first visit to her home I heard his account of his experiences in Britain in 1943 and 1944. He remembers that it started with twin shocks. Shock number one was that his unit, all black, were to sleep in tents, while the men of the white unit nearby were stationed in relatively comfortable barracks with adequate protection from the British weather. Shock number two, much greater, was the dearth of black girls in the rural Midlands. 'Hey, I don't see no coloured girls,' one of his friends had exclaimed. 'What are we going to do for girls?'

'Well, I love girls,' Walter laughed. 'I'm gonna get me a girl. I don't care what colour.' And he did. The small-town places of entertainment went in for segregated evenings, but there was none of that nonsense in the big dance halls of Birmingham. So that's where Walter and his friends headed at weekends. It was on the steps of these establishments that he first saw Janet's mother, petite, attractive – and white.

'I caught up with her before she went inside and asked, "Are you accompanied by anyone?" When she said no, I asked if we could go in together and maybe have a dance. She agreed to just one dance – and we ended up dancing all night. After that we saw each other every weekend. I'd come up to Birmingham and sometimes she'd turn up at the base to see me, without warning. The fellas would raise their eyebrows and say, "Lady to see you again, Walter."

'We used to have lectures on not getting serious about girls, but it's just human nature for a man and a woman who like each other to start to get deeply attached. Doesn't matter where they come from.'

Walter believed he was dating a single woman. Looking back he can see it was strange that he always met her away from her home and that she never talked about her private life. They had been going out together seven months when she provided him with yet another double shock; she was expecting his baby – and she was married with a young daughter. 'She was upset and frightened. She didn't know how she'd tell her husband. Neither did I! I was stunned, and I was angry that she had misled me. Not that I blame her for what happened. I was the kind of guy who put pressure on a girl. She'd say, "We must wait," and I'd say, "No, we can't wait. How do you know what's going to happen tomorrow?"

'War is not like any other time. You never know what is going to happen from one day to the next. You make up your mind to have a good time while you can. It was hard for married ladies. Janet's mother didn't do nothing others weren't doing. Their husbands were away, sometimes for up to two years. They didn't even know if they'd be coming back. They got lonely.

'I pulled myself together and offered to do what seemed like the best thing – to send the baby to my family when it was born, and have it brought up in the States. It seemed to me that would be best for everyone and I wanted to do right by the child.'

He contacted the American Red Cross, who agreed to help. Then he wrote to his mother. 'I know I should have told her the truth like a man, but I come from a very religious family and I knew she'd be shocked and hurt.' So he concocted a story about a death-bed promise to a dying comrade to take care of the child his girlfriend was expecting. 'My mother didn't buy it. She picked up on the truth right away. But however disappointed in me she was, she'd have taken in the baby.'

Whether Janet's mother would actually have parted with her anyway is unlikely but before any arrangements could be discussed, and shortly before the birth, Walter was posted to France. A few months later he received a letter from Laura's husband who had arrived home unexpectedly from active service. 'It was a polite letter,' Walter recalled, 'explaining that he was going to bring Janet up as his own. "My daughter will not be leaving England," he said. "My daughter!" I was impressed. I don't think, in his position, I'd have done the same.'

Even so he worried about his daughter, 'about the little black child growing up in a white family. Would people be kind to her? It would have been different if she was with my family. She wouldn't have been a white child in a black family. Her colour wouldn't have singled her out. We vary a lot in colour. I'm the darkest in the family. My sister is lighter than Janet.'

Back in America at the end of the war he tried to make up his mind what to do next. 'Should I get a job, try to go back to school? The war disrupted men's lives, made them restless. I decided to re-enlist. In all I spent twenty-three years in the army. I was posted straight back to Europe, to France.'

From there in 1946, he got a 32-hour pass and came over to England to see his daughter. 'I don't exactly remember where the meeting was, but there was only Janet and her mother present, not the stepfather or Janet's half-sister. Oh, she was such a cute, pretty little girl. I felt very proud to be her Daddy and very sad leaving her. But I was happier too. My mind was more at ease. I could see she was happy and well cared for, and I was assured her stepfather was going to adopt her. I didn't want to rock the boat and I was sure I'd see her again.'

He did, but not as soon as he expected. He continued to send maintenance money, through the army, until he received another polite letter, saying, 'Janet is officially my child now and we do not think it fair that you should have to continue to support her.' She was 5 years old and Walter carefully put his collection of photographs of her, and the family's new address away. But both were sadly destroyed.

Walter couldn't remember the family's address. In desperation, when he was stationed in England in the 1950s, he went to Birmingham and drove round and round the streets in the vain hope that he'd spot – and recognize – the girl in the photographs. The miracle didn't happen. Walter went on to have a large family with his first wife, but he never forgot Janet. 'I always believed she'd find me one day. A girl has a special feeling for her Daddy.'

Meanwhile the 'cute, pretty little girl' grew up hating the way she looked, ashamed of her colour. 'For a long time I didn't realize I was black,' Janet said. 'Nobody ever mentioned it, you see, and I never saw anyone else dark-skinned. Looking back, I think that unconsciously the policy in our house was "think white" and I was encouraged to think I was exactly the same as my Mom, my adoptive father and my sister.'

Janet is unusual, even among mixed-race war babes, in that her problem was not in coming to terms with being illegitimate or the daughter of an American serviceman as much as with her colour. Her adoptive father worked in a factory and she spent her earliest years in a poor part of inner Birmingham 'where everyone knew everyone else's business and there were no luxuries like bathrooms or indoor toilets!' It sounds very much like my own childhood neighbourhood – except that all of the neighbours were kind!

'They must have known all about my background but I was never made to feel different. I was completely accepted. When we moved out to the suburbs, nobody knew anything about us and the neighbours weren't the nosey kind. It must have seemed like a new beginning to my parents. People made the assumption that I was the adopted child of both of them and they let them think that. I knew my Mom was my real mother, of course, and I think I knew from quite early on that my father was American. Just that. It was not talked about. I must have been a very naïve child because it didn't occur to me that if my sister was older than me, my Mom must have been already married when I was born. I didn't worry about things like that.'

But there was a dramatic change when Janet reached 15 and left school to start work in a factory. 'When I was a young child there were hardly any coloured people in Birmingham, but in the 1950s there was an influx of people from the West Indies. Suddenly there was colour prejudice. Notices appeared in shops and on factory gates, saying "No coloureds", but still I didn't twig that this involved me. Then I went into a shop by the factory to buy some sweets and the woman behind the counter said, "I can't serve you. Haven't you seen the notice?" pointing to the "No coloureds served here" sign. I'd seen it and thought it was a shame that people should be treated like that because they came from abroad and had different coloured skin. But I wasn't one of them. I was English. I thought she'd made a mistake or it was a joke, but of course she hadn't and it wasn't.'

She didn't tell her parents what had happened. Perhaps it was too shameful or she felt she'd somehow let them down by not being able to 'think white' strongly enough to convince the doubters. Instead she made up her mind to try harder. 'I wanted so badly to pass for white that I'd buy the palest shade of foundation and powder and spread it on thick. I must have looked ridiculous, but it was better than the alternative. I never told boyfriends I was half black. I just hoped they'd think I was a dark-skinned white person. I assumed it worked because they never asked me, but maybe they were being tactful. The only time I can remember it coming up was when a policeman said to the boy I was out with, "What's the matter, mate? Can't you find a girl your own colour?"'

Luckily Janet didn't have to carry what she saw as her shameful secret into marriage. She bumped into Paul, who had known her when they were both children and was in no doubt of her background. Not that it bothered him, though some people in Paul's family worried about what colour their children might turn out. Janet went to the doctor for a bit of genetic information on that one.

But even three beautiful children, lighter than her in colour, darker than Paul, didn't put her mind at rest. She was forever keeping them out of the sun in case they grew darker, determined that they were going to grow up white. It was the same with herself. On the sunniest day she was clad from head to toe, fingertip to shoulder, in case the sun turned her even a micro-shade darker. It was a sensitive and sensible neighbour who talked her out of it. 'She convinced me that if she and half the white population lay out in the sun trying to turn the colour I was, there couldn't be too much wrong with it!'

But she had also, by then, begun to think about her father. 'Probably the first time I really wished he was around was on my wedding day. My adoptive father did a good job, but I suddenly wanted my real father, my own flesh and blood, someone who looked like me, to give me away. And when my eldest son was born, I wondered if this was my father's first grandchild and whether he'd have felt proud if he could have held him.

'I think it was the children that gave me the urge to find him . . . looking at my eldest and wondering where he got his tremendous confidence from. And that would bring me round to thinking about myself. I was different from my family in many ways: my hot temper, for instance. I didn't get that from anyone in the family. Maybe I also wanted someone to make me feel proud of being black, proud of being the person I was – and it all came back to this man my mother had told me was called Walter and who came from Mississippi.'

And so, Janet started searching. But I'm leapfrogging decades here. Back to the past, to 1945, in another part of Birmingham.

4
'Yank's Leftovers'

The war was over after six long, weary years – and what's more, we'd won. The Americans, who'd played no small part in this victory, left and our own men came home; at least the lucky ones did. There was dancing in the streets and bluebirds over the white cliffs of Dover, and life made a valiant effort to return to normal. For most people it was a time of rejoicing, but for my mother it must have been a time of slowly and painfully fading hope as she waited for the letter from America that never came.

Around her, rituals that even Hitler hadn't managed to disrupt went on as usual. At 5 a.m. sharp on a Monday morning, Miss Spencer, stooped and shuffling, would make her way down our yard to the communal wash house, known as the brewhouse. She'd be joined by kind-hearted Mrs Lucas who kept us supplied with home-made fruit cakes, and the first wash-day shift would begin. The two women always did their washing together. It was the sort of job where four hands were infinitely better than two.

A fire would be lit under the large boiler or 'copper' and the dirty washing boiled up inside it in a strict order: bed linen first, clothing second. It would be beaten into squeaky clean submission with the aid of a 'maid' and a 'dolly tub', and then fed between the rollers of a gigantic mangle that threatened to gobble up your fingers as well if you weren't careful. By 7 a.m. the neatly patched sheets (Long Street hadn't needed the war to learn about make-do-and-mend) would be billowing in the breeze or dripping limply in the rain depending on your luck with the weather. In good time the rest of the wash would join the sheets and then it would be someone else's turn in the brewhouse.

Peace didn't immediately banish rationing nor did it do much for prosperity. People still ran out of money half-way through the week and had to resort to getting their foodstuff 'on tick' at the local shops. The bill would be settled up on pay day, which of course meant there wouldn't be enough cash to stretch to the next weekend. It was a vicious circle. You never quite caught up. Come to think of it, it wasn't all that much different from our credit-card society today.

Unlike many women, who gratefully turned over their power presses to the returning men and sought gentler employment or went back to being full-time housewives, my mother carried on with her factory job. It was the only work she knew and there was no question of giving up work. There were no welfare benefits and if she didn't work we didn't eat. It was as simple as that. At some point she abandoned the fantasy of Jack Crowley returning on his white charger – or in his white Cadillac – to carry us off to the wonderland that was America. Would she have gone if he'd asked her, I wonder? Her family, her friends, her roots were in Birmingham. She was a Brummie through and through and I find it hard to imagine her living happily anywhere else. But how different my life would have been if this dream had come true. Instead she faced the harsh reality of being a single parent, though this acceptable term hadn't been invented then. She was simply an unmarried mother with an illegitimate child, whose father happened to be a GI. And even in our rough and ready neighbourhood there were many ready to look down on her – and me.

My mother and grandmother worked side by side operating capstan machines in a grimy factory. Perhaps we all have a smell that evokes childhood for us. For some it's garden flowers, freshly mown grass or the mouth-watering aroma of bread baking. For me, it's the strange industrial smell of metal coolant or 'suds', used to lubricate factory machinery. After a day at work the smell clung to my Mum and my Nan, to their clothes and their hands and even their hair, till it seemed to be part of them.

While they worked I went to a council nursery, where I managed to pick up every childhood illness known to medical science. After a bout of measles with complications which put me in hospital for three months, Aunt Slim, Nan's sister, volunteered to look after me. Now my days were spent in a veritable palace. This house had a big kitchen, comfortable armchairs and a sitting room so grand it was declared off limits to me. It wasn't until I was at grammar school and visiting friends in the middle-class suburbs that I realized what a humble, but lovingly kept working-class home Aunt Slim's was.

Even as a small child I don't believe I had any illusions about my own house. There was no bathroom, no indoor toilet, no hot water – unless you count the kettle which hung over the black-leaded fireplace boiling merrily. From the tiny kitchen, a bare wooden staircase led up to two bedrooms, one of which I shared with Nan. This was so small that you had to scramble across one bed, covered with a mixture of shabby blankets and old coats, to get to the other. The walls with their chipping plaster were unpapered and unpainted, but I decorated them creatively by squashing any of the resident bedbugs foolish enough to put their heads above the parapet. They made a rewarding blood-red splodge.

The bugs were just one species of the wildlife sharing our humble abode. In the dark, damp cellar, reached by a flight of steep, stone steps, mice, cockroaches and spiders would scurry for cover in the light of your flickering candle, as you paddled across the flooded floor for a bucket of coal to set the fire. It was, I suppose, what you'd call a deprived childhood, but the one thing I was not deprived of was love. For the first five years of my life, I was the centre of my mother's and my Nan's lives. When I cast my mind back to bedtime in that cramped, bug-infested little room, it's not the cold and the discomfort I remember but the warmth of the house brick, heated in the fire, and carefully wrapped in old rags to warm my feet. And the feeling of my Nan's arms around me when I crept into her bed and snuggled up to her on the frostiest nights.

The people around me were almost all women and I listened to their conversations and became an old woman in miniature myself. 'Don't lean on the palings, love. You'll have them over,' my mother remembers me advising a neighbour before I was three years old. It was one of the expressions I heard regularly, often directed at me. Another favourite was, 'Come away from the miskins (Brummie for dustbin) – you'll catch the fever,' Nan's favourite warning. What fever – yellow, scarlet or even the black death – I never found out, fortunately.

The only man in my life was Uncle Ron, married to Tilly, Aunt Slim's pretty daughter. They lived at Aunt Slim's house, and I worshipped tall, handsome Ron, who looked, I thought, like a film star. When they took me out, I'd walk along proudly between the two of them and day-dream that I was their little girl and had a Mum and Dad like most of the other children I knew.

I don't know when I first began to ask questions about my father, but I knew from a very early age that he was an American soldier. He'd come to England, married my mother and had to go overseas to fight the Germans before I was born. He was killed, like a lot of other brave soldiers, in the D-Day landings. Both Mum and Nan had told me the story. They made it sound as if he had virtually won the war single-handed, and though it was a sad story, it also made me feel very proud of my father. It didn't quite make up for the gap in my life, but I knew I was lucky to have a mother and grandmother who loved me so much.

It's hard to imagine that my Nan was then only a woman in middle age, around the same age as I am now. To me she always seemed an old lady, small, slight and, sadly, toothless – the latter because she'd pulled out all her own teeth and wouldn't wear dentures. I had no idea this do-it-yourself dentistry was unusual till I grew up. In poor areas like ours, where few people could afford to go to the dentist, it was fairly common. In any case, Nan would have been terrified to let what she saw as a maniac with a drill and pair of pliars loose on her molars. Instead she waited for the tooth to go bad (keeping the worst of the pain at bay with salt or oil of cloves), then gradually worked it loose. 'Gotcha!' she'd shout triumphantly as the offending tooth finally parted company with the gum. My mother, too, had a fear of the dentist and removed a lot of her own teeth. There the family tradition stopped. I prefer to leave the job to someone with the equipment, the training and the anaesthetic.

Nan was a frail little woman who could turn into a tigress if anyone threatened or even criticized me – and that included my mother. 'Don't you touch that child,' she shouted, as Mum discovered I'd eaten the entire inside of a newly baked loaf through a hole leaving her only the crust. 'It's not her fault. It's that friend of hers, Violet, that's put her up to it.' It was always someone else's fault in Nan's opinion. When Mum objected to her spoiling me, she'd retort, 'You leave her alone. The world will knock her around enough.' I don't expect she could have guessed how soon her prophecy would come true.

But Mum too could jump to my defence – sometimes literally. I've seen her clear the garden fence to get to a neighbour who had insulted me and consequently offended her. I had no idea why this particular neighbour treated me differently, whispering odd remarks to anyone who was around or even spitting on the ground when I passed by. If my mother saw her though, she would come hurdling like an Olympic athlete across the little garden fences at the front of the houses. Then there would be a slanging match and I can still recall the confused embarrassment I felt as the eye of this storm in a teacup.

'At least I have a licence for mine,' the neighbour shouted.

'You haven't always had one!' my mother screamed back. It took me years to work out that the licence in question was a marriage licence, which the neighbour had only acquired after her daughter was born. This, by her odd reckoning, gave her the right to scorn my mother and me. Again it was grammar school and contact with other girls' families which taught me that most mothers were more genteel and not given to street brawling, whatever the provocation. Mum and Nan were untouched by such middle-class niceties; they defended their own in the only way they knew how.

Such incidents were not common. Most of our neighbours were decent and warm-hearted, and apart from lacking a father I had no feeling of not fitting in. Sooner or later I suppose, something had to happen to change that. The incident that rocked my childhood confidence blew up quite unexpectedly.

It was a bright summer's day and I was playing in the street with my friends. We were making quite a racket and unfortunately we were making it outside the house of a certain Mr Atkins, not renowned for his sweet temper. He opened his door and shouted at us to 'clear off and play outside your own bloody houses'. Like the assertive mini-adult that I was I informed him that he didn't own the road and we had every right to play there if we chose. Not altogether surprisingly he flew into a rage and began hurling abuse in my direction. Part of this, the part that stuck in my mind, went something like this: 'You're not fit to play with the other kids. Everyone knows your father is a bloody Yank. The Yanks should have taken their leftovers with them and not left the likes of you to be a nuisance to decent folk.'

Bewildered, I ran home crying. Nan was at work but Mum was there and I sobbed out my story. I wasn't prepared for what happened next. My mother's face reddened and her eyes flashed. As she half-dragged me into the street and down to the Atkins' home, I wouldn't have been surprised if she'd started breathing fire.

'Come out here and say to my face what you just said to my child, you bastard!' she shouted, banging on the front door. 'I'll kill you,' she added for good measure, picking up a brick and slinging it against the closed door with force. I stood at her side, sobbing in fear and embarrassment, wishing I'd never started this. By now the neighbours had come out to witness the spectacle. Neighbourhood disagreements were not unknown but this was spectacular. The only person who failed to emerge was Mr Atkins. Someone took Mum by the arm and gently escorted her back home. Inside, still shaking with rage, she tried to calm her nerves with a cup of tea and made me promise not to tell Nan what had happened because it would hurt and upset her.

I didn't tell Nan. I didn't tell anyone, not for a long time. But I never forgot that moment – the first time I heard my father, the brave American soldier, referred to with scorn as a 'bloody Yank' and myself as 'Yank's leftovers'. At the back of my mind, I'd known there was something different about me. There were whispers, odd looks, conversations that stopped abruptly when I came into a room. Except for the neighbour who was so proud of her marriage licence, there hadn't seemed much unkindness in this, only curiosity. Now for the first time I was the butt of scorn and disapproval, as if I was something disgusting, unwanted 'leftovers'. My mother recognized the seriousness of what had been said: it was too horrific even to let Nan know about.

Did I look different, I wondered? Was I marked in some way to show I was unfit to play with other children? A look in the mirror confirmed that, on the outside, I was more or less the same as everyone else. But inside I knew there was something that set me apart and I could never rely on being accepted again.

.

There was something else different about me, too. I had acquired a stepfather. His name was Bert and the moment he came into my life, the happiness went out of it. The first five years of my life are crowded with happy memories, but after my mother married, the good moments were few and far between, and even when they came they were blighted by the malevolent presence of the man I was supposed to call Dad but never could. I'd wanted a father so badly it was ironic that when I got one he should be like this.

Motherhood hadn't really changed the girl that Jack Crowley knew. My mother was still an attractive young woman when she took off the factory overalls and let her hair down from the turban that most of the women wore to work. She often went dancing, and while stockings were still scarce and expensive, I was allowed to help draw the dark 'seam' up the back of her legs with the eyebrow pencil. It was much more fun than colouring in books. She still dressed as well as her wages would allow and liked to top off her outfit with a 'Mrs Miniver' hat, copied from the popular film of the time. Most of all she loved the cinema, that temporary escape route from sadness and boredom. I used to go with her and soon I too would learn the trick of stepping out of my own troubled existence and into the happy-ever-after life of the characters up there on the screen.

But when I was 5 and Mum began getting dressed up and made up every evening, she was not going to the cinema or a dance. She had a boyfriend. She had been doing an extra part-time job as a barmaid and there she'd met two men, both customers at the pub, who were courting her. One was a jolly chap, always ready with a joke, but he had a serious drawback – he was an undertaker. 'I couldn't bear to think of him touching me after handling dead bodies all day,' Mum told me years later. The other suitor was a divorced man, not much older than my mother, with a fairly important job in a local factory. He was determined she'd go out with him, sending a friend to persuade her, waiting outside till she'd finished work and insisting on walking her home.

His persistence paid off. Soon she brought him home. He was introduced as Bert, a friend of Mum's. There was no hint that this man was to become my stepfather, but even so it was hate at first sight. I instinctively recoiled from this tall thin man with the brutally short black hair and the piercing blue eyes emphasized by his spectacles. I was sure the feeling was mutual and I dreaded his frequent visits. Even the fact that he bought my first bicycle didn't make me like him any better. I think I even knew then, though I wouldn't have been able to put feeling into words, that this was a gesture to impress Mum.

The wedding took place almost without me noticing. I wasn't taken to it, but suddenly one day Mum came home wearing a wedding ring and Bert was moving in to stay. Mum must have been happy in those early days of marriage, I suppose, but if she was, she was the only one. The happy atmosphere in the little house disappeared overnight.

Bert didn't seem to like Nan any more than he liked me and he very quickly moved upstairs, taking Mum with him. Their bedroom became a sort of bedsitter where they spent most of their time. I stayed downstairs with Nan, whom he treated as an unwelcome guest in her own house. He begrudged her every scrap of food she ate. I remember Mum cooking Christmas dinner and having to sneak Nan's portion down to her when Bert wasn't looking. It wasn't long before the rows started. Bert would come home from the pub ready for an argument with Mum, and it seemed to me that I was always the cause of it. Huddled together in her bed, Nan and I would hear every word of it.

'Why the hell should I support another bloke's kid?' he'd begin. 'Don't think you can stop working. I'm not going to work my fingers to the bone to keep some bloody Yank's leftovers.'

Nan would hug me and tell me to take no notice. 'That man isn't fit to lick your real Daddy's boots. If your father could have met you he'd be proud of you. He'd love you very much.' I hung on to those words. I knew that my father had been gentle, kind and good, all the things Bert wasn't. I used to imagine what it would be like if he was alive now. He'd sit me on his knee and tell me about America. And when it was tea-time we'd all sit around the table together, Nan too, like real families did. I wished there was a photograph of him so that I could make the fantasy more real, but there wasn't so I had to make do with what Mum and Nan told me about his looks.

I day-dreamed a lot. It was another way of escaping reality. Occasionally I'd pretend that my father hadn't died after all; that there had been a big mistake made and he turned up at our house to teach Bert a lesson for being horrible to me. I knew this couldn't really happen, but that didn't stop me gazing at American film stars from the front row of the stalls and trying to decide which of those faces my father should wear in my day-dreams.

Later on there was a more practical reason for allocating him a film star's face. After marriage my mother had a different surname from mine. So, when he arrived, did my brother, Raymond. This puzzled the children at school. It made them ask questions and single me out in a very uncomfortable way. Somehow the story Mum and Nan had told me, while I believed it totally, didn't seem enough to impress my classmates. To be able to hold my head up and feel every bit as good as them, with their loving Daddies at home, I had to produce a living, breathing father or a good cover story.

Since there was no way of producing a real man, a photograph was the next best thing. The first step was to flick through my mother's glossy *Picturegoer* annuals to find a suitable candidate. Jeff Chandler, an actor who turned up a lot in Westerns, was the lucky man. I liked his crinkly smile and his greying wavy hair, but most important of all was the way that hair grew. My father, according to Mum, had a widow's peak, a hairline dipping down to a small v-shape at the centre of the forehead. So did I – and so did Jeff Chandler. I cut out the picture, glued it to a piece of cardboard and popped it into a small, transparent plastic wallet. It must have made a convincing photograph, at least to children my own age. Nobody quibbled or hooted with laughter when I took it out in the playground and explained that this was my American father and he was fighting in the courts to have me go and live with him in his luxurious home.

Lying in bed at night, listening to Bert vent his anger at my very existence, I wished more than anything in the world that my story was true. I never blamed my mother for getting married. As I grew up I realized that a husband and family were what most women aspired to. She couldn't have been expected to condemn herself to permanent single parenthood, but marrying that particular man she inadvertently condemned me to a miserable childhood.

Strangely, my stepfather's cruelty didn't put me off the whole idea of fathers. It just made me long even more desperately for a warm loving man I could call Daddy. Nor did Bert's perpetual scorn totally demolish my confidence. Instead it gave me a determination to succeed at anything I tried, so that he could be proved wrong. Long after Bert had gone the trait stayed with me and it was to stand me in good stead when faced with the American military establishment telling me there was no way I could trace my real father.

It's a moot point whether childhood suffering is worth the strength of character it is said to build. I certainly wasn't able to see any silver lining to the clouds in 1952 when Nan became ill. I can still see her now – and still feel the same lump in my throat I felt then – as she walked out to the waiting ambulance, her handbag over her arm, her head, under the felt brown hat, held high. I had been assured that she would soon be home from hospital and I was trying, with all the will-power I could muster, to be grown up about it and not give in to the sadness and fear I felt.

Bert stood by the open window as she left the house and I stood beside him as he had ordered me to. Then he did something that even by his standards was bizarre. He began to sing, a loud cheerful song that carried down the yard. 'You sing too,' he ordered, 'show her you're happy she's going.' I looked at him in horror but made no sound. He grabbed my arm and pinched me, harder and harder, till I began to sing the words in a very quavery little voice. 'Louder,' he urged, hitting me to make the point. I cannot remember the name of the song nor the tune but I'll never forget the awful feeling of betraying a person I loved so dearly. Nan never looked back but she couldn't have avoided hearing Bert's voice and she straightened her back and drew herself up to her full five feet with dignity. Maybe she never heard my small voice over his, but for a very long time I remained sure that she had and that she went into hospital believing I was happy to see her go.

It was the last time I saw Nan. I was too young to be allowed to visit at normal times, but special arrangements had been made for me to visit one Sunday afternoon. On the day preceding this big event, a message came and my mother had to rush to Selly Oak hospital. She took me with her and I was left with a kindly porter, colouring in a book, while she went to see Nan. She returned looking upset, but assured me that my visit the next day would still go ahead. That was all I cared about. Next morning I was up early, willing the hours to pass quickly. At lunch-time a policeman arrived at the door and took Mum aside for a whispered conversation, while I lingered anxiously in the background. I was aware now that something was terribly wrong. When he left, Mum came over to me in tears. We wouldn't be able to see Nan, she said. She had gone to Jesus.

The information and all it implied did not sink in straight away. It seemed hard to believe that I wouldn't be able to see Nan today; impossible to believe that I would never see her again, or hear her voice – 'Come away from the miskins' – or snuggle up to her in bed for reassurance when my stepfather droned on and on about my failings. I knew I should cry. That's what you did when someone died, wasn't it? Then you felt better. I tried to force the tears, but they wouldn't come. All I could feel was blinding anger, but I didn't know who I was angry with. It was a wet day and I remember running out into the street without a coat and finding a bomb site where a falling bomb had left a deep crater. I crouched inside this crater soaked to the skin and shivering, peering upwards to try to see Nan in heaven. How wicked I must have been, I thought, for God to take away my father and now my Nan, the one person who loved me whatever I did, however badly I behaved. She would even have forgiven me for singing the day she went into hospital once she knew that Bert had forced me. But now I'd never be able to explain or say I was sorry for being so weak that I gave in to his bullying.

The tears came then and wouldn't stop. I felt I had nobody now. My mother had Bert and my baby brother and she didn't need me. I was completely alone.

.

Life went on. I couldn't imagine how it could when Nan wasn't there. How could the sun rise and the stars come out and people carry on about their business when such a very important person had gone? For everyone but me the enormous gap left by her going seemed to fill up quickly. I missed her every day and every night for a long, long time, but gradually, even for me, the sadness grew less intense. I learned, because I had to, to stand up for myself without her help.

The only person who was happy with the situation was my stepfather. Now he could take over the whole house and rule the roost properly. Raymond, my half-brother, was too young to care either way. Poor little Raymond. I resented him for taking my mother's attention from me and I was not very kind to him. As he grew from babyhood to childhood, Bert became almost as nasty with him as he was with me. He'd never liked little boys, he said. So Raymond was often sent to bed without his tea for the smallest misdemeanour, just like me. But unlike me, he always got a snack from Mum who smuggled him up something 'because he's only a baby'. I was expected to grin and bear the hunger pangs.

At the back of my mind, I knew that I was not, as I'd imagined at the height of my grief, surplus to requirements now that Mum had another child. But I did feel she had let me down somehow; that she was a bit of a traitor. Admittedly she tried to stand up for me when Bert started bullying me but I couldn't understand why she didn't solve the problem by just throwing the horrible man out. After all it was her house now, not his as he seemed to imagine.

In fact she had tried to evict him on a few occasions, but he always came back, drunker and more belligerent than when he left, once with the vicar in tow to plead on his behalf. It was not a happy marriage. 'I made the wrong choice,' my mother told me ruefully once. 'I'd have been better off with the undertaker.'

We used to go to the pictures together, something we loved. I could lose myself completely in the film. When the lights came up and reality flooded back it was like waking reluctantly from a lovely dream. I think it was the same for Mum. Her dread of going back to our little house was as strong as mine. I could tell by the tension in her body as we approached our yard that the same thoughts were running through her mind. What mood would Bert be in tonight? Was he going to be all right – or would he start arguing and laying down the law? Mum would grip my hand tight as we walked through the door and we'd wait for a minute, sensing the atmosphere, like vulnerable wild animals in dangerous surroundings.

Those were the days of grammar schools, when the 11-plus examination provided the brighter children with the chance of a good education and, if they were lucky, a job beyond the dreams of most people in Long Street. It could be an escape route from poverty for children from my background, but it wasn't for such a mature reason that I desperately wanted to pass the 11-plus. No, it was because my stepfather had laughed at the very idea. I was far too thick, he said; Yanks usually were. With that remark he guaranteed that I would work as hard as was humanly possible to get in.

When the offer of a place at Waverley Grammar School arrived my mother ran through the yard, waving the letter, shouting, 'She's passed! Our Shirley's passed!' The neighbours were almost as excited as she was. People rushed up to congratulate me. It was as if I'd achieved something for the whole neighbourhood and they were proud of me. Now, surely, Bert would have to eat his words and give me a pat on the back, however grudging.

Did he? He glanced at the letter without a flicker of emotion. 'Arrived today, did it? The blokes at work whose kids passed heard weeks ago. Someone must have dropped out and left them with a spare place. She's only got in by the skin of her teeth.' How silly of me to think he'd ever admit I'd done well. It didn't matter really. I didn't want his praise; I just wanted to prove him wrong and I'd succeeded. I thought of Nan that night; of how she'd cuddled me and told me that my real father would be proud of me. I wasn't sure where I stood on the subject of heaven, but if there was one I hoped that both she and my father were there looking down. I knew they'd both be proud of me.

It was one thing passing the exam, another finding the money to pay for the expensive uniform and sports equipment I was expected to turn up with on my first day at the new school. Family and friends rallied around as they always did in emergencies. A bus conductress friend of Mum's cut up a pair of her old culottes to make me two skirts. Aunt Tilly bought me a gym blouse and a tennis racquet for my birthday, and we found a pair of second-hand hockey boots in the rag market. They were two sizes too big, but I'd grow into them.

There were various administrative procedures connected with changing schools and one of these involved taking my birth certificate into my primary school shortly before I left. I had to ask Mum for this several times before it appeared. Even then it was handed to me inside a sealed envelope addressed to my teacher. There was something odd in my mother's behaviour that worried me. Anxious not to be embarrassed in front of my teachers I decided to check it out and tore open the envelope on my way to school. I made sure I was alone as I unfolded the document and ran my eyes across the information on it. I spotted the offending sections immediately. Under 'name of father', there was a small dash, under 'Mother's maiden name' was Lily Ross. You didn't need an 11-plus success to put two and two together. Oh, the humiliation of it! My mother hadn't married after all – and what about my father? Why wasn't his name here?

My heart thumping with the shock of what I'd discovered and guilt at what I was doing, I tore the certificate into tiny pieces and stuffed it down a drain. I told Mum I'd lost it. Instead of nagging me about my carelessness as I'd expected, she went to the Register Office and came back with a shortened version, the kind with no space for humiliating details. I suspect she guessed what had happened. I kept the new information to myself for a few weeks, turning it around in my head, trying in vain to find a different, more acceptable interpretation. When I couldn't, I waited till Mum and I were alone one day and blurted out the question: 'Were you and my father really married?'

She didn't seem terribly surprised. She gave a little smile, which years later I interpreted as meaning, 'Oh, dear, she's getting too old to be palmed off with fairy tales. I'd better change my story a little.' No, she admitted, she and my father hadn't got round to the actual wedding before he was killed, but they had been engaged. I can remember breathing a sigh of relief. The spectre of illegitimacy hadn't been wiped out but it wasn't quite as bad as I'd feared. Being engaged was almost as good as being married in the circumstances. I told her I wanted to know more about my father, and with a soft, faraway look on her face, as if she was recalling a lovely romantic film she'd once seen, she began to speak.

She told me his name for the first time – Jack Crowley, though he liked to spell his first name in the French way, Jacques, probably because his mother was French. He'd been dark and handsome and I looked a lot like him. He'd come from the state of Idaho and had been born in the same town as Lana Turner, the film star. She'd loved him very much, she said, and when a telegram arrived shortly before I was born to say he'd been killed on D-Day, she was heart-broken.

It wasn't a lot of information, but it satisfied me at the time. I understood why my mother had told the little white lie about being married. It was to protect me. There were now a few more details to add to the picture of my father, and a new plan was forming in my mind. When I was older I would go to America and find my grandparents. Imagine their faces when I introduced myself as the English grandchild they didn't know they had. Of course I'd have to learn French to communicate with my grandmother. It never occurred to me that she would have learned English! This ambition gave me the impetus I needed to excel in French during my first couple of years at grammar school. When the teacher praised me, I explained that I had a French grandmother. 'That must be why your accent is so good,' she said, obviously assuming I spent many happy hours in conversation with the lady in question!

Sadly, none of the plans and hopes I had for the future when I started grammar school were to come to anything. I left, without taking any exams, at the age of 14. Whether the system had failed me or I failed the system I'm not sure, but I never really fitted in. We couldn't afford all the things I needed and I always felt like the poor relation. I never brought my friends home, though I was invited to their houses, usually in the leafy suburbs. I thought the place where I lived might have shocked them and, if I'm honest, I was becoming a bit ashamed of my mother in her crossover pinnies, with her hair in dinky curlers. I'm sure there were other children at the school whose parents considered themselves working class but they were still different from us, and I was at an age when such things mattered.

None of my friends in Sparkbrook had passed the 11-plus. They had all gone straight to the local secondary modern. This had placed an insurmountable barrier between us which perhaps only someone who was a schoolchild in this period can understand. You only had to appear in your uniform – secondary modern schools in general had no uniform – to be greeted with scornful calls of 'grammar grub' and 'snob'. My old friends refused to play me with once I was 'on the other side'. I became a difficult pupil, always disrupting lessons and making a nuisance of myself. If you can't compete in the other ways, like wealth and status, you have to have something going for you. Being the 'naughty girl' of the class was a kind of status – and it helped relieve the boredom. The headmaster didn't put up a fight to keep me when I asked to be transferred to the secondary modern school.

I felt much more at home there. The work demanded no effort at all and there was the added advantage of being able to leave at 15 instead of 16. Higher education had completely lost its attraction for me. I had already changed schools when Mum had her third and last child, my half-sister Patricia. For years I'd longed for a little sister, but Mum had made it clear that she had no enthusiasm for providing one. Then one evening she told me she was going to the doctor's surgery because she hadn't been feeling very well, and asked me to come with her. She emerged from the doctor's office looking shocked.

'I'm sure you're a witch,' she told me. 'You've wished this on me!' She was six months pregnant. Though she'd already had the two of us, the possibility hadn't occurred to her. No wonder it took her so long to realize she was pregnant with me.

Pat, like the rest of us, was born at home. I was there when Bert came home at lunch-time and asked, 'Has she had it yet?'

'Yes,' I said, knowing his feelings about miniature males, 'it's a boy.' He turned away, not even planning to go upstairs. 'I'm only joking,' I said. 'Mum's had a little girl.' He was up the stairs two at a time. I'd never seen him so excited. From that day, Pat was the apple of his eye, his 'little angel'. He was bewitched. When he was with her, he was a different man, a besotted father. But unfortunately the magic didn't extend to anyone else in the house. Whatever Pat wanted she had, irrespective of what sacrifices had to be made – a musical teddy bear, a big rocking horse, two bicycles because the first one turned out to be too big.

If anything, Raymond and I were treated even worse than before the baby's arrival. Raymond lived in fear of his father. Once he accidentally broke the elaborate frame surrounding a photograph of Pat, and Mum had to tell Bert she'd done it, to save Raymond from a beating. I didn't even have to do anything wrong to be punished. In direct contrast to his actions with Pat, I only had to want something to be deprived of it. I liked to watch a pop programme on our recently acquired television set, so he'd take the plug off and put it in his pocket before going out to the pub to make sure I couldn't see it. Sometimes my mother, risking electrocution and combustion, would stick the wires in the socket and we'd watch the black and white screen nervously, ready to jump up and disconnect it when we heard his footsteps. Worst of all, I wasn't even allowed – in Bert's presence – to touch the baby sister I'd longed for. It was as if I was tainted, or 'unfit' as the objectionable neighbour, Mr Atkins, had put it all those years ago and might somehow infect this beautiful baby.

With Pat's birth I was forced to recognize something. I'd always believed that the spitefulness and cruelty my stepfather showed to me was all there was to him. Seeing him with Pat, it was obvious that there was another side to him. He could be warm and tender and loving. Somewhere inside the callous exterior there seemed to be a human being fighting to get out. I'd watch him playing with her, showing her off proudly to the neighbours, and I'd feel an unexpected pang of regret. If he had shown me even a fraction of the affection he lavished on Pat, my childhood could have been so different. But he'd chosen to reject me from the start and I couldn't understand why. Raymond was a boy and, however irrational, that was Bert's reason for not taking to him. But I'd been a pretty little girl of 5 when he met me. True I'd been wary of him, but I could probably have been won over, if he'd tried. But he didn't try. What was so unlovable about me? Was it who my father was, rather than what I was? Did he always see me with 'Yank's leftovers' stamped across my forehead and think with jealousy of the first man my mother had loved?

Bert's dearest wish was to see his little angel grow up. He never made it. When Pat was only 3 years old, he died of a heart condition. He'd been in hospital and came home, a very sick man, aware he didn't have long to live. Before his death he apologized to my mother and Raymond for the pain he had caused, and they forgave him. He asked to see me, but I refused. I could neither forgive nor forget. I didn't go to the funeral. I stayed at home to look after the little angel he wouldn't let me touch while he was alive.

.

I was 17 when my stepfather died and my life had changed dramatically. At the age of 15, I left home and went to live with Betty, a friend of Mum's. She and her husband were a lovely childless, older couple. It would have been wonderful if I had been able to live with them from an early age, but it was very strange walking into their lives at 15.

Still, it worked quite well for a few months. I'd just left school and Betty got me a job in the office where she worked. Then, sadly, Betty had to go into hospital for an operation and it wouldn't have been seemly for a teenage girl to live alone with her husband. So I moved on again – this time to my Aunt Tilly's. That didn't work out too well. By now she had two children and there wasn't much spare space in her two-bedroomed house. Another friend of Mum's offered to have me and I packed my bags once again, like a nomad.

It was a very disruptive period of my life, but anything was better than living with my stepfather. My mother agreed that leaving home was for the best. Indeed it was she who found me the lodgings, always locally and with friends or family so that she could keep an eye on me. But I still occasionally felt a twinge of resentment that I was the one who had to move out of my home.

Somewhere in the midst of this toing and froing I managed to meet the person who was to bring stability and security into my life – though you'd never have predicted it from our wobbly start. His name was Barry McGlade and he was a tall, gangling 18-year-old, with a cheeky face and matching attitude. I met him, of all the romantic places, at the local off-licence. I'd walked down to buy some pop; he'd come over from nearby Balsall Health, a district that made Sparkbrook look up-market, with his cousin Raymond who fancied a girl down our road.

'Haven't I seen you somewhere before?' he asked, a chat-up line that was past its sell-by date even in 1961. He told me he was an apprentice electrician – which was true, and that his car was in for repair – which certainly wasn't. He didn't earn enough to buy a bicycle.

Barry was my first real boyfriend. There had been other brief flirtations, but when I was at home, Bert had seen to it that no boy stayed around long. I was, like a lot of girls of the time, an innocent who acted as if she knew it all. My sex education was severely limited and what I knew I'd gleaned from a schoolmate called Anne, who used to regale the class with tales of her sexual adventures, real or imaginary. Every class has a girl like Anne – or used to in those less enlightened days.

I couldn't ask my mother anything. The subject was taboo with her – and remained so until her dying day. I'd already had a terrible fright when a boy had kissed me at 14 and I was certain I'd be pregnant as a result. My first period came as a total shock and sent me wailing to my mother, convinced I had some terminal ailment. Her attempt at an explanation was so confusing that I went away convinced this was a once-only event in a woman's life. Imagine my horror when the same thing happened again a month later!

I don't blame anyone else for what happened next, but given my unhappy background, my loneliness, my need for warmth and closeness, I suppose it was inevitable. You can almost see me written up as a social worker's classic case history. Barry and I began to experiment with sex and the experiment went wrong – or perhaps it went right! I became pregnant. I wasn't sure at first and my shame kept me from going to the doctor, but I'd mustered enough knowledge to know the obvious signs. It didn't seem possible. According to Anne, there were people doing what we'd done several times a night, with such skill that bells rang and the earth moved – and they didn't end up with an unplanned pregnancy. It didn't seem that our inexpert, alfresco fumblings in the Lickey hills could have resulted in such a life-shattering event.

Each morning I would wake up, willing my body to prove I was mistaken. It never did. I was terrified. I couldn't eat and I couldn't think. This one enormous anxiety blotted out everything else. Years later I realized this was how my mother must have felt in May 1945, when she found herself pregnant and alone. It might as well have been 1945 for all the help that was available to an ordinary girl in that first year of the swinging sixties. Abortion was just something you heard wealthy girls could have in Harley Street clinics. Or something the poor and desperate risked in an unhygienic back-street hovel. Perhaps I was lucky that Anne didn't seem to know any back-street abortionists when I was driven to consult her. Instead she recommended worm cakes. These alarming looking tablets from the chemist were taken to get rid of worms. In large doses, she assured me, they had the same effect on babies.

Well, not on this baby, they didn't and secretly I was relieved. I was beginning to feel a sneaking attachment to this small being I was now certain was growing inside me.

I told Barry. 'Oh, well, we'll get married then,' he said. He was always easy-going, if unromantic. I breathed a sigh of relief. Now that it was settled I could see that what I had regarded as a disaster was the answer to my prayers. Marriage was a way of escaping from my stepfather for good. A wedding ring endowed instant adulthood. No longer would anyone be able to tell me what to do. I could come and go as I pleased, no questions asked. Marriage equalled freedom. I'd no longer be billeted on all and sundry. Now I'd have a home and someone to love me, and soon there would be a lovely little baby who would be all mine. With Barry's casual proposal, fear and dread turned instantly to delight and anticipation.

We were married at Birmingham Register Office on 27 July 1962, with just Mum and a friend as witnesses, no guests, no photographer. There was time for a drink in a nearby pub afterwards and then we went back to Barry's parents' home, where his mother had made sandwiches and got in a bottle of sherry. It was not the sort of wedding little girls dream of. Barry's Mum knew I was pregnant but I hadn't told my own mother. Because of my age, she'd had to sign a consent form and she'd been reluctant at first. 'You're not in trouble, are you?' she asked.

'Of course not,' I lied.

'Go on, sign it for God's sake,' Bert had cut in. Anything to get rid of me. It did occur to me that this was history repeating itself, but Mum had been older and engaged when she fell pregnant and the circumstances were different. My mother's and father's relationship, I felt, had been somehow special.

Barry and I moved into a dreadful bedsitter that cost 4 guineas a week rent, half his wages. Trying to manage on what was left over was very difficult before the baby was born and impossible afterwards. We were like two kids playing at being married, playing at house, and not doing it very well. There was no money for food and I couldn't cook anyway. We used to visit our families around mealtimes and hope there would be enough for us. There usually was.

We had nothing for the baby, but again the families rallied round. Mum gave me Pat's cot and mattress. Baby clothes were donated by a neighbour who'd had a baby a short time before. Barry's Mum offered us her old pram, but she'd been keeping coal in it, and I didn't fancy putting my newborn baby in there, however well it was cleaned out. Aunt Tilly saved the day by buying us a decent secondhand pram. Mum only found out I was pregnant, though she obviously had her suspicions, when she arrived unexpectedly one day and found me knitting baby clothes. 'I thought so,' she said, but I still couldn't give in and admit it.

'I'm pregnant now,' I insisted, 'but I didn't have to get married.' Of course when Martin was born, she knew the truth. She could add up. To give her her due, she accepted it well. There were no recriminations.

Our independent living didn't last long. We soon admitted defeat and moved into the McGlades' already crowded house. Married life was turning out to be a shocker but motherhood was something else. I held Martin, he looked up at me with these big, wondering eyes and I fell in love. Here was my very own precious little human being. Nobody could take him away from me. Nobody could tell me not to cuddle this baby. I learned how to look after this little stranger by trial and error. Don't most first-time mothers, whatever their age?

Being a mother came more naturally than being a wife. It hadn't taken long for my fantasy of escaping to freedom to collapse. I hadn't realized that marriage carries its own restrictions, that a husband is every bit as likely as a parent to want to know where you are going and what you are up to. Though he was the absolute opposite of my stepfather in character, Barry had, in a way, taken Bert's place and I began to resent him. Why should I have to consult him over everything? Who did he think he was? One half of me was a responsible wife and mother; the other an unruly teenager pushing against the boundaries the grown-ups had created.

Both Barry and I felt that we'd sacrificed our youth, and if my life had followed the expected pattern of the imaginary social worker's case history, there would have been a divorce before I was into my twenties. But there was a strong bond between us and, somehow, we weathered those early storms. I soon tired of Barry's Mum telling me, however kindly, how to look after the baby, and insisted we move in with my mother instead. Back I went once more to the house where I was born: Barry, Martin and I in one bedroom; Mum, Pat and Raymond in the other. But my mother was just as bad as Barry's. She tried to take Martin over and spoiled him dreadfully – probably like my Nan did me!

One day the ancient bedroom ceiling fell in just minutes after I'd moved Martin off the bed. It was the final straw. We got in touch with the Housing Department and after much deliberation, they gave us a council flat. It was in a horrible place and we had nothing to put in it, but it seemed like a gift from heaven. We moved into this bare empty place and started to collect bits and pieces of secondhand furniture to make it into a home. For the first time I began to feel settled and able to put down roots. Really, this was the start of our married life. We had hoped for a brother or sister for Martin, but unfortunately it didn't happen, and we accepted it just wasn't to be.

I won't say it was all plain sailing from then on. Barry and I actually split up for a year and I moved back to my mother's with Martin who was then about 7. The resentment at losing out on our teenage years had finally driven us apart, and for that one year we both made rather desperate attempts to recapture the free, fun-loving times we felt we'd been cheated out of. While Mum baby-sat, I dressed up and went night-clubbing, meeting new people, having a good time. Then one day it hit me that perhaps I was only playing at having a good time and that not one of the new people was a patch on Barry. Fortunately he'd reached a similar conclusion about me, and we got back together again, not much older but a great deal wiser. I've never regretted that separation. If it hadn't happened we would not have realized how much we value each other and I doubt we'd have been together today.

.

Never, at any time in my life, were thoughts of my father far from my mind, but for a few years he was definitely relegated to the back burner. This is a familiar pattern for us war babes. During our teens and twenties we are too busy forming relationships, pursuing careers, starting families, paying mortgages – in short, too busy living – to have time for much else.

Often it's when a child is growing up and you catch on his face a glimpse of something that he certainly didn't inherit from either side of the known family, that you are jolted into thinking, 'Who is he like? Could it be my father?' So it was with Martin. He had brown eyes like Barry and people said that otherwise he looked like me, but there was some part of the mixture that couldn't be traced to either of us. I'd gaze for ages at my child, particularly when he was asleep, and wonder who he was. Did my father have the same set to his mouth? Were the fleeting expressions that crossed his face reflections of his French grandmother? I would be overcome by a wave of sadness because it seemed I would never know the answer.

My father might have remained nothing more than a sad ghost from the past, which came to haunt me, momentarily, in my son's face, had it not been for the school history project. When he was between 6 and 7 years old, Martin came home from school very excited about a lesson they had had on the war. They'd been told to ask their parents and grandparents about the subject. It was going to be a class project. I glanced at his exercise book with no more than motherly interest and a date leapt out at me from the page. In childish but clear figures, my son had written '6 June 1944 – D-Day'. I pointed out, as tactfully as possible so as not to discourage him, that he'd got the wrong date. Indignantly, he insisted he hadn't. Miss had written it on the blackboard and Miss, of course, was infallible.

Warning bells were beginning to toll gently at the back of my mind, but I quelled them with logic. Even teachers make mistakes. When I took Martin into school next day I made a point of seeing his teacher and mentioning that there seemed to be some confusion over the date of D-Day. Surely it should be 1945? Definitely not, she assured me cheerfully. That's what the library books said. I went straight round to the library to check out some of those books myself. She was right. All those years I'd believed – because Nan and Mum told me so – that my father had died on the D-Day landings of June 1945 which would have been three months before I was born. Now it seemed that, miraculously, he had died fifteen months before my birth. However you tried to rationalize the figures they didn't add up.

The warning bells were clanging deafeningly now. Why had I been told such a pointless and blatant lie? When and where had my father died? Had he, in fact – and I hardly dared let myself acknowledge this thought – had he died at all? Once again I confronted my mother. Once again, she took it calmly, giving that little 'here we go again' smile. She didn't look like a woman who thought she had done wrong.

No, she admitted in response to my questions, she didn't know exactly where, how or when my father had died. The story they had told me about D-Day was just to keep me quiet and stop me asking questions. I was shocked but trying to make some sense of the new information. 'So how did you find out he had been killed?' I asked carefully. 'You said you got a telegram?'

The telegram, it turned out, had been another little fib. Only wives received telegrams of that kind and my mother and father hadn't even been engaged. That had been another little embellishment to keep an inquisitive child happy. It seemed as if nothing I'd been told about my father was to be believed; in particular the one central fact: 'So you can't even be sure that my father is dead?' I said, trying to keep my voice steady.

'I've no proof,' my mother admitted reluctantly, 'but I'm sure he is. Otherwise he'd have got in touch with me.' My mind was racing. There must be dozens of reasons why any young man would fail to contact a girlfriend, even when they weren't separated by a war and an ocean. They might not be particularly nice reasons but they had to be considered. He hadn't, she said, even known she was pregnant.

'If you have no proof of my father's death, he could still be alive.' I felt like a small child carefully building up a tower of bricks, prepared at any minute to have them knocked down. But my mother had to agree, reluctantly, that this was possible. She genuinely didn't seem to see that it made a great deal of difference either way, and couldn't understand what I was getting so worked up about.

I watched her uncomprehending face and felt like grabbing her and shaking her. All those years she'd made me live with that hateful man, that travesty of fatherhood, when I might have been able to find my real father. And she couldn't even see the damage she'd done. I made my mother tell me the whole story or at least the bare bones of it, and I wrote down everything she could remember. I was caught in a heady mixture of excitement and anger. I kept thinking: I can't believe this. I have a father after all. But why did I have to waste so much time before I found out? In my euphoria, I didn't doubt that he was alive or that I would be able to track him down. I made up my mind there and then that one day I would find him, no matter how long it took or what it cost.

The discovery that she'd lied to me did something to my relationship with my mother. That initial surge of anger I felt never quite dissipated while she was alive. It wasn't until after her death that my attitude softened and I began to see the story through her eyes. I could appreciate then what a hard time she'd had and why she believed it best to tell me a few white lies rather than the harsh truth. I could even understand why she had 'killed off' Jack Crowley. It was the only way to put him, finally, out of her mind so that she could get on with life. Death was less painful to cope with than desertion. I think she actually grew to believe her own story till I set out to rake up old memories and prove her wrong.

I had a few attempts at phoning the American Embassy soon after that conversation, but it was hopeless. The calls had to be made from a public phone box and I ran out of money and got cut off as I was passed from person to person. I didn't know what to ask and I didn't know how to be insistent when people fobbed me off. I got nowhere, but I wasn't downhearted. At the back of my mind I knew the chance would come to find my father. I just had to bide my time and be ready when opportunity knocked.

5
Not the Only One

I grew up believing I was a one-off, the only child in Birmingham – in the whole of Britain, if my imagination had stretched that far – with an absent American soldier for a father. Had it been a subject openly discussed I'd probably quickly have learned otherwise, but so much secrecy and so many half-truths surrounded my parentage that I had no way of getting it into perspective.

Of course there were thousands of GI babies growing up in Britain and in many parts of Europe in the post-war decades, most of them equally convinced they were the only ones. Some of them were aware of their origins from early childhood but for most it was a skeleton in the family cupboard, which emerged by accident or in distressing circumstances like a family row. With hindsight a lot of them could pinpoint clues picked up from seeing a document not meant for their eyes or from snatches of conversation overheard and never fully understood. Once they knew, the whole complicated picture began to fall into place. But always there was one vital piece of that jigsaw puzzle missing – their father.

No two lives are identical and, though we have a lot in common, our childhoods and the ways in which we found out about our background vary tremendously. A rare few felt they 'always knew' but several did not make the discovery until they were adults. For many there was a deeper-layered mystery to uncover than mine. I always knew that Bert was my stepfather. A great many people who have contacted me were brought up to believe that their stepfather was their natural father, either because they were born as the result of an affair when their mother was already married, or because mother and stepfather had married when they were too young to remember and no one saw any reason to enlighten them.

Some had relatively happy childhoods. For others, like myself, those supposedly 'happiest years of your life' were marred by a bad relationship with a stepfather. Not that the wicked stepfather was universal. Some war babes remember the man who brought them up with affection and gratitude. Strangely it doesn't, in general, seem to be the married men whose wives were unfaithful while they were away at war who necessarily turned into the unkindest stepfathers. Perhaps because it takes a tolerant person anyway to forgive and forget, or they remember wartime peccadilloes of their own – or perhaps, knowing the little cuckoo in the nest from babyhood, they developed fatherly feelings for it. More often it was the stranger who met and married the mother when the young child was already on the scene, who seemed to have trouble with acceptance. As a child in this latter category, Joe from Cornwall, whose GI father was black, recalls that his stepfather treated him 'with rejection, violence and total disregard'.

Sue, whose mother, Nancy, is interviewed in an earlier chapter, felt rejected twice – by the man her mother was married to when Sue was born and, later, by her mother's second husband. 'My stepfather was a very cold man. His natural daughter, my younger sister, was the apple of his eye and he had no emotion left over for me. I didn't understand why I was pushed out until I was 12. I was having a bad time with my stepfather and my mother told me the truth about my real father. She thought it would be something to fall back on when my stepfather was particularly awful and it did help a bit.

'I used to think, "If my real Dad knew how I was being treated, he'd be down on him like a ton of bricks." The thought that he was out there somewhere got me through the absolutely bloody awful teen years. I always knew I'd try to find him one day, but I put it off because I was so afraid of being rejected again. How could I be sure he'd want to know me? It wasn't until I had the security of a happy marriage and a family of my own that I dared risk the search. By that time I felt I could cope with whatever rejection I got.'

But perhaps the memory of childhood I've heard expressed most frequently is some variation on this by Len from Leicester: 'I didn't feel unloved. My stepfather cared for me in the best way he could, but something was missing. My half-brothers and sisters – you could see they belonged. They took after our mother or their father. But I didn't seem to take after anybody. I just didn't fit in.'

Heather By contrast, Heather, who also comes from Leicester, was, and still is, close to her stepfather, Arthur. Heather inherited her Mexican-American father's dark colouring and was mystified as a child, as to why her fair-skinned brothers and sisters looked so different from her. Her mother, Dolly, explained this away, rather creatively, as the result of leaving her out in the sun too long when she was a baby.

Heather accepted this until the night, aged 11, she was woken by a heated argument between her mother and the man she had always known as Dad. The argument culminated in Arthur telling his wife to 'clear off to America and find your boyfriend, Richard – and take Heather with you'.

It was clear to the 11-year-old, huddled at the top of the stairs, that her stepfather was saying this Richard was her father. She crept back to bed, numb with shock, trying to make some sense of the information. 'The only Americans I knew were servicemen stationed at a nearby Base, and I'd never heard of my family having any connection with them.

'I didn't tell anyone, it was just too upsetting. I tried to convince myself I'd misunderstood, but I knew I hadn't. One result was that I became very resentful towards Arthur. My mother didn't leave. That row was just one of many, and life carried on as before. Arthur continued to treat me exactly as he always had, as if I were his own child. He was a good father, but I was growing into my teens and there were the usual bits of rebellion and rows with parents. I turned all my resentment on Arthur. When he'd tell me off it would be on the tip of my tongue to say, "You can't tell me what to do – you're not my Dad." But I never said it.'

The first time she had a chance to do anything about the secret locked painfully inside was at 14. A couple of older girls were going to a dance at the American base and she persuaded them to take her. 'I don't know what I hoped to achieve. I suppose I thought I'd walk in, spot a man who looked exactly like me and know he was my father. The older girls didn't want me tagging along anyway. When they met boys they liked, they left me sitting in a corner alone. An American serviceman came over and sat beside me. I was terrified but he was very kind. He said: "You shouldn't be here; you're not old enough."

'He was so nice I told him the whole story and he explained that the GIs who'd been here during the war went back long ago. I was disappointed but I was glad I'd met a real American. He seemed so nice and I thought, well, maybe my father, wherever he was, was a nice man too.'

At 15 Heather left home to live with the family of her best friend. She wasn't away long. Her mother left her stepfather and he pleaded with Heather to come back and help look after the five younger children. This she did until she became pregnant at 16 and married her boyfriend. It was while she was expecting her daughter that she knew she had to find out more about her background, and whose genes she was passing on to her unborn child. It took a lot of determination to confront her mother, now remarried, with the angry words she'd heard five years earlier.

'My mother was amazed that I knew and had never mentioned it. She wanted to know why I'd kept it secret and I couldn't answer that. I didn't know why myself. It wasn't a traumatic experience – that had happened when I was 11 – and Mum was happy to tell me about Richard. He'd been the love of her live.

I'm sure if she'd had the opportunity, she'd have left Arthur – they were already married when she had the affair – and gone with Richard. But he was shipped out, not even knowing she was pregnant. She had no worries about me trying to find him if I wanted to.

'It was Arthur who objected. He was very hurt when I told him I was going to try and find my father. He thought it reflected on him and didn't see why I was interested in this total stranger when he'd done his best to be a real dad to me. I tried to explain to him that I loved him as much as if he were my flesh and blood. Finding my biological father wouldn't alter that but I needed to know who I am.'

Ray Between the ages of 18 months and 8 years Ray, from Blackpool, lived in a children's home. With no family to help her, his mother had found it impossible to earn a living and look after him. So she'd placed him in care until such time as she could cope. When that time finally came, she was married with another son. Ray thinks the decision to have him back may have been partly forced on them – certainly on his stepfather – by the fact that the home was closing down. 'My stepfather didn't seem to want me around. I always felt he was pressured into having me and that he resented it.'

For seven years he had seen very little of his mother so it was like moving in with strangers. 'I remembered her with blonde hair. When I came out she was a brunette. I didn't really know her and I knew nothing about my background. Our relationship almost had to start from scratch.

'Within months of me joining the household my mother had told me that my stepfather was not my real dad. All I felt was relief that this man who treated me so badly was not related to me. It was a very unhappy marriage – a horrible environment to be in. There were fights all the time and even though my mother went on to have three more children it was inevitable the marriage would break down. It did when I was in my teens which forced me into the position of being the "man of the house" and meant I had to take on responsibilities and help out till the younger ones were grown up.

'I think Mum told me about my father partly to make me feel a bit better, but also to prepare me for remarks, like Yankee b—, flying in my direction. We were still living in the same area as when I was born, so there were no secrets. Everyone knew who my father was, and they'd let me know it in their own way.

'As the months and years went by I gradually found out more about my father by asking questions, the way children do. The problem was – I discovered much later – that my mother's story was a very romanticized version of reality. For instance she told me he was a daredevil pilot when he was an aircraft-maintenance man. She made him into a war hero.

'I suppose you can't blame her for fantasizing a bit when you think what the reality of her life was like later – or even before. She was 21 – my father, Brett was a year younger – and already had a failed teenage marriage behind her when she met him. She never told him that she was pregnant. I think she felt there could have been no future for them, his home being so far away and her still officially married. She probably viewed the affair as something like a summer romance that would run its course and end. Only this ended with the problem of a baby to look after.

'The biggest fib though was that my father had been killed in the war. She told me she had been informed of this by the authorities and she let everyone in the neighbourhood believe it too. I suppose it was a neat way of tying up the story, and it saved face with the neighbours. There would be no questions about why he hadn't stood by her.

'I grew up completely accepting he was dead. It wasn't something I thought of questioning until I met Sue, who became my wife. She was always quite nosey and she'd say things like, "But how does your Mum know? How can you be sure he's dead? Wouldn't it be lovely if he wasn't and you could find him?"

'I used to say, "Don't be silly." But as it turned out she was right.'

Kay Kay found out that 'the man I'd always known as Dad was not my father' in the worst possible way.

'It came out in a family row when I was 16. It certainly stopped the row. It was very strange. There was no follow-up, no explanation, just the bald fact left hanging in the air.

'I didn't know what to think. If this was something my mother had invented just to get at me in the heat of the moment, surely she'd tell me when she calmed down. And she didn't. I remember telling my Gran and she said, "Oh, take no notice. Your mother made a mistake."

'When nobody spoke about it again I just knew I had to find out the truth. I went to the Register Office and asked for my birth certificate. They looked up some records and then I was taken into a room and told to sit down. An older man who looked quite important was fetched. He asked if I knew that the name on my birth certificate was different from the name I was now called by.

'I said I'd wondered if it might be. They were very kind to me, these strangers, but I felt so upset. All my life I'd thought of myself as a certain person and now I was being told that person didn't exist. I felt as if I didn't exist.'

Maria Like Kay, Maria from Evesham in Worcestershire found her life turned upside down as the result of a few angry words in a family quarrel.

Maria, an artist, grew up in a family she believed consisted of her parents, her two older brothers and her sister, Eileen. She was the youngest child by ten years and much as she loved them, always regretted that her parents were so much older, and consequently more old-fashioned than her friends' parents. By the time she was 16 and attending art college, her brothers and sister had married and left home.

One day when the younger brother was visiting an argument developed – 'just the meaningless sort of squabble brothers and sisters go in for. I adored him but we didn't always see eye to eye. At one point when he was laying down the law, I said something like, "Who the hell do you think you are anyway?"

'And he replied, "I'm your uncle, that's who."

'There was a moment of total silence and then his wife started to say, over and over, "Oh, my God, oh, my God . . ." I couldn't understand what was going on and I suppose my mother, who was also in the room, must have decided she'd have to come clean.' The truth was that Maria was the child of her 'sister' Eileen, and a GI named Tom. Her 'brothers' were her uncles and the couple who had brought her up, her grandparents.

'It is impossible to explain the shock of finding out that everything in your life has been a lie,' she says. 'What upset me most was that everybody – family, friends, neighbours – knew the truth. Everyone, that is, except me. I felt bitter and angry about being deceived by so many people. It was such a bad age to find out. If they had picked the right moment and told me at 7 or 8 years old, I'd have accepted it, but at 16 you are so emotionally unstable anyway. I immediately saw myself as an unwanted baby, dumped on my grandparents who had no choice but to put up with me.

'I did go to see my real mother who was married with a family. My memories of what we said are hazy. She was very angry that my brother had blurted it out, but really the responsibility to tell me was hers. She was as much to blame. I was really very disturbed. I packed my bags and left home. I got myself a job in a holiday camp on the south coast.

'I used to phone home and my grandmother would cry and plead with me to come back, and eventually I did. I still thought of her as Mum of course. The same with my grandfather; he was Dad. I loved them as parents. I loved my mother too, but in a different way – like an older sister, I suppose.

'We were never really close and when I decided I wanted to know more about my father and maybe try to find him, it was very difficult to talk to her. It was never the right moment. Her husband and children were always around, and she made it clear, without having to say so, that it was the last subject in the world she wanted to talk about.'

The hesitancy some of us feel about approaching our mothers for information or an explanation astounds people who have never been in this situation. They would have rushed in with a list of questions at the first sign of intrigue, they insist. But it just isn't that easy.

If you find something out as a child it's probably because you've overheard a conversation not meant for you, poked your nose into private papers or, like me, opened a sealed enveloped addressed to someone else. Voicing your suspicions is a confession to wrongdoing and likely to land you in hot water. You are the guilty one, not the parent keeping the secret. It's also very frightening to find out something that turns your image of yourself and your family on its head. To probe deeper threatens chaos. Better hang on to what you know for sure and shove the troublesome skeleton back in the cupboard. If you ignore it perhaps it will go away.

Those are the problems for children who don't have the power, anyway, to demand explanations, but what about those who find out or start to have their suspicions as adults and still hesitate to ask? Sometimes, but not always, they are people who do not have a very close relationship with their mother. Discussing a sexual relationship with a son or daughter, even after the event, is not something that many mothers feel happy about. And these were not relationships with a happy ending. Some mothers give out such strong vibes about their reluctance to recall the past that it seems cruel to try and force them. Some people prefer to suffer themselves rather than risk distressing their mother.

Take John G, for instance, a businessman from Lincolnshire. He only found out when he was about to apply for a passport and needed his birth certificate. His mother warned John's wife that he would find a different name on the birth certificate from the one he'd grown up with. Did he go round to his mother for further information? Not for years – 'I was very busy getting my business off the ground.' Not in fact till he'd had a nervous breakdown. 'I was under stress anyway and I think the business with the birth certificate and wondering about my father pushed me over the edge.' Even then he had to 'pluck up the courage' to talk to his mother about the past.

The reluctance might be something to do with British reserve. Carol, now happily reunited with her father, found out about her background by reading some private papers of her mother's when she was 15. It was clear from these that the man she had believed to be her father and who no longer lived with them, had belatedly (seven years and two children after the event) divorced her mother for adultery with Carol's American GI father. She never mentioned what she knew to her mother.

'I didn't feel I could ask my Mum questions about such a personal subject – but a strange situation arose. She seemed to assume that somehow I knew the whole story, though nobody had told me and she never spoke about it. It was only ever mentioned obliquely to other people, never directly to me.' Carol was over 40 before hearing about my search prompted her to question her mother. Now that she's met them she says she can't imagine any of her American relatives ever being that inhibited.

John C

It took John C more than twenty years to get round to discussing the past with his mother, but then John's situation is different from most. He grew up in a children's home, knowing neither his mother nor his father. It was obvious that he was of mixed race but he didn't spend much time agonizing over his roots. He was too busy surviving, he says. And survive he did. Now divorced and bringing up his two children, John is a designer of computer systems and a labour councillor in Hull.

It wasn't until he was 18 and about to leave the home that he was given his birth certificate and saw, for the first time, his mother's name and address at the time she'd placed him in care. She had lived in a village near Sheffield, and John says it was curiosity that drove him to call at the house that had been her home. His first attempt ended at the garden gate when he lost his nerve. Five years later he went back, knocked on the door and found an aunt, his mother's sister, still living there and delighted when he introduced himself. His aunt took him to see his mother, now married with a large family.

'At first she seemed pleased to see me,' he recalls, 'but when I was leaving she said, "I don't want to see you any more, John." Apparently I was the image of my father, even around the same age, and it brought back too many sad memories. I was disappointed but not heart-broken and I accepted her decision. She was, after all, a stranger and if I'm honest, she was not the sort of mother I'd hoped to find. The house was a bit scruffy and I suppose with a houseful of kids to look after, so was she. I was very thoughtless and judgemental then.'

It was twenty years before they met again, but John kept in touch with his aunt and with the half-sister he'd met while visiting his mother.

Organizing anniversary celebrations for the Home where he grew up, he discovered that he was entitled to his records from the time he was placed in care, aged 6 weeks. In these forty-year-old papers he found the name of his father, Jack, and the fact that he had been a 24-year-old American. Through unofficial channels (chatting to the older locals around the area where he was born) and official ones (the American Embassy), he discovered that his father had been a member of the US 8th Army Air Force, based in Wrothley. Like most of us fed a little information, John became completely hooked.

'I found I really wanted to know all about this young man. I was surprised how involved I became. It was like a detective story but the one person with all the clues, my mother, didn't want to know.' While he was in the area he called to see his aunt. 'And who should be sitting in her front room, having a cup of tea, but my Mum! I thought she'd run off immediately, but her attitude seemed to have changed over the years and she was willing to talk to me. She's a widow now – maybe that made a difference.

'I told her I wanted to find my father and she agreed to help. That was less than two months ago. We are slowly starting to build up a relationship and I've come to think of her and care for her as my mother for the first time. Each time I see her she tells me a little more about my father and my birth and the dreadful time when she had to give me up. She says she sat up all the night before, holding my little hand and crying, but there was no other way. She was only 18 and her father insisted.

'Talking about the past is painful for my mother. She and my father were in love. He knew she was pregnant and they talked about her going to join him in America when she was 21, but they both realized it wouldn't work with the attitude to mixed marriages.'

At the time of writing John has only recently embarked on the search for his father. 'I'd never given him much thought till I learned a little bit about him and suddenly he became a real person to me. Hearing my mother's story has made me want to know his side of it. It must have been hard for him leaving her here, knowing what she'd have to go through.

'I feel no resentment towards him or my mother. They were both young people in a situation they couldn't control. I'd love to meet him and bring him back to Yorkshire to see my mother and the places they knew together. If a father-son relationship developed that would be a bonus, but basically I want to meet him and tell him that I understand what it was like for him.'

Marilyn Marilyn from Birmingham was the first person to contact me when the story of my search first appeared in a local paper. Poor Marilyn! I listened as she poured out her story and thought she must be mad. Who was this woman claiming to be in the same position as me and what was her game? That there was another war babe living a few miles away took a while to sink in. When it did I was delighted. We each had someone to talk to who really understood. However sympathetic family and friends are, they can't put their hand on their heart and say, 'Yes, I know how you feel.'

Marilyn grew up the second child in a family of five. There was never a hint that the man she called Dad regarded her in a different light from her brother and three sisters. She fitted in in every way, even to looking 'the image of my mother. Only my unmanageable, gingery hair singled me out – nobody else in the family was lumbered with that.'

She remembers stumbling on her birth certificate when she was a child and thinking it odd that her father's name was not on it. When she started work in the nearby chocolate factory and needed the certificate, her mother found a shortened version with no space for details.

She married Keith when she was 20 and had two daughters. Her 'father' died in 1972 and soon after her mother had an operation and came to live with the family to recuperate.

Marilyn said: 'One night when I came in after the late shift at the factory, I could see she was a bit drunk. I made us some coffee and came in to sit with her, just the two of us. Out of the blue, she said: "I've got something to tell you."

'In that instant I remembered the birth certificate and I knew it was about my father. She told me that my real father, Glenn, was a GI she'd fallen in love with while "Dad" was away during the war. If I ever wanted to see a photograph of him, she said, she'd left one, and some letters, with my aunt.

'I was very shocked. My first reaction was to be angry because nobody had told me. A lot of the family knew, including my older brother, who'd been a toddler when my mother and father met. Next I thought about my stepfather. My wedding day flashed before my eyes – the way he'd proudly walked me down the aisle – and I remembered what a good grandfather he'd been to the two girls. And all the time he knew I wasn't his. I just felt sorry I'd never have the chance to thank him.

'My mother and I never spoke about the matter again, strange though it may sound. The next day she was withdrawn and uncommunicative and it didn't seem the time to bring it up. It never did seem the right time. She died not long after.'

At a family get-together shortly before her mother's death, Marilyn's uncle, the man who had brought her father home and introduced him to her mother, asked if she'd like to have a talk with him about her father. 'But I was still in the denial stage and refused,' Marilyn recalled. Soon after, her uncle died, leaving only one close family member of that generation, her aunt, who didn't want to talk about an incident that had caused a great deal of family trouble.

Marilyn didn't admit to herself that she wanted to talk about it either for two years – 'during which time it preyed on my mind and I suffered a bad bout of depression. Finally I asked my husband if he'd fetch the photograph and the letters – one to her, one to my uncle – that Mum had left with my aunt. As I looked at the writing paper, fragile with age, I was terrified of what I might find.'

In fact she found a love letter from a warm, caring man, who knew all about her and wanted her mother to get a divorce and marry him. What she'd feared had been a sordid affair turned out to be a touching love story with a sad ending. The pleasant-looking man in the colour photograph had unmanageable, gingery hair!

We searched America for Marilyn's father, Glenn, of Wilmington and Ashtabula, but sadly he has remained elusive. Marilyn says: 'I can't say I was looking for a father-figure, it was more that my life was like a jigsaw with a piece missing which I wanted to find. After several years of being obsessed with trying to trace him, and the disappointment of once believing I'd found him only to be let down, I've given up. I've stopped searching but of course I haven't stopped hoping. I still dream of getting a call from a man who says, "Hi, Marilyn, this is your Dad." We can all dream.'

<u>Mick</u> Wolverhampton social worker, Mick, still lives in the terraced house from which his father used to pick up his mother in his jeep in 1944. His mother never married but continued to live in her parents' home and brought him up single-handed. Later Mick and his wife, Sheila, and son, Derek, lived with her but despite this physical proximity mother and son spoke very little about George, the young GI with whom she'd had a short, wartime romance.

It was only after his mother's death in 1989 that Mick found out more than the basic facts about his father. As a young child he believed he'd been killed in the war. 'I didn't ask questions. I suppose I assumed he was English. When I was around 12 or 13, we were watching a programme about America on the television and my mother told me that my father was American. It was quite deliberate as if she'd been waiting for the opportunity. I quite liked the idea. It made me a bit special in some way. I still assumed, because she hadn't told me otherwise, that he was dead.

'It wasn't until a few years later that I worked it all out. I asked my mother if my father had been killed and she said, "No, he's alive." She was quite embarrassed about it by then and not very forthcoming.

'I didn't press her but I remember thinking, "That makes me a bastard." It's not the sort of thing you tell people – or wasn't then – and I kept up the pretence at school that my father had died in the war. My mother and I didn't talk about the subject in any depth again. As I got older I think she became more embarrassed about it. She also became more guilty, blaming herself for having made a mess of her life and for having to bring me up in a certain amount of poverty as a latchkey child because she needed to work.

'She worked for a small company as a sort of clerk/housekeeper. I've been told that she was an office manager and a very confident woman prior to my birth. The stigma and shame of having an illegitimate child and the poverty and social problems of single parenthood (she told me she'd chosen not to marry because of her responsibility to me) made her feel inferior and beholden to people. She was always saying, "Don't do that, what will people think?", which used to make me very angry as an adolescent.'

Like many of us, Mick thought, on and off, throughout his life about the possibility of finding his father. 'But I had neither the money nor the knowledge to do it. Maybe there was something more too. Something held me back while my mother was alive. As she got older I felt she would have liked to talk about him and so would I, but neither of us made the move. By that time we weren't very close. Not that we didn't get on or I didn't care about her, but there was a barrier between us when it came to emotional things. I kept putting off talking about it until it was too late, something I now deeply regret.

'I always knew that I'd try to find my father one day and knowing me, my mother knew that too. She talked to Sheila quite a bit. She told her that she had letters from him and from his sister, written between 1944 and 1946, and that she was keeping them for me to read.

'The first thing I did, the very day after she died, was to get the letters down. It was a very emotional experience reading them. Suddenly George was not just a name but a real human being. I discovered that he'd been sent from England to France without knowing my mother was expecting me. He'd had a very rough time in the war and was hospitalized and sent back to America. When he knew about me he wanted my mother to go to America and marry him, but she didn't. She might have told me the reason if I'd asked, but now I'll never know. By 1946 he'd married someone else. The last letter is one from my father's sister telling my mother about the wedding. How did she feel then? Something else I'll never know.

'I went through the letters carefully, systematically noting down everything they told me about my father – date of birth, regiment, where he'd served, etc. Immediately after the funeral, I drove over to the big reference library in Birmingham and started my research.

'I went through the telephone directory for Boston to find all those who shared my father's surname and got a map of the city to look up where he had lived. It was very exciting, like being a detective. I've no doubt that it was also part of my mechanism for coping with the grief.

'In the library I also met an assistant who gave me the name of a certain Shirley McGlade – someone she thought might be able to help me!'

6
Starting to Search

One morning in 1972 I opened a copy of a daily newspaper and found myself looking at a spread on American film stars and where they came from. I glanced over it casually – my passion for the cinema had faded – and my eye landed on one name: Lana Turner – born Boise, Idaho, it said. The place meant nothing to me, but what was it Mum had said? 'Your father grew up in the same town as Lana Turner.' She hadn't remembered the name of the town and it had registered in my mind only as another tiny nugget of data on my father to add to my small store. For some reason it had never occurred to me that the information could be put to a practical purpose, but now, courtesy of the British press, I'd accidentally stumbled on my father's home town.

Barry, Martin and I were living with Mum and my half-sister, Pat, in a suburb of Birmingham at the time, and my first task was to check with Mum that my father had really told her what she claimed about the actress and their common home town. I didn't want to appear suspicious but I'd been told so many lies, however white they seemed to my mother.

Mum was indignant. Of course she was telling the truth and she saw no reason to imagine Jack Crowley had made it up either. After all, he wasn't boasting that he was the star's best friend. He hadn't even claimed to know her. It was incredibly exciting; the first clue I'd had since discovering that my father could, possibly, be alive. That newspaper article rekindled the urge to find him which had been dampened down by the trials of everyday life. It also led me up a blind alley and delayed the search by years. How was I to know the papers had got it wrong? Those were the days before I had any personal contact with the media, when I believed everything I read in newsprint. Soon after, I made the first of my trips to Birmingham Reference Library, which would become almost a second home a decade later. I wanted to find out a bit about Boise and the address of its town hall.

What did I expect when I sent off my urgent letter to the town hall? At the very least, I suppose, confirmation that my father had lived there and clues to where he might be now; at best, his present address. I was blessed with optimism in those days. The polite reply stated simply that they had no records of a Jack Crowley ever having been born in Boise. I greeted this letter with tears of disappointment and disbelief. Had I foreseen how many similar disappointments and rejections I'd get before actually finding the man I'd probably have given up there and then. As it happened, I wasn't totally disheartened once I'd got over the shock. Maybe my father hadn't actually been born in Boise but had moved there as a child. It should still be possible to trace him if I knew how.

I decided I'd contact the American Embassy. Surely they, of all people, would know whom I should approach. I had rung the place once before, immediately after Mum had admitted that my Dad hadn't died in the D-Day landings after all. But I'd been in a public phone box – we didn't have a telephone of our own – and I'd been confused, emotional and uncertain of the facts. It was obvious I was getting nowhere and I'd put the phone down in frustration. Now, though, I had a useful bit of information to go on and I felt more confident.

The chap I spoke to was pleasant and helpful. He advised writing to the Pentagon. Of course, I thought, go right to the top. If anyone could help me trace my father, that was the place. The letter went off. Weeks passed; weeks of slowly diminishing hope, as I checked the post eagerly every morning for a letter bearing a US stamp. It never came. The Pentagon obviously had other fish to fry. The disappointment turned to stubbornness. I wasn't going to be defeated this easily.

Back I went to the American Embassy. The nice man was as sympathetic and helpful as ever. He gave me the addresses of another couple of governmental departments in the States that I could try. This time my request for information and advice elicited a response, though not quite the one I'd hoped for. I received a couple of very official-looking forms, packed tight with questions: what was my father's date of birth, his social security number, his service number? Was he now married, and if so what was the name of his wife and his wife's parents? It must have been obvious that if I had the information they were asking for, I wouldn't have needed their help. I'd probably have been able to find my father myself.

I didn't know whether to laugh or cry but in the end it was anger that was my main emotion. How dare these faceless civil servants treat me like this? I imagined them in their skyscraper offices, reading my letter and seeing not the human being behind it but an irritating little problem to get out of the way. Send her these forms – that'll shut her up. She'll never be able to get the information we are asking for. We won't be hearing from her again.

They were right of course – at least for a while. I did try filling in what small amount of information I had and leaving the questions I couldn't answer, but the forms just came back marked 'insufficient information', which made me more angry than ever. I didn't exactly give up but I didn't get anywhere useful either. At intervals over the years that followed I would telephone the American Embassy to see if they'd had any new brainwaves. Unfailingly polite, they passed me from department to department, from person to person, like the proverbial buck. I suspect now they'd had other queries like mine and didn't quite know what to do with us. The policy seemed to be to fob you off, shift you on to some other agency as quickly as possible – anything to get you off their backs.

My certainty that I was going to find my father had been shaken. I was beginning to realize what I was dealing with – the US bureaucracy, solid as a brick wall against troublesome individuals like me. Some kind American at the Embassy wasn't going to take pity on me and go out of his way to help me find my Dad. Just the opposite. As a young girl the neighbours had treated me like someone from another planet because my father was American. Now the Americans didn't want to know me either. I was an alien on both sides of the Atlantic. At least that's how I felt on the bad days. There seemed no point in bothering.

It seems incredible, now I'm a battle-scarred veteran, that I almost gave up after such a small fight. But I didn't have the confidence, the knowledge or the sheer bloody-mindedness then to take on the bureaucrats, let alone the American government. I hadn't built up enough of a head of steam about my rights to do anything very effective. It wasn't till I saw how other people in the same position were being treated that I got angry and stubborn enough to refuse to take no for an answer. It's easier to fight for a cause and for other people than for yourself. It's not quite British, somehow, to make such a fuss about your own needs.

Yet if there was a time, outside of childhood, when I needed a father around, it was during those years. I left my home and my husband briefly and went back to Mum. My marriage almost split up. A lot of the time I was unsure of what I wanted myself, being pulled this way and that by the needs of others. I badly needed someone around who could be honest, unselfish and strong, but with my interests always at heart; just the sort of person I imagined my father would be.

For a while I thought that what I wanted was my freedom, the chance to enjoy the carefree single life I'd missed out on. I'd gone from childhood to marriage and motherhood, without a breathing space. There had been no time for dancing and dating, for being young and foolish and proud of it.

But you can't turn back the clock. There was no way I could pretend to be fancy-free and 16 years old again, and I quickly discovered I didn't even want to. There was never a mention of divorce. After my childhood I could never have deprived Martin of the father he loved. Not that Barry would have let me cut him out of his son's life. While we were apart, he visited so often we saw nearly as much of him as when we were living together. Nor did I lose contact with Barry's family. They were always welcoming, wanting to see me as well as their grandson. Barry's father took me to one side. 'I know you never had a father, Shirley, but I'm your father now. If that lad of mine has been playing you up, tell me and I'll give him a clip around the ear.'

My mother certainly thought Barry had been 'playing me up' and was not hesitant about telling me. Whatever her motives – and I'm not sure she understood them herself – Mum played a big part in bringing about the separation. She disapproved of Barry spending so much time at the pub with his mates. I wasn't too keen on it either and it was hard to make allowances for the fact that he too had had to settle down at an age when most men have nothing more pressing on their minds than whose turn it is to get in the next round. We were always short of money and had very different ideas about dealing with the stuff. Barry thought you should save up patiently for what you wanted; I had a touch of the 'live now, pay later' philosophy and wanted at least the basics on hire purchase. I've come round to Barry's way of thinking over the years, but looking back, it was easier to take the high moral ground over whether we should have an automatic washing machine when you weren't the one struggling with piles of dirty laundry.

'You wouldn't be hard up if you came back to live with me,' Mum would say. 'You could go out to work. I'd look after Martin. You know how much I love having him. And Pat and I would baby-sit if you wanted to go out in the evening.' As the arguments with Barry increased, the offer became too tempting to resist and I moved into the new council house.

Maybe Mum really did believe I would be better off with her, but she had other, more selfish motives too. She was lonely. One child, my brother, Raymond, had flown the nest already. Pat was growing up fast. Even more than me, I suspect, she longed to turn back the clock; to be a mother at the centre of a family that needed her. What she was trying to recreate, I think, was the family life she had enjoyed in the days before Bert, when the family circle had consisted of grandmother, mother and dearly loved child. Despite the poverty, despite the stigma of having me, that had probably been the happiest time of her life.

Pat was an extra bonus, a lively teenager, but there was no room for a grown man in Mum's ideal family – and who can blame her after Bert? It may sound odd but she had nothing personal against Barry, nothing that wouldn't have applied to any man I'd married. In later years he got on well with her, better than me sometimes. Unlike me, Barry would never lose his temper at a cutting remark and he never bore a grudge. But at that time in her life she was creating her own little fantasy and Barry had no place in it.

There was probably another reason for Mum's determination to have Martin and me around. The agoraphobia that eventually left her housebound was just starting to show itself, though neither she nor I recognized the symptoms. Already she was developing a horror of being alone. She'd started looking after the little boy of a neighbour, less for the small income than for the reassurance of having even a small child around. Some days she would keep Pat away from school, and when I moved in with her, she would do the same with Martin, against my wishes.

I had no idea that these apparently irrational feelings had anything to do with a condition which I thought – if I thought about it at all – meant a fear of open spaces. The terrifying panic attacks when she stepped outside the door were some distance in the future, but at some stage while I was living with her, Mum became aware that there was something seriously wrong. When it had a label and she realized she wasn't the only person in the world with these fears, she told me how frightened she had been in those early days. 'I thought I was going mad,' she said. 'I was afraid to tell the doctor in case he had me locked up.'

We weren't apart long before I realized that, whatever our difficulties, I didn't want a life without Barry – and if there were pleasures for him in his enforced bachelorhood, they soon palled. We might not have been 100 per cent successful at being married, but we were total failures at being separated. Before long we were seeing so much of each other it seemed pointless to continue calling it a separation. I think all I really wanted was a break and a chance to check the grass wasn't greener on the other side of the kitchen sink. Now I was ready to go back home.

But it wasn't that easy. Seeing her every day it had become too obvious to ignore that Mum wasn't well. She was totally dependent on having me around and I couldn't bear to abandon her to her fears and anxieties. Nor did I want to abandon Pat. I knew what would happen if I were living elsewhere and only dropping in a couple of times a week. Mum would start to depend emotionally and practically on Pat, keeping her at home for company, and my poor little sister would be weighed down with responsibility well before her time. She was a young woman now. She should be out having a good time, doing all the things you never get a second go at if you miss them first time round – as I knew to my cost.

Good-humoured as ever about life's little ironies, Barry solved the problem. He moved in with us, with no complaints from Mum, by now well aware of her own difficulties. Once again we were living in cramped conditions, though nothing like as cramped as the house in Long Street, which had been pulled down with all its memories, good and bad.

Barry and I discussed the possibility of asking the council to rehouse us in a house big enough for two families. Despite everything he had no reservations as long as I was happy and knew what I was taking on. Mum could improve but she could also get much worse and I was the one who would have to look after her.

In 1975, after a series of battles with the council's housing department, that were useful early training for different battles to come, we all moved into our house in Woodgate Valley. This is a large overspill estate on the south-west tip of Birmingham, a rare place not spoiled by the 1960s passion for grey tower blocks. If you take a short walk up the road, even now, you can find yourself in unspoiled countryside that might be a million miles from inner-city Birmingham.

I loved it. I'd take the dog for long tramps across the fields, as much for my pleasure as his. And sometimes, on a warm summer's day, I'd look up into the endless blue above, feeling strangely comforted and telling Snowy: 'See that sun up there? Somewhere, thousands of miles away, it's warming my Dad. And when he looks up, he sees the same sky as me. I don't know where he is, but we're part of the same universe.' Snowy didn't look at all interested, but who else could I tell? Any sane human being would have thought I was crazy. Or so I believed until I started to meet other crazy people who'd had the same experiences and spoken very similar words – usually to the dog, the cat or the budgie. We called ourselves the War Babes!

.

1984 was the year that changed my life, but there were no warning signals as I drifted towards my fortieth year. Our son, Martin, was grown up and virtually off our hands. To our regret, he'd remained an only child. It's a bit of a dirty trick for fate to play, plunging you into motherhood when you are still virtually a child and depriving you of any further chances when you're a grown woman. But that, as they say, is life, and I tend to believe it's mapped out for us by someone with an unfortunate sense of humour. The little accident that brought Martin into our world now seemed like my greatest stroke of luck. Otherwise maybe I'd have remained childless.

There had been no luck where my mother was concerned. Her agoraphobia had worsened, though at least now it had a name and she knew she was far from the only person suffering its uncomfortable symptoms. Eventually we got her into a day centre for people with similar problems, which gave me a breather, but persuading her on to the minibus for the centre some mornings was a major diplomatic exercise. She was okay once she got there but getting ready and going out to the vehicle parked outside the door was more than she wanted to cope with some days.

Before the place at the centre became available I'd had to give up secretarial work. Anything that took me out of the house was incompatible with Mum's condition. She wouldn't stay in the house alone and there weren't enough neighbours and friends with time on their hands to come in and sit with her, though she could be happy and talkative when she had company. There had been times when I'd had to take her to work with me and there are limits to how much of your domestic problems you can expect the boss to share. So I'd taken Hobson's choice and stayed home, doing some childminding and short-term fostering for the council. I liked having children around. They livened up the house.

As part of her therapy, Mum was supposed to try little outings on her own, but there always seemed to be a reason why she couldn't do it today and tomorrow would be a better day to start. Sometimes I got irritated and felt she wasn't trying, but when I saw her in one of her irrational but very real panic attacks, I couldn't feel anything but sympathy. She would come down to the shops with me. As long as she had my arm to hold on to, the attacks, the fear that she would not be able to breathe and would pass out, could be kept at bay.

'Whatever would your Dad say if he saw me now?' she'd ask me occasionally as she hobbled along. 'He'd never believe I was the lively girl he knew.' The fact that she wouldn't recognize him either never occurred to her. She had aged, but safely protected in her memory, Jack Crowley was still the dashing handsome soldier from 1945.

In the house there had to be someone with her always and she couldn't bear doors to be closed. 'Don't lock the bathroom door. Something might happen to you and I wouldn't be able to get in to help you,' she'd say, when she meant, 'Something might happen to me and I wouldn't be able to get in.' I could rely on at least one anxious visit per bath. Wherever I went she would follow, growing panic-stricken if I'd gone upstairs for a minute without her noticing and she imagined I'd left the house.

It was hard work but we got by. We'd even managed to start buying our house, though we were beginning to rattle about inside it a little now that Pat had married and Martin was out at his girlfriend's as often as he was home. Barry was still working as an electrician. He'd been made redundant from his old job, and in the interval before he found another we'd resurrected an old pipe dream of ours, the possibility of running a pub. Wouldn't it be nice, we mused, to be able to work together, our own bosses, making a good income, and having a non-stop social life into the bargain? Belligerent drunks, demanding owners and an eighteen-hour day didn't figure in our dream – but neither did me being struck down with a devastating illness and finding myself with a voluntary 'job' that threatened to take over my life. The idea might have died a natural death if Barry had settled well in his new job, but he didn't and we started looking seriously at the possibility of becoming tenants of a pub.

The first clues that 1984 was going to be a memorable year came in March via another newspaper article. This time it was in the *Sunday Mercury*, a long-established Midlands paper – a piece about American GIs who'd been stationed in the region coming over to celebrate the fortieth anniversary of D-Day. I read it several times, the familiar feeling of hope building up again. I told myself not to get excited. It was a million-to-one shot that my father would be booked on one of these tours, but I had to find out. If I could get hold of the name of the tour operators involved they would be able to tell me.

First thing Monday morning I rang the reporter who'd written the article and asked him for the tour operators' names. He must have been blessed with a good nose for a story because he clearly found it an intriguing request. Why did I want to know? Personal reasons, I told him, but he wasn't satisfied and kept probing. Eventually I was driven to explaining, prompted by encouraging questions from the other end of the line.

To my amazement he said it was a great story and he wanted to use it: 'You mean write about me?' I was astounded that anyone would be interested in reading about me and my background, and on second thoughts, I wasn't sure I wanted them to. I was certain Mum didn't. But it was only a local paper and I didn't have much choice. What the reporter was offering was a straight deal – I could have the name of the tour operators if he could use the story and a picture.

Oh, hell, what was there to lose, I thought. I said yes, put the phone down, took a deep breath and broke the news to Mum. To say she was against the idea was putting it mildly. For the rest of the week she was running around like a chicken with its head chopped off, wailing, 'Oh, my God, the neighbours! Everybody will know about us now. They'll cut us dead in the street. How could you do this to me our Shirley?'

She was right that it would be news to the neighbours. Out here, away from the confined, nosey neighbourliness of her youth, Mum was just another respectable widow, living with her daughter. Nobody paused to wonder whether that daughter had been respectably conceived all those years ago. It wasn't something I broadcast, but I certainly wasn't ashamed of it. I had half-forgotten how indelible my mother's brand of shame was. The sexual revolution, the women's movement, the changed attitude to women having babies outside marriage had all passed her by completely. That sort of behaviour might be all right for today's women but not for her. At the back of her mind, she could still hear the whispers echoing all the way from Long Street and the scorn about Yank's leftovers.

The following Sunday, there it was, on page three of the *Mercury*: an article and a big picture. I thought Mum would have a fit. 'Look what you've gone and done. Nobody knew our business, now it's all over the paper. We had such lovely neighbours, respectable people. What will they think of us now?'

To be honest it did seem as if I'd got a dud deal – a photograph which distorted my face and turned my nose into a bulbous blob, and I'd drawn a blank with the tour operators. My father's name was not on the list of Americans coming for the celebrations. As far as I was concerned, having 'our business' in the paper wasn't going to make a scrap of difference either way, apart from upsetting my poor mother. The story would be glanced at, thrown out and forgotten. Today's newspaper didn't even have the distinction of becoming tomorrow's fish-and-chips wrappings any more, but that was no consolation to Mum.

Our first trip to the shops after the article appeared was an ordeal for both of us. I had to nag Mum to get her out of the house at all, and she slunk down the road, her collar turned up, her eyes cast down, praying we would meet no one we knew. Given the chance, I'm sure she'd have preferred to go round the supermarket with a paper bag over her head. When the first person approached us with, 'I saw you in the paper . . .', I thought she was going to have one of her turns. But the woman went on, hardly pausing for breath, 'Fancy your Dad being an American, Shirley! Why ever didn't you say? What a lovely story, Lily, so romantic.'

It took a long time to buy a few groceries, interrupted as we were by a continuous round of questions and good wishes. 'What a lovely story. I hope you find your Dad' was the gist of it. There was no disapproval or criticism, only interest and surprise (though I have to say that these were women and I've had much less sympathetic reactions to my story from men old enough to have lived through the war years).

If I was surprised at the warmth, Mum was astounded. After the initial shock, she began to blossom. She'd answer the questions about how she met my

Dad and eventually she began to volunteer information. 'He was a lovely chap, a real gentleman. I know he'd want to meet Shirley if he knew about her.' It was probably the best thing that could have happened to her. For the first time in forty years, the layers of shame and guilt and embarrassment fell away and she was able to talk to people outside the family about that very important time in her life. The world didn't see it as a sordid little episode after all but as she herself had always felt it to be: a brief but unforgettable love story. You could see the relief on her face.

7
War Babes

That article, which I thought would have no effect on my life, started a ball rolling which hasn't stopped since. Immediately afterwards I had an extraordinary phone call from a woman I thought at first to be some sort of copycat freak. 'She's claiming her father is a GI just like mine and she's also been trying to find him,' I whispered to Barry, with a smile of disbelief, my hand across the mouthpiece. 'I supposed I'd better humour her.'

That was Marilyn, who only lived a few miles away. She was nervous and excited and probably a bit sceptical about my claims, since she'd never heard of anyone in the same boat either. But as we talked it became obvious that she was genuine. We circled warily for a while before welcoming each other with surprise and delight like long-lost sisters. It hit us immediately that if there were two of us there had to be more – 'Maybe a dozen or more,' Marilyn suggested. We talked of trying to find these other people and forming some sort of group.

By now two local television stations had picked up the story and contacted me. Both wanted me to appear on their evening news programme on the same night, at the same time. I said yes to the first, the BBC Midlands, so Central Television asked if they could send a reporter and camera team to the house and record a piece.

And that's how I came to be sitting on the living-room floor, beneath a battery of lights, a map of the United States spread out in front of me, pointing to my father's – supposed – home town. It was the first but not the last time there would be television people in the house, disrupting my life and moving my furniture around. I still couldn't see it leading to anything useful, apart from local notoriety, but Mum loved it once she'd extracted a promise that they wouldn't ask her anything or put her in front of the cameras. At least she wasn't at risk of being alone in the house.

In the period between the Central team leaving and the taxi arriving to take me to the BBC Pebble Mill studios, I had to get ready and, like every woman in such situations, I didn't have a thing to wear. In desperation I settled on a bright red dress and a friend lent me her black hair lacquer to colour in my hair at the temples where it was going grey.

I was in the studio for two hours before going on air and I was absolutely petrified. This was a live programme. What if I said something stupid or lost my powers of speech entirely? There was no way we could pause and start again. The few minutes on air were among the most terrifying of my life. If anybody had told me then that I'd soon, of necessity, become a regular broadcaster, on both sides of the Atlantic, I'd have laughed. As far as I was concerned this was a little interval of excitement in my otherwise quiet life and, shaking like a jelly in the television studio, I was beginning to wish it was over.

If nothing else, it amused the family. At home, Mum, Martin and half the neighbourhood had gathered around our television to catch the dual perform- ances. In the middle of which, Barry, who'd been out at work all day and unaware of the whole business, walked in expecting his evening meal, only to be told, 'Ssh . . . our Shirley's on the telly.'

They videoed my live performance so, unfortunately, I know what I looked like. There I sat, my face and dress identical shades of scarlet, one ear sprayed black where I'd nervously missed my aim with the lacquer aerosol – a giant tomato with blight. Nobody in the house had heard a word I'd said during the interview, they were too busy laughing. Except Barry, who saw beyond the farce to the wider implications and remembers thinking, with a sudden premonition, 'Oh, my God, what has she started here?'

The telephone began ringing that night and didn't stop for weeks. Shortly after the television programmes, several national newspapers picked up my story and ran interviews and articles of their own about my search for my father. Now the unremitting phone calls, followed by letters, were coming in from every part of Britain, all saying the same thing: 'My father was a GI too. Please help me find him.' Or occasionally it would be a mother, begging me to help her trace her wartime lover for her son's or daughter's sake. I didn't even have time to be astounded. Nobody in the house did. Nor was there time to cook, clean, eat, hold a conversation or go to the toilet. The moment you put the phone down after one long, often emotionally draining call, it rang again.

I didn't have the heart to take it off the hook, knowing that at the other end was someone desperate to talk to a kindred spirit about a situation they'd feared till now was unique. It was a good job that the neighbours knew our story. It was only by having volunteers to man the phone occasionally that I ever grabbed a bite to eat. Even Mum, who a few weeks before would rather have died than discuss her dark secret, could be heard exchanging stories with these strangers who soon seemed like old friends.

I laughed with Marilyn about our estimate of a dozen like ourselves. I was now sure there were thousands – all of them trying to reach my number, all convinced, thanks to the power of publicity, that I was the one who would guide them to their fathers. Overnight it seemed, I'd become an expert, a saviour even. No use protesting that I was as ignorant as they. 'We must start a group,' people were saying, and I agreed till it became clear that what they meant was *I* must start a group. I'd been elected spokesperson and group-leader without ever volunteering for the job, when all I'd ever wanted was to find my own, elusive father.

I've tried to work out, many times since, exactly how I became the high-profile leader of a pressure group and, quite honestly, it was by accident. I just stood there and the whole thing grew around me. I was – still am, to my way of thinking – a very ordinary housewife who happened to be in the right place at the right time. I could, of course, have turned my back on the pleas for help. There were times, I'm sure, when the American military establishment wished I had. But if that had happened, there would have been another Shirley McGlade, someone else along to do what I've done. It had to happen. It was an idea whose time had come.

I never actually thought of us as a group, with a title, but a newspaper called us the War Babes and the name stuck. It seemed suitable; we were still fighting a war of kinds. It's since been pointed out to me that in America 'babes' has different connotations but it's established now and we couldn't change it if we wanted to. The only time it caused me embarrassment here was when a group of us were appearing on a television programme. We were waiting in a public room to be called for the show and a young production assistant appeared and announced loudly, 'Will the War Babes come this way, please?' You could see people's eyes adjusting to knee level as they looked around for these tots who were going to follow her. And their amazement when a crowd of middle-aged men and women stood up and lumbered, rather shamefacedly, after her.

You'd have to have had a heart of stone to listen to the stories I was hearing and not have plunged right in and tried to help. I think it was the mothers who touched me most. They'd say: 'My daughter doesn't know I'm ringing. I don't want to get her hopes up, but she wants so badly to find her father and I'd love to be able to give her his address.' Or there might be an elderly lady with a note of desperation in her voice.

'Every time there's a programme on the war, my son has me sitting in front of the television in the hope that I'll spot his father in one of the old newsreel shots.' With the D-Day anniversary celebrations coming up, there were a lot of old clips of wartime events, all in black and white, so grainy you wouldn't have recognized your best friend on it.

The mothers would always tell me that theirs was a true love story and I'd say, 'Don't worry, I know.' I'd never believed the relationships between American servicemen and British women were a joke, or the attitude that the girls who got involved with the GIs were the kind who would do anything for a pair of nylons. In those days it was the good girls who ended up holding the baby. The others were smart enough not to get caught or knew how to get rid of it if they were. I've always had respect and sympathy for the mothers and those phone calls confirmed I was right. When I talk to War Babes who were adopted, I tell them not to condemn their mothers for giving them up. Life was a lot different then. Welfare benefits were few and hard to get. As my mother always said, either you worked or you starved. If you were a young girl with an illegitimate baby and your parents said you must have it adopted, you had no choice. Without my Nan, my Mum would not have been able to keep me.

And then there were the war babes themselves. Sharing feelings and experiences with those other sons and daughters (mostly daughters – far more women than men have contacted me) of GIs was amazing after a lifetime of isolation. We talked about the need to know who we were and of the hope of finding a real father out there who cared about us and approved of us. With some you felt instantly close. It was more like rediscovering an old friend than meeting someone new. You could tell each other the unvarnished truth, without holding back for fear of being thought foolish or slightly nutty. Your family and friends try their hardest to understand but they can't empathize the way someone who has been through the same experience can.

I was talking to people who'd tell me, 'I sometimes think I'm crazy,' and out would come a story that varied only in detail from me talking to the dog and imagining my father sharing the same sky. Or they'd tell of weeping and praying like a small child: 'Please God, help me find my Dad.'

'Don't worry,' I'd say, 'that's normal. Or if it's not, quite a few of us are off our heads!' I could talk – and laugh – about my obsession with Stratford-upon-Avon. Barry must have been heartily sick of the place. Every sunny weekend, I'd suggest, casually, that we drive the thirty or so miles out there.

'Again?' he'd say. 'Wouldn't you like to go somewhere else for a change?' Of course I didn't want to go anywhere else. It wasn't Shakespeare that was the attraction, nor the timbered buildings, and the swans on the Avon didn't rate a glance. I went to see the American tourists who flocked there in the summer. Or rather, I went to hear them. I loved American accents – still do – whether they are from the North, South, East coast or West. To me these voices from so far away were a thread connecting me to my father. To Barry's embarrassment I'd follow people around the town and into souvenir shops, pretending to examine the pottery and postcards as I drank in every word, phrase, nuance of speech. There was always the possibility that one of them might know my father, might even be my father, though even to me that was pushing coincidence too far. I never approached or tried to speak to any of them – for which Barry was no doubt grateful. Just to hear their voices was enough.

Obsessed? Certainly. Crazy? Probably. But now I was being introduced to several other outwardly sensible law-abiding middle-aged citizens who understood my craziness.

Of course, not everyone who rang was prone to bouts of such strange behaviour. Neither were they all lovable. Having a GI father is not an absolute guarantee of a sweet nature. There were the grumblers and the moaners and the ones who expected they only had to snap their fingers and that I – supported by my hordes of secretaries and researchers, no doubt – would instantly find their fathers. 'I gave you all the details six weeks ago, and I haven't heard back,' they'd say crossly.

'You and a couple of hundred others,' I'd say, trying to keep my temper and my head.

One of the funniest things was the image some of the callers seemed to have of me as the high-powered head of a business organization with, no doubt, lip gloss, shoulder pads and a power suit. 'Could I speak to Shirley McGlade, please?' a nervous caller would ask on the other end of the line.

'Speaking,' I'd answer and there would be a pause.

'You mean I'm through to Mrs McGlade? I didn't expect you to answer the phone yourself.' The more publicity I had the more calls of this kind came in. How I wished I could have lived up to their fantasy. The reality was me, in whatever clothes I managed to throw on in the morning before the phone started, racing around trying to run a home and be a half-way decent wife, mother and daughter, while this enormous new and exciting task was taking over my life.

The thought had crossed my mind of turning what I do into a business, charging a fair and honest fee to help people trace their fathers. Many people had suggested it. But somehow even the thought left a bad taste in my mouth. It would have been adding insult to injury. By the time they contacted me, most of these people had been ripped off and shoved around in various ways. I cared and I wanted them to know it. I couldn't possibly have asked for a fee for my time and attention.

After I'd had my first taste of publicity in the United States with an appearance on NBC television, the deluge of mail arriving from private detectives offering their services for exorbitant fees convinced me even further that I was right. My help had to remain voluntary. That way nobody could ever accuse me of being in this for any reason other than that I believed in what I was doing. Besides, businesses are complicated. They demand time and energy be put into such dreary activities as keeping accounts and satisfying the tax man; time I'd far rather spend being an agony aunt to the sad, or sharing the excitement when I phone someone and say, 'I think I've found your father.'

It wasn't easy to manage financially in those early days, though. In fact it's never been easy, but at the beginning there was absolutely nothing coming in and lots of letters and phone calls going out. In addition basic office supplies had to be bought. I'd cleared out the tiny spare bedroom and decided to use it as an office – though certainly not the sort of office my more impressionable callers were visualizing. Because I couldn't afford a typewriter, I wrote everything by hand, until I developed what I took to be writer's cramp (a mistaken diagnosis, but more of that later). Then I bowed to the inevitable and bought a typewriter from a neighbour's catalogue paying for it the only way I could, a small amount each week. Barry couldn't complain; this was even more of a necessity than a washing machine in the early days of our marriage.

Everything else had to be paid for out of what I could save from the housekeeping and what extra Barry could contribute. He tolerated this well but would have a little explosion now and then, and complain that I was neglecting my family for total strangers. Then I'd ease off for a little while, and try to stay away from the office and fuss around him, Martin and Mum a bit more (though if anyone was enjoying these new contacts, it was Mum). But I'd be hard to live with, twitchy, nervous and bad-tempered, suffering withdrawal symptoms from my War Babes. Before long, by unspoken agreement, I'd be back with them again, letting the dust pile up and forgetting about mealtimes.

Necessity toughened me up over money. I simply couldn't afford to be oversensitive about the subject. It occurred to me, reading the Sunday papers one day, that if journalists were willing to flash cheque books about for all sorts of unsavoury stories, the least they – or rather, their proprietors – could do was to make a donation to War Babes, by way of a small fee for any interview I did. From then on, I made it a rule: no donation, no story. It annoyed some journalists – particularly those on the posher publications who considered it an honour for you to feature on their glossy pages – but once I explained the situation, most could see my point.

When I fix up an interview for any of the War Babes I always ask for them to be paid. Sometimes this can make the difference between someone being able to afford to visit an elderly father quickly or having to save up for the trip, when, to be brutal, their father might not be around that long. Occasionally I can fix a straight swap, as I did for Len, who urgently wanted to see his 85-year-old father for the first time. The BBC, shooting a documentary, wanted to film someone meeting their father; Len couldn't afford a trip to the USA. I brought them together. Satisfaction all round.

The other skill I developed was scrounging. If anyone could get me envelopes, typing paper, pens, I'd ask them to. If they had access to a photocopier, I'd persuade them to do some copying for me. I made it clear to everyone, War Babes included, that unused postage stamps were always useful. Anything which could be useful in keeping the group off the rocks, I was willing to beg, borrow or steal. I had no shame. I'm sure people began to dread meeting me but I was getting together a useful little office. Common sense decreed that I would have to reverse the charge of telephone calls to people whose fathers I was tracing, and that when there was a charge for a certain piece of information – checking for a driver's licence, for instance – the person concerned would have to pay this small cost. But I'm proud that I've been able to continue as I started, running a voluntary service. It's lovely when you find a father sometimes and get a big bunch of flowers from a grateful son or daughter. I have occasionally thought that £10 in the kitty would be far more useful, but a sniff at the bouquet has banished the thought. There's limited pleasure in sniffing a tenner and it probably wouldn't last as long as the flowers.

When the calls started coming in, I had no idea how I was going to find anyone's father. I hadn't done too well with my own, after all. But then there were no experts on this subject. Most of us who'd tried had come up against the same stonewalling by the American military establishment. Someone had to have a go and it might as well be me. My head was swimming with people's life stories. The first thing I had to do was to get the information down on paper. I asked everyone who rang in to write, giving me all the details they had on their father and everything relevant on their mother and the relationship. I went out and bought a large ledger-sized notebook and allocated each person a number and a page for details. It wasn't long before I reached number 300.

What they knew about their father ranged from everything but his present address to nothing, not even his name. I couldn't hold out much hope for the latter category, but I kept them on my list in case when we became better known in America, some of the fathers might contact me and say, 'I'm looking for my child. Her mother's name was —'

A clear picture began to emerge, and what was most interesting was that, despite our superficial similarities, there was no typical war babe. They came from all backgrounds and all parts of Britain (additionally a few contacted me from Continental Europe). Some were black, most white; some had been adopted as babies, others grew up with just their mother; a few had been brought up by relatives but many grew up with a stepfather and step-siblings. A few had parents who had been married and somehow lost contact; other parents had been engaged. Some of the fathers had lived with the mothers at the time of the birth and afterwards; others had left Britain totally unaware they were about to become fathers. Some fathers had been welcomed by the mother's family; others rejected outright. Some fathers had maintained contact after returning to the States, others hadn't. In a number of cases, the father's family had written and exchanged photos. Some affairs had been brief, but many had been long – or as long as the movement of troops in wartime permits.

It was fascinating watching these jigsaws of other people's lives build up, like seeing history come to life. I also felt I was beginning to get organized. My secretarial training helped, but what kept me going was a fair bit of common sense, acquired over the years, and the determination of a British bulldog. People had often remarked that once I get my teeth into something, I won't let go. They didn't always mean it as a compliment – quite the opposite sometimes – but it was a trait that was to prove invaluable when the going got tough and the world seemed to be determined to keep us from our fathers.

But there was something else too that was keeping me going in the years ahead. I was angry. Sympathy and empathy can inspire you to great efforts, but red-hot anger is a wonderful fuel for the fighting spirit.

The object of my anger was, again, the American government. I discovered that many of the sons and daughters had, like me, written to the government departments suggested by the American Embassy. They had been sent the same forms to fill in, but unlike me, some of them had the information they were asked for. They knew their father's birth date and place of birth. They had his home address, though obviously it was out of date. A few had parents who had been married and could produce marriage certificates, plus birth certificates containing their father's service number. And still the bureaucrats were saying no, we can't help, we can't give you information even if your father is dead. 'Insufficient information' was still being given as a reason, though it was plainly untrue if they carried out a proper search. The other explanation centred on a fire in the 1970s which destroyed many records, including, invariably, those you were asking for. What they omitted to mention – and I didn't discover until later – was that they had alternative records, which could reveal the same information. The last-ditch excuse was the Privacy Act, which seemed to prevent them giving out any useful information . . . or so they said.

The unfairness of what I was hearing horrified me. Even if I'd been able to fill in every line on my forms, I'd have been building up my hopes for nothing. They would still have refused to help. I really hadn't, at that stage, given much thought to the Privacy Act or the Freedom of Information Act or any of the other laws that would become familiar to me in the years to come, but I recognized a mean deed when I saw one. I was not going to let the American government or the military establishment or whoever get away with this. If we couldn't find our fathers with their help then we'd find them without it.

Getting started was surprisingly straightforward in the end. I honestly believe that God doesn't send you a burden he doesn't think you can carry. I wouldn't have been able to cope with this one a few years earlier, but although it could have seemed like bad timing in view of the illness that was waiting in the wings for me, I was ready when it came. Things just seemed to slot into place. I investigated the resources of the central library and found they had most American telephone directories on microfilm. This was my first line of attack when I knew a man's home town. I would spend eye-straining hours in front of the microfiche writing down the addresses and phone number of everyone with the right surname and first name or initial. There might be six or sixty; it depended on the name. My heart sank every time I was faced with a Williams or, heaven help us, a Smith. All the possibilities would have to be written to and, as often as not, you drew a complete blank. If you were lucky, one of the people you'd contacted might be a relative. If you were very, very lucky, a reply might come back saying, 'Yes, I'm the man you are looking for.'

Sometimes, after hours at the microfiche my eyes grew so weary I stopped seeing straight. Regrettably I delayed one woman's meeting with her father simply by seeing only three figures of a house number when there were four. I'd had a tiring day. Sometimes a wrongly spelled surname caused the problem. I searched high and low for Maria's father with no success. It wasn't until she found the announcement of her parents' engagement in a wartime newspaper that we realized why. Her mother had accidentally changed just one letter in her ex-fiancé's name. Once that had been corrected it took only a quick rummage through the telephone book for Maria to locate her father.

Probably the quickest find I ever clocked up was Carol's father. She'd been carrying his name and address around with her for ages, convinced he'd have moved home long ago. She came to see me, prepared for a long haul. It took exactly as long as picking up the telephone and dialling International Enquiries.

He wasn't at the same address – he'd moved a few miles down the road – but his son still lived there. Carol left in a state of shock.

The telephone directory method had its uses but it could be fairly hit-or-miss. It was a boon to discover that with a name and a date of birth to go on most State Departments of Motor Vehicles would do a driver-licence check and release a home address if there was one. It was even more useful when I found friends and supporters in America, who could do it from their end more quickly and accurately than I could from England. There was also access to American electoral rolls, carrying names and addresses, as here, and City Directories, held in public libraries in many small American towns, could provide similar information.

I learned as I went along. Several of the people on my first list of members had made attempts to trace their fathers themselves and though they had failed, they had succeeded in gathering a valuable hoard of information which they passed on. 'If a man was in the Navy, you can try this . . .' someone would say and I'd jot it down or add it to the store of bits and pieces in my head. I was surprised at how much I'd picked up myself from my seemingly abortive conversations with Embassy staff, about the way the system worked, and then there were the historians and military experts who contacted me after bouts of publicity with advice on sources of information and books to read.

Of course some of the suggestions turned out to be duds. The newspaper which I'd been told would trace people if you applied as a group never even got back to us. The letters to the senators – one in each State – didn't advance our cause one jot. Those who replied quoted the Privacy Act, which they assured us prevented information on our fathers being released. George Bush, then Vice-President, wrote back insisting that I had already met with officials at the American Embassy where it had been explained to me that my information was insufficient and outdated. This simply hadn't happened. The Vice-President had confused me with someone else. But we were up and running, tracing fathers without the help of officialdom on either side of the Atlantic. It was a slow, arduous process which could have been made relatively quick and simple if the American government hadn't been so pig-headed, and there were lots of people I couldn't help. But it was a start.

People often ask me about the first person I ever traced, and yes, I do remember him, though the order starts to blur after that. Oddly, he wasn't even a father, but an ex-fiancé. One of the first people to contact me was a single, childless woman from the north of England. She too had a GI to trace and she wondered if I would help. I didn't see why not.

During the war, this woman had become engaged to an Italian-American. I'll call them Sally and Joe. They were very much in love and made the kind of dramatic pact wartimes tend to inspire: that if they were separated and didn't marry each other, neither of them would marry anyone else. Sadly they were separated. Joe was shipped out suddenly and Sally lost touch with him. She didn't have his address but knew the name of the small town he came from in New York State. She had tried to be sensible and put this wartime romance out of her head, and had, once, almost succeeded. She had got as far as arranging her wedding, but called it off at the last moment because she felt she could not walk down the aisle with another man after the promise she had made to Joe. The memory of that relationship had haunted Sally all her life, growing stronger, if anything, as the years passed. By the time she read about me, she was desperate to know what had happened to Joe and to make contact with him, whatever the outcome.

I tried, without success, to trace Joe in his old home town. He'd obviously moved on. The question was, where to? I sat down and thought about it and asked myself where would I have moved to if I were Joe. It was my first attempt at putting myself in the other person's shoes and using my intuition, a trick that's proved useful in my searching ever since. If I were to move from Birmingham, I decided, there was a good chance it would be to one of the towns nearby. Why should Joe be any different? I got in touch with Sally and suggested she get a map of Joe's state, draw a circle around his town and start looking him up in the telephone directories for the small towns inside the circle. She did – and found him. He hadn't moved far from home.

I'd love to be able to report that Joe too had remained single and that he and Sally rushed into each other's arms and lived happily ever after, but real life let me down there. Joe was happily married, his promise long forgotten. Sally was disappointed and honest enough to admit it, but she was also extremely relieved to know the truth and to hear at last what had become of him. She wrote to him and to his wife, who proved to be very understanding, and claims that she can now sleep at night, instead of tossing and turning, and going over a promise made in the heat of the moment so very long ago.

8
I Think I'm Your Daughter

There's an old saying that troubles come in threes, and though I hesitate to label War Babes as one of my troubles, it was capable of causing me some heartaches in 1984. Trouble number two came hot on its heels, heavily disguised as a treat. In June, when I was still fielding calls night and day from people trying to trace their fathers, Barry and I got an offer we couldn't refuse – the tenancy of a traditional old-fashioned pub in Birmingham's picturesque jewellery quarter. If I'd been honest I'd have admitted it was the right job at the wrong time. When we'd originally decided we wanted to run a pub, War Babes hadn't been thought of, and here it was threatening to become a full-time job if I let it.

Barry wanted us to have the pub. So did Martin, who was set to become one of our barmen, and my sister, Pat, who would be doing the cleaning. Even Mum was looking forward to lending a hand where and when she could, and the great advantage was that I would be able to work on the premises and still keep an eye on her. It was going to be the family business. Everyone was looking forward to it and there was no way I was prepared to be the wet blanket who lost us the opportunity because of my own selfish interests. Besides I'd never been afraid of hard work and I didn't doubt I had the energy to do both. I might have done too, if it hadn't been for trouble number three, waiting round the corner to pounce when I least suspected it.

Luckily we weren't planning to sell the house. Pat, her husband and their little girl, Ruth, were moving in, for a while at least. It would give them a chance to save up a deposit on a home of their own, and we'd have resident caretakers. We transferred our furniture to the living quarters above the pub and they moved theirs in.

We moved on a Thursday, and on Sunday morning I woke up in agony, my hands gnarled and twisted into claws. I didn't know what was wrong with me, but it was terrifying. I'd seen old ladies with hands like mine and never given a thought to the pain that went with it. In their case I knew what caused it; arthritis. But that was something only old people suffered from, wasn't it?

It wasn't quite out of the blue. There had been a few aches and pains, mostly in my right hand, over the past weeks. Writer's cramp, brought on by all the letters I had to write by hand, I'd assumed. The doctor had diagnosed a probable pulled muscle but suggested I have blood tests done 'just in case'. In case of what I wasn't sure, but most of the test results had come back and apparently I had nothing serious.

I couldn't do a stroke of work on Sunday – what use is a barmaid who can't pull pints? First thing Monday morning I phoned the doctor's to make an appointment, and discovered that I hadn't had the results of all the tests yet. There was one which had just come in and the doctor wanted to see me about it. We left Martin to open up while Barry drove me to the surgery – and that's when I was told that I had rheumatoid arthritis.

It didn't mean much to me at the time. I was almost relieved there was a name for the terrible pain in my hands and that they could be treated and restored, more or less, to normal. If I'd realized then that what I had was a progressive and painful disease that could leave you crippled I don't know how I'd have reacted. Taken to my bed? Abandoned War Babes? Given up the idea of the pub and asked Barry to take me home? The latter might not have been a bad thing in view of how it turned out, but I heard what I wanted to hear and left the surgery with hope. I'd been told that the arthritis could get worse, or that, because I was young, the disease might burn itself out quickly. And that's what I preferred to believe.

I was in constant pain, but running a pub is like being on the stage. Whatever you are doing five minutes before the doors open – even if you are in the middle of a murderous row with your husband – you go down there smiling like a pair of deliriously happy turtle doves. If you are in pain, you keep it to yourself. Nobody goes out to the pub to hear the landlord's wife crying. They come to be cheered up and if there's any crying to be done, the customer does it and you offer the shoulder and the hanky.

For nearly a year I managed to keep all the balls in the air – serving in the bar, doing the catering and still finding fathers, though not nearly as many as I'd have liked. If nothing else I deserved an Oscar for the public smile I kept in place. Towards the end of that time I was getting up and down the two rickety flights of stairs to our living quarters on my bottom, and down a floor to the toilet at night the same way. I was taking prescribed drugs, but not, I know now, ones strong enough to help much. Perhaps they wanted to see how my body would cope before putting me on anything stronger. I'm almost grateful now that I was allowed to experience the worst of the pain. It's stopped me grumbling about the constant everyday aches that are an inevitable part of the condition. I know it could be very much worse.

Finally, almost as an encore, I slipped three discs, probably as a result of the distorted way I'd been holding and moving my body to try and minimize the pain and keep going. I was now in total agony and unable to keep up any pretence. Barry had to carry me upstairs and to the toilet. The doctor came in and gave me the strongest pain-killers he could find, but explained that I would have to wait until Wednesday for an appointment at the Pain Clinic. That was Saturday and with the wonderful sense of timing that seems to run in our family, Mum got ill and started bringing up blood on Sunday. She was rushed to hospital, crying because she was worried about leaving me; while I lay on the settee crying because I couldn't look after her.

I was kept in hospital – a different hospital from Mum – on Wednesday, and poor Barry found himself the main player in a farce. He was trying to run a pub, while visiting two invalids in different places, doing their washing and bringing in all the things a bed-bound patient needs. Inevitably he got muddled and I ended up in Mum's very unsexy winceyette nighties. Goodness knows what she was wearing.

It wasn't going to work. Barry and I both knew it now. My arthritis wasn't going to burn itself out, magically, overnight. I'd got the short straw, the other alternative. I was going to get worse. And that's what has happened, but it has happened so gradually that I have had time to learn to cope with each new stage, and to come to terms, as much as you ever do, with something like this. I've had to accept that I have a disability now and that I will never be able to do the things I once took for granted. I've learned to take note of what my body is telling me and not to push it beyond its limits, because if I do it will pay me back with days or weeks of pain and immobility when I can't do anything at all. Back in 1985, in a hospital bed, all this philosophical stuff was the last thing on my mind. I just wanted them to get the pain under control and to get out of there fast.

Mum came out of hospital, still ill and with no definite diagnosis, and went to live with Pat and her family back in our house. When I was deemed ready I left too and went back to the pub, but not for long. 'That's it,' Barry said, 'dream over,' and handed in his notice. It was a sad day. It could have worked if I had my health, but now it was out of the question. I cried, not really because we were leaving, but because I'd had enough. All I wanted was to go home to my own dull, cosy little suburban house. Someone else could take the stage and charm the boozers of Brum.

We moved back in gratefully and for a while, until Pat and her husband found a place of their own, lived with two families and two sets of furniture crowded together. Even so, it was heaven. Walking carefully, in my new slow and rather sedate fashion, I made my way to my little box of an office. There were some colourful postcards from America to stick on the wall, sent by people who'd found fathers and gone over to meet them. There weren't many but I knew there would be plenty more. They gave the room a jaunty air and acted as a reminder of why I was sitting in there for hours on end, while the sun shone outside or the rest of the family were roaring with laughter at a telly sitcom downstairs.

The requests for help had piled up while I'd been away. Pat had forwarded messages and letters but I hadn't always been able to deal promptly with them. The fuss had not quietened down. Journalists still wanted to interview me. Each time someone found a father, their local media wanted a story, and every piece of publicity unearthed a whole new set of people whose fathers had been GIs, and who'd thought they were the only ones. I was finding fathers, and contrary to the gloom merchants on this side of the Atlantic, who said I'd wreck families, and the American government which was determined to protect these men's privacy, whether they wanted protection or not, the fathers were greeting their long-lost children with open arms.

Of course I was aware we were dealing with a sensitive area and so were all the war babes, though I made a point of emphasizing it to them in case their enthusiasm made them impulsive. People were strongly advised never to telephone out of the blue and say, 'Hi, Dad, this is your son/daughter,' or words to that effect! For a start Dad was an old man and the shock might not do him any good at all. And even if his heart was up to it, his nerves might not be and there was every chance he'd slam the phone down and refuse to discuss the matter further. At the very least you'd be getting off on the wrong foot.

Then there was the family to consider; a family possibly in total ignorance about your existence. He might not have told wife or family that he had a child. He might not, like my father, have had any idea himself. The person on the other end of the transatlantic line, answering to your father's name could very easily be a son with the same name. To have his father's past slung in his unsuspecting face in this manner could cause a major family rift, though most American half-brothers and half-sisters accept the news very well when it's delivered sensitively.

What applies to the telephone applies equally to the letter. I open the mail in our house and could well identify with the wife who casually slits open a letter addressed to her husband, to learn in the first line that he has a child in England she knew nothing about. Nobody with a grain of sense rushes headlong into an emotional minefield like this. You go in carefully, gradually, testing the ground before every step.

Early on, with finding my own father in mind, I'd worked out a plan. When making contact with my father – if I was ever lucky enough to find him – I was going to be a little economical with the truth. I would say – and this is what I did when I first telephoned him – that I was a younger member of a British family who had known him during the war, and just wanted to renew contact. That way I could check I'd actually got the right person and could choose my moment to announce the whole truth. I used the same cover story when approaching ordinary people who might be able to help with information that would lead me to my father – possible friends or relations or just people with the same name picked from the phone book. Aside from not incriminating him if these people happened to know him but nothing about me, the scheme also worked.

People have tried it both ways, so there are informal comparative studies, which show that if you write to someone, admitting you are trying to trace John Smith, who is your long-lost father, they simply don't want to be involved. But if you confess only to being a member of a family who knew him, they are happy to provide every bit of information they can muster. The same applies if you say you are an amateur genealogist, trying to trace American members of your family, or someone hoping to organize a reunion in your area of old wartime GI comrades. Both have been used as successful cover stories, though, personally, I feel happier sticking closer to the truth. Well, I *am* a younger member of a family who knew Jack Crowley during the war. I also made a point of writing back to people who had helped me, after I found him, and explaining the truth. They were invariably pleased for me. One couple said they'd guessed, because my supposedly casual letter hadn't hidden my real desperation to find this man.

Having made allowances for the shock our phone calls were going to cause to our fathers, what really astounded me were the number of men who seemed barely surprised. Some sounded as if they had been waiting for the call for forty-plus years, rendering subterfuge unnecessary. Take Paula, for instance, whose mother Helen's relationship with Ben I've already written about. Paula was one of the earliest people to contact me. Her mother, a miner's daughter, had always spoken warmly of the military policeman with whom she'd had a long relationship and expected to marry. The day before Paula had read a newspaper story about me and War Babes, she and her mother had been talking about how sad it was that her efforts to find him had come to nothing and there seemed to be no avenues left open to try.

'It seemed like an omen,' Paula told me on the phone from the Yorkshire village where she lives with her miner husband and three children. Paula was the unfortunate lady whose reunion my tired eyes set back two years when I misread a number on the microfilm of a telephone book. When I did find the correct number and phoned it through to her one Saturday afternoon, she responded with a familiar mix of excitement, disbelief and terror.

'I kept looking at this number,' she told me afterwards, 'and trying to believe that if I dialled it, it would put me in touch with my father. I couldn't quite believe it. It seemed impossible after all these years. My hands were shaking when I picked up the phone, and then, suddenly, there he was, as clear as if he was standing beside me.'

Paula had already written to a large number of people with the same surname as her father and was an old hand with the cover story. Having established he was the Ben who'd been stationed in Sheffield, she told him she was from an organization which traced GIs who'd been in England during the war, and that some people here wished to get in touch with him.

'I'd barely got out the words when he said, "Is one of these people Helen —?" (giving my mother's maiden name).

'I thought, I hope he hasn't got a weak heart, and said, "I'm Helen's daughter."

'"That makes you my daughter too," he said. I was speechless but so relieved. I'd been prepared for complicated cat-and-mouse games and breaking the news very gently.

'He was just delighted I'd made contact,' Paula said. 'He wanted to know all about my mother and the rest of the family. He'd known my mother nearly four years and knew them all. His wife had recently died and he was rather lonely. I don't think I could have come into his life at a better time. He said he'd wanted to find me for years but didn't know how to go about it and he was extremely annoyed when I told him how the American government had refused to give me his address.'

In fact, Ben was one of the men who gave an affidavit to support the War Babes' legal case when we were trying to force the US government to release more information on our fathers. In it, he says that he loved Paula's mother very much and wanted to keep in touch after the war, 'but due in part to her family's intervention we eventually lost touch'. He had often thought of his daughter, he adds, and wished that he knew where she was, but had no way of finding her. 'I was surprised to learn that the American government refuses to release addresses of American fathers to their overseas children. If I had known my daughter was trying to find me I would have wanted the government to give her the address, or at least to notify me of her enquiry. I do not consider her contacting me to be any kind of invasion of my privacy; on the contrary it has been a source of great joy.'

The joy was mutual. Paula, who could ill afford it, ran up a steep telephone bill making regular calls to her father. 'What else could I do? I had a lot of time to make up for. He spoke to my mother on the phone too. She was very happy I'd found him but we had to be careful not to hurt my stepfather's feelings by going on about him. Mum feels no bitterness about the past now, though it hurt her deeply when my father didn't come back for us after the war – something her family seems to have played a part in.'

In 1986 Paula went to visit her father, then 73 years old, in Baltimore. He'd last seen her as a tiny baby. 'We'd exchanged photographs, of course, but it's still not the same as seeing someone in the flesh. When I got off the plane I had to go through Immigration with half a dozen other people, so most of the crowd had dispersed when I walked into the reception area. I saw him instantly. He was small, Jewish-looking, with dark, olive skin. We looked nothing alike. The only thing I seemed to have inherited from him is his double chin – and he could have kept that!

'I had wondered if I'd feel awkward, but I felt completely at ease with him, and with his friends. He was retired of course, and not in the best of health, but he had a good life. Most days he met his cronies from the old days for a chat and a game of cards. His apartment block had a swimming pool and a sort of community centre where they met. His ex-daughter-in-law, his son's first wife, had remained close and she kept an eye on him.

'He showed me all the sights around town and introduced me to everybody. I'd link my arm into his when we went out. It felt good, completely natural and very satisfying to be together.'

By the time they met, Ben had become a gentle and rather fragile old man, but he'd had a colourful life. For years he'd been manager of a burlesque theatre, the equivalent of our better class strip club with glamorous dancing girls. He'd been in prison for tax evasion and was regularly fined when one or other of the girls in his show removed a garment too many. Far from being shocked, Paula was tickled to bits to have such a lovable rogue for a dad.

'He was larger than life, like a character out of the movies. He knew everybody who was anybody. There are pictures of him with all sorts of famous people. He was obviously very attractive to women and though he was only married once, had loads of affairs, including a couple with famous strippers. But he told me the relationship with my mother was different and that he had never cared for anyone as much as he had for her.'

Paula only managed to see her father once. He died without ever returning to England to see Helen and meet his grandchildren. Paula's half-brother – she has two – phoned to tell her the sad news. 'He'd gone to play cards with his friends and was suddenly taken ill. I knew he hadn't been in good health but it was still a shock. I'd hoped to see him again. It left a gap because he'd become part of my life in a short space of time, but at least I knew him for a while.'

There was one question she never asked him – what exactly had happened after the war to stop him coming back to Yorkshire for her and her mother. 'I wanted to know, but the last thing I wanted to do was to hassle him or make him feel guilty for something that occurred so long ago. I kept hoping the subject would come up naturally, but it never did. And then, suddenly, it was too late. But at least I know that he never stopped thinking about us.'

By the end of 1985 I'd traced a dozen fathers. It was very satisfying when you found someone but it was painfully slow going and there was no way round this while the American government refused to help. Having to work from such a distance complicated even the simplest investigation. I knew it would be very valuable to have helpers in the States who could check on the spot but I hadn't worked out how to locate such people. I presumed most people there felt, like their government seemed to, that we were a nuisance and an embarrassment, something unpleasant left over from the war. Some days I looked at the long list of names awaiting attention and felt completely disheartened.

'At the rate I'm going, our grandchildren will inherit this job,' I remarked to Barry.

'They'll be a bit late,' he replied. He was right, of course. Time was running out for these men, most in their late sixties and seventies. Finding them was a matter of urgency, which made the delays even more frustrating. Still there was no other way of looking at it. Twelve fathers found meant twelve happy men and women who'd found them. I envied them, for I was no nearer finding my own father and my hope of ever doing so was at its lowest ebb. When the publicity for War Babes first started, I'd had a letter from an American girl who was in this country trying to trace her English mother. She wasn't asking for help but offering information; the address of an American organization called the Adoptees Liberty Movement Association (ALMA). Adopted children in America do not have the right, as they do here, to information on their real parents when they reach adulthood, and ALMA was set up by an adopted woman, Florence Fisher, to offer support to others in the same position. Not unlike War Babes but on a much larger scale. By the time I became a member of the group, as an individual trying to trace my father, it was nationwide with branches in every State.

The most useful bit of help provided by ALMA is the Search Buddy. He or she is a volunteer based in the State in which you are searching, who will check every source of information for you. I was incredibly lucky – or so I thought at the time. My Search Buddy, Beverley, actually lived in Boise. She knew the town well and was very hopeful that she would locate Jack Crowley, or at least someone who knew where the family had moved to. I virtually held my breath while she began her search. This was it. Surely I couldn't get this close and fail to find him. Yes, I could! Beverley searched all the public records and asked a lot of private questions. She knew what she was doing. I was not the first person she'd helped by any means. In her own words she 'turned the town of Boise upside down' in her efforts to locate my father – and came up with a blank.

'No way,' she told me, 'does this man come from Boise. There must have been a mistake.'

It was the worst slap in the face I'd received so far, the end of all my hopes. There was no place to go from here. I couldn't understand it, and I began looking at poor Mum with renewed suspicion. Beverley had suggested there had been a mistake. Mum was the only one who could have made that mistake. Suppose there hadn't been a mistake but Mum had deliberately misled me? Wasn't it possible that my father had not been an American but an Englishman, and that she didn't want me to find him? She could have made up this whole elaborate story, complete with GI's name and State, to put me off the scent.

I put this theory to her once. Only once – the explosion of annoyance and distress that I should think such a thing made me feel so guilty I didn't take it any further. It was only an idea anyway, bred of desperation for an explanation. Mum had lied to me in the past about my father, but she'd always stuck by the basic details, and when I thought about it, she didn't have the imagination for such elaborate flights of fancy. So I tried to put all thoughts of my own father out of my mind and concentrate on other people's fathers. Perhaps this was what I was meant to do in life and my own Dad had only been a way into the life's work mapped out for me by fate. It was reassuring, but not reassuring enough. However I tried to rise above my own needs and petty feelings, I did feel cheated. I'd long ago learned that life is not necessarily fair, but somehow this seemed particularly unfair.

I think Barry believed that my personal search had ended and was rather relieved that he wouldn't have to live any longer with my 'ups', when I thought I was getting close to my father, and my 'downs' when I turned out to be wrong. I'd come up against brick walls before, but this one was so solid and so high that there seemed no way around it. My hopes of finding Jack Crowley had rested on the belief that he grew up in the same town as Lana Turner. If he wasn't from

Boise after all, he might be anywhere in the United States, the ultimate needle in the haystack. I had no other clues to pinpoint him. I couldn't see what I could do next, but at the same time I couldn't quite give up hope and by the end of 1985, this conflicting mixture of emotions was making me anxious and depressed.

In the end it was Barry, worried about me, who suggested the last-ditch all-out attempt to winkle more information out of Mum. 'I don't think she'd deliberately keep anything from us,' he said, 'but there's probably a lot of stuff tucked away at the back of her mind that's half-forgotten. Why don't we sit down with a pen and paper and ask her a few questions to get her talking? You know she'll go on for hours about the war and your father once she gets started. We'll make notes. You never know – something useful might emerge.'

It was worth a try and Mum was more than willing. She wouldn't pass up a chance to talk about the good old days with an audience hanging on to her every word. Barry insisted we go about the exercise properly, so we got books out of the library for research purposes, including one on American uniforms and badges. Maybe we could find out what my father's rank had been.

When Mum got to the bit about trying on Jack Crowley's jacket and the material being lovely and soft and the colour of our carpet, Barry came in with, 'Were there any badges on it?' A little badge with US on it, she thought, probably others. "What about his shoes? Did he wear boots or shoes?" Shoes, she thought; boots wouldn't have looked right.

'There were three stripes on the sleeve,' she said suddenly, 'and something under the stripes, but I don't know what.'

That was about the extent of the new information and it didn't look promising. We took a break to make a cup of tea. Barry was still sure there was more in her subconscious but the only way to get at it would be to have her hypnotized and regressed and neither of us fancied suggesting that to her at the moment! There's a limit to how much you can ask of an old lady, even your mother.

Mum talked on for hours more. 'Just let her ramble,' Barry had said and she certainly knew how to do that, but it was all stuff we'd heard many times before. It ended with the oft-repeated quote from Jack Crowley! 'I came from the same town as Lana Turner but I don't have to tell girls that to impress them.' It had clearly made a big impression on Mum, it was one of the things she was absolutely certain about, and it took us back to where we started, right in front of that impenetrable brick wall.

I'd had enough. It was late, I was tired, we were getting nowhere. I wanted to go to my bed, and poor Mum must have been worn out. We decided to sleep on it, and I was very nearly asleep when Barry sat bolt upright in bed: 'Your

Mum is certain that Jack Crowley came from the same town as Lana Turner, isn't she?'

'Mmm,' I muttered, trying to cover my head with the bedclothes.

'But why are we so certain that Lana Turner came from Boise?'

It was as if someone had turned on a 100-watt electric light bulb. I was suddenly wide awake. 'Because I read it in the newspaper.'

'Exactly!' my husband said, with heavy sarcasm. 'And we know you can believe everything you read in the newspapers!'

I certainly knew journalists got the facts of my life wrong at least as often as they got them right. Since they'd started writing about me I'd become a divorcee in one paper, acquired three children in another, turned up at several different addresses and been quoted as saying all manner of things that had never escaped my lips. But somehow the possibility that the same mistakes could have occurred with a film star had never crossed my mind.

It was the end of my sleep for that night. I was busy planning how I'd fit in a trip to the library tomorrow when Barry had time to spare between jobs. There had to be a biography of Lana Turner somewhere on the public library shelves of Birmingham and I had to find it immediately. I couldn't believe I hadn't thought of this before, and why had Barry waited till now to come up with his brainwave? It was so obvious. I wouldn't even let myself think the other alternative – 'What if she doesn't come from Boise after all?' A chink was opening up in the wall. There was hope again.

The good news was that there were two biographies of Lana Turner; the bad news, that they were out and would have to be ordered. They took ages to come in. The initial excitement had all but evaporated and the doubts set in when I got a call to say both books were now available at the library. Mum was out at her day centre, so Barry took me round, and drove home at unusual speed with me clutching both books in my arms like precious cargo. I handed him one as we stepped over the threshold and we sat down immediately in adjacent armchairs and started reading. We reached the appropriate place at almost the same time.

'Wallace,' Barry shouted, leaping up. 'That's where she was born. That's what it says here. What does yours say?'

'Wallace,' I shouted back, almost unable to believe it. 'It's in Idaho, like Boise.' I was on my feet too, searching around for one of my maps of the USA, spreading it out on the table. And there was the town of Wallace, hundreds of miles north of Boise, close to Canada and surrounded by forests. That fitted in with Jack Crowley's story of being a lumberjack. It was all fitting together nicely.

How many times before had I thought that only to be disappointed? But this time it was going to happen. I'd make it happen.

It took an effort of will to come down from my high and start the systematic, detailed checking. First step was the central library and the microfiche check of the phone book for Crowleys. Those I found and contacted didn't know my father – well, I never thought it would be that easy – but I did establish that this was the centre of the forestry area and picked up the address of Idaho Forest Industries. I wrote, using my usual cover story, and asked if they had ever had a Jack Crowley on their workforce. They hadn't, but the chairman of the board kindly had all the Crowleys in the area contacted on my behalf for clues. Again, nobody knew the man in question.

The three other forestry companies I contacted had no record of him either but one of them explained that a lot of fly-by-night companies set up business, but lasted only a short while and didn't keep records. My father could have been with one of those. Already one trail had run out. It looked like being a long haul.

Around that time I had a call from a reporter with National Public Radio in Washington State, an American-based Englishman called Steve Webbe. He wanted to interview me by telephone about my own personal story, for an early morning programme. I was happy to do the interview – we needed all the American publicity we could get – as long as we only used my father's first name. I didn't want him hearing of my existence for the first time on his radio and expiring into his cornflakes with shock or something.

I liked Steve immediately. It was clear that he understood and empathized with my feelings. He continued to chat to me after the interview had finished, explaining that he had an adopted sister and had helped her find her natural parents. 'If there's anything I can do to help,' he said and it was obvious he wasn't just making an empty gesture in the expectation of being refused. By coincidence I'd just, that morning, received a letter from the postmaster in Wallace. He didn't know my father but he knew an elderly lady, who'd now moved away and who had talked about a Crowley family who'd lived in the town. There had been a Mrs Crowley – no father was mentioned – and two sons, Jack and Ted. It was a tentative connection, but it did suggest I could be on the right track.

'There's only one thing you can do to help me,' I told Steve. 'Find my Dad.'

'Do you really want me to?' he asked, a little surprised by such a tall order.

'Yes please,' I said. If you were going to be cheeky, you might as well be really cheeky. 'I've been looking in the wrong place for so long. Now I think I'm on the right track but I can't face doing it alone. I need some help.'

'OK,' he said. 'Tell me exactly what you've got so far and leave it with me for a while.'

That was a Tuesday in March 1986. I trusted him to get back to me, but I didn't expect it to be for a long time. I knew from experience how drawn-out this searching business could be. Steve rang the following Sunday. He'd been in touch with a friend, a teacher, and he'd got hold of the high-school records for Wallace dating back half a century. There, in black and white, were the names and birth dates of my father and my uncle Ted, as well as the name (Cecile Rose Crowley) and address of their mother. There was even a photograph of my Dad in a school play.

A classmate who'd graduated the same year as my father still lived in Wallace, but Steve hadn't managed to get him on the phone yet. When he did, he hoped to find out exactly where Jack Crowley had moved to and make contact. He had planned to wait until he'd spoken to the classmate before phoning me, Steve said, but he had to share the excitement with someone. I couldn't thank him enough. What he'd achieved so far was absolutely wonderful to me. I might, as Barry warned, trying to calm me down, have a long way to go yet, but this was the first time that anyone outside my family had acknowledged that Jack Crowley actually existed.

Steve assured me he'd call back when he had something else to report. I begged him to let me know everything, however small. I was trying very hard to prepare myself for a long wait, and any titbits of information would keep me going. It was the following Saturday night when Steve's next phone call came.

'You're not going to believe this,' he said, 'but I've just been talking to your father for two hours.' He was right, I couldn't believe it. It had happened so fast, it took my breath away. I was prepared for almost anything but not for this. It was only as Steve continued talking that it began to sink in. 'He's a fantastic person,' he enthused, 'a really nice guy. I didn't tell him about you, not the truth. I told him I was doing a programme on war brides and had been speaking to a family in England who asked to be put in touch with a Jack Crowley if I happened to come across him.'

Dad, I found out later, had been totally bewildered as to why someone doing a programme on war brides should have stumbled on him, but had been too polite to question it. He has this ability to sound totally unruffled on the other end of a telephone when he's actually in a state of shock. It came in very useful when I first revealed my identity. He'd chatted to Steve about the nursery he ran in Sacramento and the bonsai trees he grew and sold there, and charmed him.

I must have sounded as shaken as I felt because Steve insisted on knowing if there was someone with me before giving me Dad's phone number. 'I don't want you to phone him right away,' he said. 'You must sit down and think it through before you do anything. Remember, Shirley, Jack Crowley doesn't know you exist. You don't want to spoil it. You can get this far and still blow it.' He was right of course, and I give other people exactly the same advice, but it's hard to follow. I did sit down with Barry – I had to before my legs gave way – and talked about it.

'It's fantastic news,' Barry said, 'but it's late and I think you should sleep on it and ring your Dad tomorrow when you've pulled yourself together.'

'No,' I insisted, 'I've got to hear his voice tonight – even if I just let him pick up the phone and say, "Hello" before I put the receiver down.' Barry pointed out that this was rather childish and not very considerate and recommended his cure-all, a good night's sleep, again. I dug my heels in. Maybe I was childish, but how are you expected to be when you've just found your Dad at the age of 40?

'Well, do it if you must,' my long-suffering spouse sighed. He looked very much as if he was planning to leave and go up to bed.

'Don't go,' I begged. 'I might need you. But don't listen either or you'll put me off.' By the time I'd made my way back into the hall to use the phone I'd worked out where I wanted Barry – in the living room, on the other side of a half-open door, not listening but ready to come to my aid if I shouted for his support. Why would I suddenly need assistance? I wasn't quite sure myself, but I wouldn't have ruled out a fainting fit in my state of nervous excitement. I'd also worked out an excuse to give my father for phoning. I'd run through the story about being a member of a family who'd known him and then pretend I hadn't got his full address and ask for it so I could write to him. I dialled the number, praying he was as nice as Steve had said. A woman answered. I almost put the phone down but forced myself to ask to speak to Jack Crowley.

A nerve-wracking pause and then a warm man's voice said, 'Hi.' I told him I was phoning from England and he said, 'Gee, all the way from England!' The voice was just as Mum had said: polite, quiet, gentle, friendly, American, of course, but without the 'twang' that had offended British ears. I badly wanted to tell him the truth but this wasn't the time, so instead I asked him all these questions partly to check that he was the man I (or my family) was looking for, but mainly because I couldn't bear to let him go. He seemed so close and I wanted to hang on to him for as long as possible.

I asked him if he had once been engaged to a girl called Lilian Hughes, which amazed him. 'She up and married someone else,' he laughed. I told him his parents had been divorced and that his mother was French. 'French-

German,' he corrected. I said I could understand him keeping quiet about the German part during the war. Then I asked if he'd been a lumberjack. He hadn't but he'd worked in the forest industry, he said, and I thought, 'Lie number one!' Did he live near Lana Turner when he was young, I wanted to know. In the same town, he said, then quickly added that he had never met her.

'Can you dance?' I tried.

'Yes, I can,' he said quickly.

'But could you dance in 1944?'

A little laugh. 'No, I wasn't much of a dancer in those days.'

'I heard you weren't,' I said, joining in the laughter.

'How do you know all these things?' he asked, sounding amused and curious but not at all alarmed. He seemed completely relaxed about a strange woman ringing him from England knowing minute details of his life, though he says now that he was astounded.

'I told you,' I said, 'my family knew you.' I mentioned my Uncle Albert, because, apparently, he used to talk to Albert for hours, but he couldn't remember the name. Nor the name Slim; nor Ross, my mother's maiden name.

Auntie Slim used to love to organize a sing-song at her house and they had one the Christmas my father was here. They'd all sung his favourite song, 'Indian Love Call'.

'Yeah, that used to be my favourite,' he laughed. 'You know more about me than I know myself!' That was true in a way. I knew he'd spent Christmas 1944 with my family, but he had no recollection of this. He insisted he'd spent it in Oxford. It was the first discrepancy, and combined with the fact that the names of my family meant nothing to him, it was very worrying.

I thought, 'Oh, no, he can't be the wrong man after all this.' So much else fitted. He sounded so right. I told him I thought it too much of a coincidence for him not to be the man I was looking for. Maybe, I suggested hesitantly, though I was pretty certain of my facts, a member of my family had got the thing about Christmas wrong. Could I write to him?

'Sure,' he said, amiable as ever. 'Have you got my address?'

'Well, that's what I rang to ask you for, actually,' I lied.

He asked, rather belatedly, for my full name and I was about to say Shirley McGlade, when it struck me I'd had some publicity in America and he might have heard of me, so I changed the surname in mid-sentence to Ross.

It was when I put the phone down it hit me. My Dad! I'd been talking to my Dad! I felt as if I was floating six feet above the ground. So what if he had forgotten a few facts after forty-two years. There was no doubt in my mind that I'd found my father.

I wrote to him immediately, reiterating most of the information I'd given him on the phone and sticking to my story. My family had talked a lot about him, I explained, and I'd wondered what had become of him and decided to find out. It struck me that if, for some as yet unspecified reason, I couldn't break the news that I was his daughter, perhaps I could get to know him as a friend. I kept the letter as light and friendly as possible, refusing to let my pen communicate the sense of urgency I felt. This man was still a stranger, still capable of being frightened off by the wrong move.

Even so his letter arrived only a week later. I opened it roughly, urgently, and a black and white photograph fluttered to the ground. It was a picture of Jack Crowley in his uniform, taken when he was in his twenties and a match for any of the good-looking film stars I'd gazed at as a child while trying to imagine what he looked like. My first thought was, 'But I know you.'

I showed it to Mum who looked at it for a long time. 'Oh, yes, that's him,' she said with that faraway look that told me she'd been transported back to the war years. I tried to tell her my strange feelings about the photograph; that I knew the person in it as if he was a familiar member of the family. 'Of course,' she smiled, 'go and look in a mirror.' I did, but I couldn't really see me in the other, black and white face. People tell me I look like my Dad and there is definitely a resemblance, but not enough to make me feel that instant sense of familiarity. It was my mother-in-law who explained the mystery. I went up to see her – I was visiting regularly anyway because my father-in-law was seriously ill – and took out the picture to show her, without explanation.

'Good God,' she said, 'what's our Martin doing in an army uniform?'

I went home to make the most important phone call of my life. I can remember every word, every pause and silence of that call. I'll go to my grave with it etched on my brain like some celestial film script. But there were altogether more mundane worries on my mind as I prepared to make the call. Barry was hurrying out to visit his sick father and I thought, He'll kill me when he sees the phone bill!

Mum was there and I positioned her behind the open door, as I had done Barry with the previous call, for moral support. 'If I can't talk to him, you'll have to,' I told her, ignoring her protests. I was timing the call to catch my father home alone. It should be around 9 a.m. in Sacramento and he'd told me in the letter that his second wife, Rhoda, worked at the local college. He'd retired from his job as an aeronautical engineer but had taken up a second, less stressful occupation, the growing of bonsai trees, azaleas and orchids.

My stomach was churning. It was all-or-nothing time. I'd decided I couldn't keep up my pretence any longer. I had to tell this man the truth, whether he rejected me or not. He seemed relaxed and happy to hear from me. 'Was it me your family knew?' he wanted to know immediately, and I assured him it was.

'Are you alone?' I cut in quickly before he could comment further. I'd already discovered how chatty he was and I didn't want to have to fight my way into a pleasant chat with my dramatic announcement.

'Yes, just me and the dogs.'

'You're not wearing a pacemaker, are you?' I asked, trying to make light of it but half serious. I really did worry about the effect of the shock I was about to deliver on a man his age. He laughed off the idea and started to ask me about something in my letter. 'Please,' I cut in, 'don't talk for a minute. I've got some news for you. I think I'm your daughter.' As in all the best farces, he didn't quite hear. He does have a hearing loss.

'You're what?'

'Your daughter.'

There was a pause before he said. 'Oh, my God.' Then, 'Are you dark?' It was only afterwards it struck me what a strange turn the conversation took at that point. I looked down at my arm. It wasn't something I'd thought about. 'Quite dark. I go brown easily in the summer.'

'Do you know your great-grandmother is Crow Indian?'

'I don't know anything about myself – and I feel quite sick,' I said, clutching my stomach.

'Why?'

'I'm scared.'

A reassuring little laugh. It felt as warm as a hug. 'How can you be scared of your own father?' It was amazing. He just accepted it. He says now that he felt disbelief and shock; well, it didn't come across to me. It was just as if he was at the top of the garden path and I held out my hand and he came to me.

And then we got down to details. He obviously wondered who my Mum was and when I told him he admitted he didn't remember her. Even when I sent a photograph, all he could say was that she looked familiar. This was hard for me to accept and Mum was understandably shattered and very, very annoyed. The man who'd been the love of her life couldn't even remember her.

'You give me that phone and I'll tell him a few things to make him remember me,' she hissed in my ear. Afterwards I had to calm her down, and try to find an explanation.

'Look, you had me around all the time. You couldn't forget,' I told her. 'He was just a young GI away from home. He probably had quite a few girlfriends.' (He's assured me this isn't so, but he was so good-looking and, from what Mum says, so charming, that I tend not to believe him.) He'd also been injured in battle, which had damaged his hearing, possibly caused temporary psychological shock and affected his memory. My father recalls very little about the war and his part in it.

I ended the first conversation as my father's daughter by asking if it was OK to write to him. 'I realize you are married and have two sons and the last thing I want is to upset your family,' I explained. 'Shall I write care of a box number or a friend?'

He didn't even pause to think about it. 'Not at all. This is something which I think should be out in the open. I'm going to tell my wife when she gets home and I'll tell your brothers when I'm in touch with them. You just write to me at home.'

9
Friends in America

S hortly before I found my father, I had a call from Sy Pearlman, Head of News at NBC television in New York. He'd read about War Babes in the *Guardian* and wanted to send a film crew and do something on us. This was the sort of publicity I'd been hoping for, exposure that would get our cause across to the American public. It was all very well being a household name in this country, but that only brought in more 'babes' and no fathers. This promised to alert the fathers to the fact that we were out here looking for them.

With my weakness for American accents, I'd probably have agreed to almost any proposition Sy Pearlman put to me on the phone. Why is it that all American males sound about thirty and seriously dishy? When he arrived to see me in advance of his interviewer and crew, Sy was nothing like the pin-up boy I'd imagined, but he was charming and I enjoyed his visits to my home. Not as much as Mum enjoyed it though. She was like a teenager meeting her favourite pop star. A real American male in our house – the very idea put her in a tizz. It was almost like having her very own GI back. Jack Crowley had a lot to answer for.

She insisted on cooking Sy a real, traditional British lunch of roast beef, cabbage and potatoes; it was obvious from the shocked expression on his face that this was not his staple fare. He explained that he never ate a big meal in the middle of the day and simply couldn't manage this mountain of Brummie stodge. Mum forgave him anyway.

Sy talked to me about my own personal story and explained that he would like to include a few other War Babes in their film as well. He also went into some depth about the way the American government had treated us. A couple of days later, a film crew and an on-screen reporter, John Cochran, arrived. They filmed Pheasey Farm, where my father's wartime camp had been, and me, standing in a howling gale on the steps of Birmingham's public library. Then it was back to our house where Lorraine and Maria were waiting to tell their stories. They looked relaxed and smart, their make-up newly applied and not a hair out of place.

After my sojourn on the library steps, my nose was glowing red, I had a cold sore on my lip, my hair had the pulled-through-a-hedge-backwards look and the wear and tear of the day had done little for my arthritis and my temper. As I hobbled into position in front of the cameras, I kept thinking about my Dad seeing this. I'd lost much of my self-consciousness about appearing on television. I realized from experience that the viewers were not sitting at home, eyes glued to the spot on your chin or the odd bit of hair sticking up on top of your head. They had better things to do with their lives and you were lucky if they were watching with half an eye while they ate their tea or read the paper or had an argument. But this was different. This was the first time my father would see me and he'd be watching with both eyes. I hoped he wouldn't disown me!

Between the first approach by NBC and the time they arrived to make their film, the miracle had happened. I'd found him. This added an extra spice as far as the television company was concerned. They wanted me to take part in a link-up between the States and London, 'meeting' my Dad for the first time on camera. I didn't have to think too deeply about it before saying no. It was early days in the relationship. I hardly knew this lovely man I had the privilege of calling Dad; nor he me. It would be a bit presumptuous to assume he wanted to be identified with me before several million television viewers and have his private past turned into a highly public present. I wouldn't risk doing anything that might stunt the relationship in its infancy, so I declined and told myself there would be another time, another way. Maria agreed to step into the breach.

Maria, you may remember, was brought up to believe that her grandparents were her mother and father. The truth – that her sister, Eileen, eighteen years her senior, was her mother and an American GI her father – emerged in a family argument when she was 16.

I met Maria following an appearance on local television. She lives in Worcestershire with her husband, George, and their son, so we're in the same television area. She phoned me and we had one of those mammoth talks that only two war babes who've newly discovered each other, can have. Nobody in the family had wanted to talk much about Tom, her father, but over the years she'd amassed a useful amount of information. She knew her parents had been engaged – there had been an announcement in the local paper to prove it, though Maria had only heard about this. At the time of her birth, her father had been in France but was expected to come back and marry her mother when the war ended. This never happened. He wrote saying that the authorities would not allow him to return.

Maria's grandparents – and, presumably her mother – were unhappy with the situation and the grandparents tried to contact him through the American authorities. They didn't hear from Tom but a letter arrived from his wife, explaining that he had two children and was not in a position to marry anyone! 'Not a very pleasant letter apparently,' Maria said. 'You can imagine what a shock it was to my mother.' It must have been about this time that the family hatched their plan for the grandparents to bring up Maria as their own, releasing their still teenaged daughter to a fresh start and minimizing the shame.

Maria was aware that her father came from Chicago and we tried to trace him in the obvious way, in that city's phone directories. Disappointingly there was no one at all under that name. I gave her the information I had on other sources and we kept in touch while she embarked on a search.

It proved fruitless until Maria decided to go into the library and look up the copy of the newspaper containing the announcement of her parents' engagement. She hoped it might provide an additional clue – and it did, in a totally unexpected way. She discovered that her mother had given her the wrong spelling of her father's name, substituting an 'e' in the middle instead of an 'o'. Her husband, who was with her, insisted they should check the phone books under the new spelling – after all they were already in the library and only had to take the escalator to another floor. Maria herself didn't have much hope that one little letter would make a difference. 'Apart from anything else, I couldn't believe he'd still be in Chicago after all this time. When the girl behind the desk asked whether we wanted north, south, east, west or central Chicago, I had visions of us being stuck in front of the microfiche for a week. Picking an area out of the air I opted for central.

'George started fiddling with the machine and I was taking my coat off and preparing to settle down beside him for a long wait when he suddenly said, "He's here." I thought he was joking, but there it was, right near the start. George wrote the number down on a piece of paper and I held it in my hand all the way home, just looking at it. Now I had it, I didn't think I'd actually use it. It suddenly struck me that I couldn't bear to speak to my father. I mean, how do you ring someone and say, "Hello, I'm your daughter," after forty years?

'But George wouldn't let me get away with that, not after all the searching. He said he'd ring, and he did, and got my half-brother who is disabled and lives at home with my father. George didn't say who he was and my brother said that his father was out and suggested ringing back in about an hour.

'Exactly an hour later, George phoned again, with me standing nervously at his elbow. I heard him ask if that was Tom G— and whether he had been stationed in Birmingham during the war, and then he said: "I've got someone here who wants to speak to you." He handed me the phone and I suppose I must have said something. Almost immediately my father said, "You're Maria, aren't you?"

'He seemed delighted to hear from me. He told me he'd tried to trace me through a private detective when I was 18. He said he'd written to me and the letters had been returned unopened. My grandmother might well have done that. I don't imagine she'd have wanted anything to do with him. We made the phone call on a Tuesday and the following Saturday I had a letter from my father. Among other things he said how much he'd loved my mother and how he still loved her, which, to be honest, I thought was drivel. How can you claim to love someone you haven't seen in forty years?

'He wanted to get in touch with my mother. I think he had visions of picking up the romance where he left off, because his wife had died a few years earlier. I'm sure he still thought of Mum as a pretty 18-year-old. When I sent him a photograph of her, he stopped asking for her address. My mother wouldn't have wanted to know. She never tried to stop me finding him, although she didn't exactly flood me with information. She was incredulous that I'd managed it, but she doesn't want any contact.

'My father also told me in the letter that there hadn't been a day when he hadn't thought of me. I thought, Well, that's very nice but why didn't you do something about it, then? I suppose I felt he was in the wrong and was surprised that he didn't seem to feel any guilt about it.'

But these reservations didn't stop Maria from wanting to meet her father, and she was happy to accept the chance of appearing on the television link-up. Perhaps she felt that seeing this man, whom her mother had told her looked like the singer, Andy Williams, would make her feel closer to him. If so, it was a mistake.

'He looked absolutely nothing like the way I imagined,' she said afterwards. 'The photographs he sent me must have been taken years earlier. I was so shocked when I first saw him, I gasped, "Is that him?", and they left it in. I really wished they hadn't. I didn't want to hurt his feelings. He was much older than I expected: he's 78 now. I don't think he ever told my mother that he was 13 years older than her.

'The link-up wasn't an easy situation to handle. It was difficult to know what to say, though my father had less trouble with that than me. He talked about my half-sister and her wonderful house. At the end, I was left with the impression that he'd talked an awful lot about money. He did say, in front of 27 million viewers, that he would come over and visit me and my family next year, but that never happened. I think he was talked out of it by a member of the family who took a dislike to me without ever having any contact with me.

'My father and I still maintain contact but not as much as we used to. He doesn't like writing and he doesn't always phone when he says he will. I have to keep reminding myself that he is an old man and not always well.'

Did she, I wondered, regret contacting her father? 'No, finding him was incredibly exciting, quite a thrill. It was something I'd hoped for since I was 16, something I had to do. But in some ways it has been disappointing. My own fault, perhaps. Knowing so little about him, I built up this image, gave him certain attributes. I always thought we'd be alike. The fact that I'm artistic, for instance. People have said to me, "I bet you get that from your father."

'It was disappointing to find out he'd been a central-heating engineer before he retired. As he said, the only thing he ever painted was the outside of the house. And I could never stop feeling angry about the way he'd left my mother and me in the lurch, or the fact that he had told her a pack of lies, not least that he was free to marry her. I've talked to him about this and he says that his marriage was unhappy and he was very much in love with my mother. But then he went back to his wife and they had a third child.

'I'd still like to meet my father, but I don't know how it would be. I've seen other war babes meet their fathers in front of television cameras, and they are hugging each other and crying, in a very emotional state. I can't believe that for me it would be like that.'

I suppose it would be too much to hope that there wouldn't be the occasional son or daughter who simply doesn't hit it off with their father – or who isn't disappointed in the person they find at the end of the long search. The surprising thing is how rarely this happens. I can count on the fingers of one hand the people who've been rejected, and there's usually a reason, like the father given a 'me or her' choice by his wife. Not surprisingly perhaps, he chose to keep his wife.

Harder to quantify are the number of war babes who are bitterly disappointed, or simply bitter, but I believe they are very few. We want to love our fathers; we've invested a lot in trying to find them. We bend over backwards to forgive and forget what, in some cases, must be seen as irresponsible behaviour towards our mothers and ourselves. They were young, we say. It was wartime. The families and the American authorities interfered. The fact that the fathers welcome us into their lives now wipes the slate clean. We don't make the same judgements as we might with a stranger who didn't happen to be our father.

Not so Maria, who admits to feeling bitterness and disappointment. She was shocked by her father's appearance and she certainly isn't the only person to admit such feelings. It may sound ridiculous, but it comes as a great surprise to many that their fathers are elderly men. They may have seen a photograph of him as a young man or heard their mother talk about this fresh-faced handsome soldier. They haven't been around to see maturity and old age creep up on those firm features. However logical you are it's a bit hard to come to terms with the difference between the man in your mind's eye and the one standing before you. Fathers don't help by picking out their best photograph to send before you meet. Those best snaps were often taken ten or fifteen years ago. But then we all do things like that and fathers are human too!

There were no shocks of that nature when I met my father, but like most people I had a fantasy image of what he'd look like until he sent me a batch of photographs. In my imagination my father was a sleek, suave, slim, grey-haired, grey-suited business tycoon. John Forsythe, the actor who played Blake Carrington in *Dynasty*, came pretty close to what I had in mind! What had inspired this touch of imagination? Very little really. Probably just a few remarks my mother made about him sounding so well-spoken, polite and well-educated. Somehow this description transported him to the boardroom, the business empire and the soap-opera lifestyle. The reality was much rounder, cuddlier and more casually dressed, and thank heavens, he wasn't a high-powered business tycoon. For me it was a pleasure to exchange the rather worrying fantasy for the more homespun reality, but for some people the fantasy is very hard to let go of.

Even harder to part with is the fantasy you may have built up of a deeply emotional reunion with the loving father of your dreams. Some people go to meet their father hoping to recoup forty-five years' worth of missed affection in one visit. Women are particularly guilty of this. They want cuddles and closeness and long reassuring talks about feelings. They need to be told that they are wanted and loved.

It can be disappointing when your father does not want to pour out his heart; is maybe a little uncomfortable at being lumbered with the contents of yours. He may be very matter-of-fact about the whole business – or appear so on the surface. A lot of men choose to avoid heavy emotional discussions whatever their relationship to you and whichever side of the Atlantic they come from. Declarations of love may not be your father's style, particularly to someone who is, however welcome and wanted, a stranger. It doesn't mean his feelings are less strong.

The first time my Dad said 'I love you,' to me was on the telephone in August 1991, even though he had written it at the end of letters. It had taken him five years and it was worth the wait. The T-shirt that arrived for me around the same time, printed with the words, 'Someone in Elk Grove [his home district] Loves Me' meant more than the most expensive gift. I wear it with pride! So I tell anxious 'babes', the openly expressioned affection may come. And if it doesn't, well, nobody promised you a silver-tongued smoothie for a father. It may just not be the man's way.

It's worth remembering that our fathers are American and Americans are different. It's easy to be lulled into a false sense of security by the fact that we both speak English, but in some ways we are still two nations divided by a common language. Nowhere is that more obvious than with money. On the whole, we don't talk about the stuff much – it's rather vulgar – and we only think a lot about it when we haven't got any. The Americans are a far more cash-conscious nation. Wealth and possessions can be openly discussed without embarrassment (something in Maria's father which worried her) and they seem to find it hard to believe they would be wanted and valued for themselves and not their bank balance. Hence the suspicion among some of the war babes' American families that the offspring might be after the family silver, or at least looking to get their name on the will.

Overwhelmingly, half-brothers and half-sisters have greeted the newcomer with warmth, but in a few cases, either protecting their father's interests or their own, they've been hostile. It's even been suggested that the British son or daughter might not be who he or she claims to be but a gold-digging imposter. I can only say they'd have to be very dedicated imposters to have collected so much information and searched so diligently. The father's name would have to be Getty or Rothschild to make it worthwhile.

A far more common source of irritation to American brothers and sisters, however, is their father's elaborate and continuous praise of the newcomer. It does happen and you've only to put yourself in their place to see how annoying it could be. It's lovely to know you are approved of – particularly for those of us who grew up with stepfathers who made their disapproval very clear – but it would be nice to keep the goodwill of the other members of the family too.

On the subject of money, I don't think I've left my father in any doubt that I want him for himself and not for what he may have in the bank. But during our earliest phone calls I think a doubt must have crossed his mind. Once, in the course of conversation, he told me, 'I'm not rich, you know.' I didn't pursue it, but I remember thinking, Well, that's OK, neither am I, but why does he feel the need to mention it? I tucked the information away in my head with all the other new details I was learning about my very own Dad, and it emerged when I was being interviewed by a woman's magazine. I knew he grew plants and I had visions of him pottering around in his garden and his old garden shed, a poor old soul, and somehow that picture was what came across in the article. I sent him the article, which both amused and insulted him. 'I know I said I'm not well off, but I'm not that poor!' he told me, rather sharply the next time we spoke.

But what of the NBC programme that opened this chapter? It went out to a vast audience across the States with, to me, totally unexpected results. There was not, as I'd hoped, a flood of fathers claiming their offspring, but there were masses of letters from all over the States offering encouragement, support and, very importantly, practical help. These were ordinary American people writing, men and women with no axe of their own to grind, who'd heard the way their government was treating us and were horrified. Their message was loud and clear: 'Don't give up. Don't let them grind you down. We're on your side.'

This was as surprising as it was gratifying to me. Because the American government had treated us like a nasty smell under the nose, I'd assumed the American people felt that way too. Now here was proof that they didn't. They didn't feel we were after our fathers' money or American citizenship; or that we would cause our fathers shame and embarrassment, from which they should be protected at any price. They seemed to understand that we had a basic human need to meet the men who had fathered us, and to believe that we had the right to achieve this if possible. Some people even got hold of my telephone number and rang to put their good wishes into words. Often they would be busy housewives with the noise of children in the background. I appreciated their kindness enormously.

Even better than the good wishes alone were the offers of help which frequently came with them. If ever I wanted anyone traced in their town or state, they said, let them know and they would do all the checking. This was just what I needed and I took several of them up on their offers, starting a chain of helpers all over the States to whom I could, and still can, turn. Some, like Mary, herself an adoptee, and Steven, an ex-army man with a lot of inside knowledge, became right-hand men and women, helping dozens of war babes to make contact with their fathers.

Each time we had publicity in America, new names would be added to my list. There weren't anything like enough people to cover every area of such a vast country, but those who volunteered have proved invaluable. It was far easier to get accurate information or have something like an obituary or a death certificate sent to you if you were on that side of the Atlantic. Even government departments seemed more amenable to requests for information from within the country and some of the helpers made excellent contacts in high places. Some of my volunteers – Lynn, for instance from Wisconsin – have become good friends. Lynn has a rare talent for ferreting out tricky information and tracking down elusive fathers. She calls herself my mole, and her undercover digging has helped bring innumerable fathers and 'children' together. I'm still reluctant to reveal her methods because although they are not illegal, they exploit loopholes in the system which could be quickly plugged if attention were drawn to them. You may think we don't need these underground methods now that the government has agreed to release information, but I don't quite trust them yet, and there will always be occasions when the official details are not enough.

Lynn was married, with two sons, when she first contacted me. Since then she had been through a traumatic divorce and, like me, has had to cope with illness and death in the family. Through letters and occasional phone calls we've got to know each other's problems. Apart from helping me to find fathers, she's supported me when I'm down and I hope I've done the same for her. I really do consider Lynn a long-distance friend now, which is one reason I don't give her name out casually to searchers. She'd be inundated. I do put some carefully selected people in direct touch with her – Mick, the social worker mentioned elsewhere in the book for example. Getting involved with an individual and being in at the 'find' is very rewarding and Lynn enjoys it as much as I do.

She says she's grown old and bold in the service of War Babes. In the early days she'd be ringing an 'alleged' father for days, trying to get him in, and when he actually answered, she'd panic and drop the phone like a hot potato. It would take hours or even days to work up the courage to try again. Now she can chat blithely, using some cover story like I do, as she checks out the information which will confirm whether or not we've got the right man. War Babes has inspired a lot of Oscar-worthy performances.

In November 1986, we had another on-camera meeting, this time between Lesley from Derbyshire and her father, Don. It was on the BBC's lunch-time programme from Pebble Mill in Birmingham, hosted by Pamela Armstrong, and once again someone else was getting the opportunity to appear because I'd backed down. Originally I'd said OK to being interviewed about War Babes and to having them fly my father in for a meeting. Then I'd started to think about it and once again the doubts crowded out the anticipated joy. It was the same old problem. Although Dad and I were getting along brilliantly on the phone and via the post, he had never suggested us meeting. Neither had I because I couldn't afford the fare to California and, in any case, I felt I should wait until he brought the subject up.

Now someone at the BBC was about to phone him and bring it up, and the idea put me in a panic. What could he say? He'd be too polite to refuse and he might feel he had been railroaded into something he didn't want. What if he went through with it and was disappointed in me when we met, or we didn't get on? This was a live show. Feelings would show, with humiliating clarity, to a few million viewers. I rang someone at Pebble Mill and caused an uproar. What was

I trying to do? I would ruin the show, and, by the sound of it, several people's lives. I thought of Lesley.

Lesley's story is one of the happiest I've been involved in, a contrast to Maria's in many ways, and Don holds a special place in my heart. Not only is he a very nice man, but he was the first GI father I met.

Lesley grew up, not unhappily, with her mother, stepfather and two stepbrothers. Her parents had been married and she kept her father's name, though her mother never talked about him to her. 'As a teenager,' she remembers, 'I'd have a row with my Mum and I'd think, "My Dad will come for me one day. I'll go and live with him." But he never came and I couldn't understand why he'd disowned me.' She had her little mementoes, including a photograph – 'He looked just like Errol Flynn' – and some wrapping paper in which her paternal grandmother had sent her a present as a little girl. It was the address on this paper – and one of my husband's brainwaves – which led us to Lesley's father.

Lesley had had an address for her father, but by the time she got in touch with me, it was out of date. We tried various agencies but without success. It was Barry, hearing about the forty-year-old wrapping paper, who suggested writing to the sender's address. It was the address of a sanatorium where Lesley's grandmother had died, and I was referred to a man whose father had been a member of staff many years ago. It was a lucky break because this man was helpful and extremely interested in what we were doing, and Lesley's father wasn't the only one he helped me find.

Lesley takes up the story:

'I was so excited when I got my father's phone number and address, I wanted to speak to him straight away. But I thought it through and decided it wouldn't be a good idea to phone. Maybe his wife didn't know I existed and a phone call from England would be bound to raise questions. I suppose a letter might do the same but I didn't think about that and I decided I'd write. It seemed a less frightening way of reintroducing myself, for both of us.

'I wrote a careful letter, not wanting to be too pushy, but putting the ball in his court, and then I waited . . . and waited. I was a nervous wreck looking out for the postman. After three weeks I began to think that my father had told me exactly how he felt without ever having to reply. He was going to ignore me. He didn't want to know. There was just one grain of hope but I tried not to cling to it. It was just possible my letter had been lost in the post. I sat down and wrote another and then I tried very, very hard to put the whole thing out of my mind and get on with my life.

'When I got a call from my husband at 3 a.m. one morning, at the old people's home where I work, it was a complete surprise. He said, "Lesley, your father's been on the phone. I've given him this number and he is going to call you. He doesn't seem to have any idea of the time here, but I knew you wouldn't want me to put him off."

'The call came through from Florida almost as soon as I put the phone back. He just said, "Lesley, this is your Dad." Apparently he'd been away on holiday and when he arrived back and found my letters, he'd picked up the phone immediately. He told me how he'd searched for me and how his wife, Amy, had encouraged him, and how thrilled he was to hear from me. I cried and he cried. It was lovely.

'We began phoning and writing. I used to think I'd soon run out of things to say, but I haven't because he's so interested. He wants to know everything about his two granddaughters and little Nicholas, Hayley's baby, who is his first great-grandchild. And he wants every detail of my life from the moment he left England when I was 4 months old, in 1945 – even my school reports.

'When she was angry with me, my mother used to shout, "You're just like your father!" – and she was so right. We're alike in looks – the same dark curly hair. At least it was dark – we're both grey now. This really pleased Dad, because his other children all look like his wife. But the resemblance isn't just physical. We even have similar handwriting. We write the same sort of letters and they both trail off and become unreadable when we're tired.'

Don is a retired mechanic, living, when Lesley found him, in Florida and now in a small town in Georgia. He loves England and its history, and he loves his English daughter every bit as much as his American children, he says. The trip the BBC offered was straight out of his dreams. He brought his daughter, Joanne, for company and moral support.

The actual meeting in a television studio may have been contrived and artificial as these things are, but it was also a moment of pure drama and very real human emotion. Don and Lesley were kept apart during the couple of hours leading up to the show, with minders to ensure they didn't wander around, or bump into each other on trips to the toilet. I was interviewed by Pamela Armstrong and Lesley talked about her experience of finding her father. Then, minutes before the end of the show, her father made his entrance and the camera swooped in on their tearful embrace. I don't think there was a dry eye in the house. In the hospitality room Lesley's daughter watched a monitor, with tears streaming down her face. Elsewhere in the building, Don's daughter watched in a similar state. Sitting a few feet away from them, I cried, mostly happy tears for Lesley, but there were a few tears of sadness for myself.

'That could have been you and your Dad, if you'd had the nerve,' I told myself, severely. 'Well, it's too late now.' I tried to console myself with Barry's words at the time that I made up my mind not to go through with it.

'Look at it this way,' he'd said, 'would you rather meet your father in a television studio in boring old Birmingham or in private, in the California sunshine?'

'You're right,' I told Barry, 'but how will I ever afford to go?'

'No problem; I'll save up,' he insisted, and true to his word, he found a small box into which he was putting a small sum each week. I appreciated his kindness, I really did, but at the slow rate the savings were growing, I'd be going to California with my pension book. And here I was casting aside opportunities for a free meeting. I must be mad!

I couldn't take my eyes off Don. With his white hair and moustache and his upright bearing, he might have still been a military man – or Colonel Saunders, the Kentucky Fried Chicken man! He came to speak to me afterwards and to thank me for helping Lesley. He put his arm around my shoulders. 'And thank you for being afraid to meet your father,' he said with a twinkle, 'because it gave me the chance to meet my daughter.'

He was the very first father I'd seen and I was quite in awe of him. Up till now they'd all been names on paper, or photographs at best. Now I was looking at a real, live specimen. I wanted to touch him to see if he was real and listen to his soft American accent. His accent was different from my father's, but there was the same quietness and softness about his voice. I wanted to take him home with me, instead of letting Lesley waltz off with him! 'Tickled to death,' was how Don described his feelings when he got home from vacation to find two letters from Lesley waiting.

'I was shocked – not because she'd turned up on my doorstep, so to speak, and my family didn't know about her. My first marriage and my eldest daughter were never kept a secret from my wife and family, but it didn't occur to me that she was trying to find me at the same time I was trying to locate her – and that she'd succeed. I was worried that she'd think I hadn't replied because I didn't want anything to do with her. So I picked up the phone, there and then, at 9 p.m. our time – and got Harold, Lesley's husband, out of bed at 2 a.m.'

What had Don been doing in the intervening years? His marriage to Lesley's mother had not outlasted the war. 'I went back to the States, like the other GIs,' he explained, 'expecting my wife to come and join me with our baby. But she refused to come over. I'm not blaming her; I guess she couldn't bear to leave her home. After a while the marriage was dissolved and we both married other people. I lost contact after four years, when she remarried and changed her name.'

He blames himself for briefly finding and losing Lesley again when she was a young woman. 'A letter from her reached me way back, before she got married, asking for my blessing. I was real pleased, but I hated writing letters and I put off answering this one. It wasn't that I didn't want contact with her or that I didn't intend to reply, but you know how it is – I had a job and a family of six children and I was always very busy trying to make ends meet. There was never a great deal of income and at that time in your life, you have to put all your efforts into raising your family.

'By the time I got round to answering that letter, Lesley had married and moved away from her previous address and my letter was returned. I can't forgive myself for losing her at that point. I tried every way I could think to locate her and my wife encouraged me.' He even wrote to Scotland Yard, but drew a blank since Lesley doesn't have a criminal record! In all, he searched for his daughter for twenty-three years.

His reaction when he heard that his government had complicated Lesley's task in finding him by refusing to give her any information was one of amazement and annoyance. 'I can only say it's a very narrow-minded bunch of politicians who make these decisions. They have no idea how people feel, what they go through trying to locate their families. We're seeing the same situation in America with people who were adopted and are refused information on their real parents, so they can't find them when they grow up.'

How did these two strangers fare when they were no longer in the hothouse atmosphere of a television studio and under the eyes of a few million viewers? 'We got on like a house on fire,' Lesley said. 'We were as easy in each other's company as if we'd never been apart.' Her father, speaking separately, gave an almost identical answer.

'She was as easy to talk to as if I'd known her all her life, like any of my other children who grew up around me. Lesley may be a grandmother now, but to me she's still my little daughter and always will be. When I walked into the television studio and saw her, I felt as if I'd have recognized her in any circumstances. She has my family's blood all right, the looks and mannerisms.'

He met, and felt instantly comfortable with, Lesley's husband and two grown-up daughters. He also renewed acquaintance with Lesley's mother. How did they get on, I wondered? 'Like strangers,' he said simply. 'There are no hard feelings, but we are different people now.'

I was doing the ironing in front of the television a week later when Don and Lesley went back on the programme to talk about their time together. We saw film of them walking through the Derbyshire countryside, hand in hand, and visiting the historical places Don loves. They looked incredibly happy and I envied Lesley all over again. Pamela Armstrong asked Don what the trip had meant to him.

'If there's a heaven,' he said, 'I've been there.' I stood there, alone, sobbing, the iron and the blouse I was using it on, forgotten. This was better than any of the Hollywood weepies of my childhood, only it was real and I'd been instrumental in bringing it about. If I'd ever doubted the value of the work I was doing with War Babes, my faith was renewed at that point. The smell of singeing cotton brought me out of my reverie. The people who imagined I was some kind of high-powered character should see me now. I was still an ordinary housewife, and not a particularly efficient one either, but even housewives can achieve miracles sometimes, and I had a feeling I'd just witnessed one.

The following year, Lesley and Harold went to stay with Don and his wife in Florida, and Lesley met more of her half-brothers and -sisters; she'd already built up a good relationship with Joanne. The closest to her in age were twin boys, but, sadly, one of them died in a car accident and the other, Greg, returned from Vietnam, like many other soldiers, with psychological problems.

'I heard from Joanne that Dad was worried about me meeting Greg, who lives at home,' said Lesley, 'but there was no need. My brother is a lovely person, a pleasure to talk to. I just feel a little sad for him. Amy, Dad's wife, is very sweet, a real Southern belle. They've told me they have changed their will to include me, which I found very embarrassing. It was something I'd never thought about, but they insist I'm one of the family now and must be included.'

Don returned for his granddaughter's wedding and plans another trip next year to see his first great-grandchild. At the time of writing, Lesley is about to embark on a visit to his new home in Georgia. They write every week; Lesley manages two letters, Don one. 'I never was a letter writer,' he says, 'but Lesley has turned me into one. I couldn't bring myself to put pen to paper, but now I sit down and turn out six or seven pages a week. What do I find to say? We discuss everything and anything, just as if we were sitting down together, chatting. I tell her about the family, about what I've been doing, even what I'm eating! I can tell her all sorts of little personal things. I love getting her letters. I want to know everything about her, past and present. Maybe you can't catch up on forty missed years but we're not doing too badly.'

He says he will always regret not knowing Lesley as a child and a young woman, but admits there is a special magic in getting to know a daughter in your twilight years. 'You've more time and freedom and a bit more cash to travel

Two of the few surviving photographs of me as a young child. No wonder that my GI father, Jack Crowley, fell for my mother (above right). Also in the photograph are Nan (left), Auntie Slim (centre), and me, age 3.

Four precious
photographs of my
father in his early
twenties, proudly
wearing his uniform in
US army camps in Utah
and Nevada.

At the Rainbow Corner, off Piccadilly, London, where US servicemen found some relaxation during the war. Jitterbugging was all the rage – it was at a ballroom in Birmingham, England where my father first met my mother. (*The Hulton–Deutsch Collection*).

With my father, Jack
Crowley, in California.
Who can doubt the joy
of this father and a
daughter, together at
last?

With another daughter
and father happily
brought together by
War Babes.

because your children are off your hands financially. It's a very special kind of relationship.'

Not all War Babes stories have such a happy ending, and it couldn't have happened to two nicer people.

10
Gains and Losses

'Is there anything you want from me?' Dad asked me during one of our telephone chats. Well, yes, I wanted desperately to come and see him, but I couldn't say that, so I asked for the next best thing.

'I want your name on my birth certificate,' I told him. Ever since the day, aged 11, I'd torn open that sealed envelope and found my birth certificate, the blank space under 'father's name' had haunted me. It seemed to say all the bad things about me that childhood with my stepfather had reinforced. Not only that initial, awful shame, that my mother hadn't been married, but that I was unwanted, unloved, fatherless. Only now I wasn't. I had a father and he was happy and proud to recognize me. I tried to explain a little of this to my father.

'Of course you can have my name,' he said cheerfully. 'Go ahead, write it in.'

'It's not that easy,' I laughed. 'You have to fill in a paternity form.'

'I'll fill in a dozen forms if it makes you happy,' he offered. The completed form came back promptly and I made an appointment for Mum and me to go to the Register Office. I was told she'd have to come along. Since she was the person who had registered me in the first place, she had to be there for the re-registering. It sounded fairly ridiculous at my age, but by now I was used to the funny little ways of bureaucrats on both sides of the Atlantic.

It wasn't the walkover of a task it might have seemed. Aside from her agoraphobia, my mother's health had deteriorated badly since she became ill while we were running the pub. She often needed support to walk and on a bad day I could hardly support myself. At times we must have looked a tragi-comic pair, hobbling along. The tragic bit was that I was slowly having to accept that I wouldn't be able to go on caring for her at home much longer. But my mind was on happier things as we waited our turn in a long queue and finally found ourselves in a bleak little office facing an officious-looking grey-suited gent. He listened to my story, looked at the forms, looked at me. What, he wanted to know, did the initial C after Jack in my father's name stand for? I had no idea.

'It could be Cecil,' I suggested. 'His mother's name was Cecile.'

The grey-suit looked horrified. 'No good guessing. You'll have to find out. We can't do anything until we know.'

Did they have a phone I could use to call America? Of course not. The next hour was spent with me and Mum crushed together in a telephone box in Birmingham city centre. A foot away a man with a pneumatic drill was digging up the pavement. Mum was pleading with me to find her a toilet, urgently, while I fed a handful of small coins into the slot. I wasn't in a good mood when I finally spoke to my Dad. 'What's your middle name? What does the C stand for?' I screamed over the noise of the drill.

'Nothing,' was the surprising answer. That mysterious C wasn't the first letter of anything but merely part of his name. Apparently lots of Americans have an initial that doesn't mean anything. I was learning something new every day – and so was the man in the grey suit. I phoned him next and explained the situation. He'd never heard of such a thing and didn't know what to do about it. He gave me a London number to phone to check if this was all right. The London contact confirmed it was OK. I rang Grey Suit who still wasn't convinced. He'd changed his tack. He now required a letter from my father explaining the C.

Somewhere around this point I lost my temper and it was perhaps lucky that the drill drowned out some of my opinions of the person on the other end of the line. I took advantage of a pause in the drilling to point out that he could contact his London office and that I was coming back to see him and expected my case to be sorted out promptly, efficiently and today. I slammed the phone down before he could argue and set off with my very distressed mother towards the nearest public convenience. One thing we had in common with America were people in authority whose sole task seemed to be to delay and frustrate you.

Mum and I had a cup of coffee, and relieved and refreshed, we started the trek back to complete our task. Grey Suit was out to lunch, so we sat near his office and nabbed him on his way back in. He was beginning to look like a hunted man, but at least the form filling could begin.

Then the questions started. He seemed to require every minute detail of my birth, and my mother's life at the time around it. I turned to Mum. 'I hope you have a good memory,' I said, 'because he's going to want to know where I was conceived next.' Mum's mouth fell open in shock. Not at the personal questions she was being asked, but at me daring to speak out in this way in front of – an office clerk! I'd forgotten her fear of public officials, however minor. After all these years she was still terrified of authority. If I'd had any fears in that direction, working with War Babes had certainly knocked them out of me.

'For Heaven's sake, Mum, he's just a clerk employed by the taxpayer. We pay his wages.'

Poor Mum. She looked as if she didn't know where to put herself. 'Your mouth is going to get you into trouble one of these days, our Shirley,' she muttered warningly. 'He could refuse to let you have your father's name on the certificate.'

Grey Suit waited for this family fracas to die down then asked more personal questions. Finally, it seemed to be done and he went away. When he came back he managed a smile. 'Right, Mrs McGlade,' he announced in a satisfied tone, 'in a few weeks' time you will be officially known as Mrs Shirley Anne Crowley.'

There was a stunned silence as Mum and I looked at each other. 'I hope not,' I said. 'I'm not marrying the guy. He's my father, as I've been explaining for hours now. It's my maiden name I want to change.'

He looked extremely embarrassed, almost human in fact. 'I'm sorry,' he muttered. 'It's an unusual request. I'm not used to this.'

'You'd better get used to it,' I said, 'and all your colleagues because I'm finding fathers all the time. There will be a lot more requests like this if I have anything to do with it.'

I went back a couple of weeks later, filled in one more form and was handed my new birth certificate. I held it aloft and looked at it. It was beautiful, complete with my father's name, nationality, occupation – all the things that had been so conspicuously absent before. It was complete and now so was I. It was the best present a father could give a daughter.

.

I got another present in March 1987. The phone rang one Sunday and it was Dad. 'Can you come over and see us in May?' he asked. I'd been waiting for him to ask for so long I'd almost given up hope. Not that I was in a position to afford the fare yet, but Barry had been saving like mad, and given an invitation I knew I'd beg, steal or borrow to get there. But it seemed I didn't even have to do any of these. Rhoda, Dad's second wife, came on the phone. They were tired of waiting to see me, she told me in her matter-of-fact way, and tomorrow she was going out to buy me an airline ticket to Sacramento. I told her I hadn't been sure my father wanted to meet me.

'Of course he wants to meet you,' she said. It seems he'd been waiting for me to suggest coming in my own good time, and didn't want to rush me. While I'd been waiting for him to mention it! I told Rhoda about my big fear – that my father wouldn't like me. 'He's your father,' she said. 'He likes you already.' It was true. He did seem to. But what was I? A penfriend, a telephone companion?

Meeting him face to face, spending days, weeks with him – that was different. Long-term friendships had failed at that hurdle, and our relationship was still new and untried. He might be my father, but he was still almost a stranger.

I thanked them both; I said I'd love to come, and it was true. It was what I wanted just about most in the world, but it was also true that it was what frightened me most.

One of my first thoughts was, 'I must tell Mum.' How I longed to be able to rush into the next room and find her there, eager for the latest instalment. But it was no longer that simple. For the past few weeks, Mum had been living in an old people's home. It hadn't been an easy decision to make, but my worsening arthritis and her increasing fragility had meant it was inevitable. Since our time running the pub, Mum had been plagued by a mystery illness which involved her bringing up blood. At first the doctors thought the problem was to do with her stomach, then they decided it lay in her lungs. We feared the worst, of course.

'Please,' I begged a hospital doctor, 'if it's cancer, don't tell her. She couldn't take it. She's not the kind of person who would want to know. She'd go to pieces.' He was sorry, he explained, but hospital policy was to be honest with patients, even if their illness was terminal. To our great relief further tests proved she didn't have cancer. What the tests couldn't seem to pinpoint was what she actually did have.

In real terms what it meant was that often I had a semi-invalid to cope with, and with my own illness as well as the demands of War Babes, I simply wasn't up to it. Mum could be a difficult patient and the strain was making me a short-tempered and poor nurse. She wasn't getting the care she deserved and towards the end of 1986 I reached a point at which I knew I couldn't go on any longer. My sister, Pat, didn't feel she could take on Mum, and the only alternative was to look for a place in a residential home. I'll admit I hadn't the courage to talk the problem over with Mum. It was too painful, too personal. I dreaded how she'd react and I was riddled with guilt, like a heartless Victorian daughter planning to send her old mother to the workhouse.

In December 1986, when Mum was again in hospital, I approached the social worker and explained the problem. I wanted a residential place, but it had to be in a home I had confidence in and it had to be local. I also wanted help in breaking the news to her.

The social worker was understanding and helpful. She took me to see a home that was virtually only down the road from where we lived. On a good day, when my knee joints were behaving themselves, I would be able to walk there in five or ten minutes. It turned out to be a very ordinary building which blended in completely with the surroundings – so completely I hadn't realized it was there – but in my guilt-induced pessimism, I still expected to walk in and find a mini-institution, packed with sad, dejected and neglected old ladies desperate to escape. Instead I found a cheerful, busy place, with bright, pretty single or shared rooms and as much freedom as each individual wanted and was capable of enjoying. Far from being the workhouse, it was like a modern hotel and I knew instinctively Mum would like it – if only she'd agree to give it a try.

The part I dreaded most was still to come – breaking the news. The social worker arranged for us to use a side room at the hospital and she, Pat and I went up to see Mum there. One of the nurses brought Mum in, looking terribly small and vulnerable in her nightclothes, as she faced this deputation. Pat had agreed that she would do the talking, but found she couldn't at the last minute. The social worker was there chiefly to offer support and so the task, as I'd feared it might, fell to me. Mum only took her eyes off my guilty face to glance, questioningly, at the others from time to time. She looked terrified, as if she were waiting for the axe to fall, for the final blow, and I was sure she was going to refuse outright to co-operate. When I'd finished she asked quietly, 'Is that all?' I nodded.

'You frightened the life out of me,' she said indignantly, her old spirit coming back. 'Coming in here like this, all serious. I thought you were going to tell me there was something terrible wrong with me. If it's only the old folks' home, I don't mind about that. I know what a strain it's been on Shirley lately. I've been thinking about it myself. I'm willing to go to this place, but I'll only stay if I like it, mind . . .'

She loved it. In some ways it's painful to admit, but moving away from me was one of the best things my mother could have done. Settling into the home was no problem. She shared a room with another lady and there was space for all her personal possessions and photographs (including one of my father). If she wanted privacy she could have found it, but being alone to my mother had, for a long time, meant fear and panic attacks, and one of the things that delighted her about the place was being surrounded by people. Straightaway she made friends and was volunteering to join in every activity available. Around the time Dad invited me to visit, she'd been offered a little job helping in the kitchen because she seemed to have improved so much. I watched this development of her personality with amazement, anxiety and pride, like a proud parent with a wayward child.

Now I was no longer worn down by the tasks of caring, I could see my mother as a person. I'd always loved her; now I remembered how much I liked her. She'd ring me, holding the phone so that I could hear a singer or an appallingly bad piano player in the background, and we'd chat and giggle like a couple of teenage pals. I'd go up to see her for an hour, arranging for Barry to pick me up, and ring to tell him to come later because I was having such a nice time. They were good times, perhaps too good to last, and I'll always be glad of them and the fact that I got to know Mum as she really was again.

I stood by the phone after I'd finished talking to Dad, wondering whether to phone the home. She'd want to know all right. I might bore everyone else in the family occasionally talking about my Dad, but Mum was always interested.

She'd never quite got over the shock of him forgetting her, though she'd tried to understand the reasons. Ultimately it made no difference to her feelings for him. Quite simply, Jack Crowley was the love of her life, the most fascinating man she had ever met. Had she known him a little longer, no doubt she'd have discovered he had his faults like the rest of the human race, but there hadn't been time for reality to intrude into their relationship and my father was enshrined for ever in her mind as the perfect man.

She didn't really like looking at recent photographs of him. That white-haired pensioner had little connection with the man in her memories. In those, Jack Crowley was for ever the handsome, black-haired soldier who swept her off her feet. She'd been delighted by his easy acceptance of me, though as she pointed out, she'd told me he would never reject me. If he was alive, that is, which, as I pointed out, she'd doubted for a good many years. This latest bit of news would make her day. I could imagine how her eyes would light up. And that's what decided me against phoning her. I wanted to see her face when I told her, and tomorrow night I was going down to see her. The news would keep.

It was 6 p.m. and I was putting the finishing touch to the evening meal for Barry and me when the phone rang. I picked it up rather resentfully. Barry was due in any minute, I was starving, and I could do without a long, complicated War Babes call keeping me from my dinner.

'Mrs McGlade?' a woman's voice enquired. 'This is Selly Oak hospital. We've just admitted your mother. I'm afraid she's had a heart attack.' It took me a few seconds to take in the words and my first reaction was that there had been a mistake. There was nothing wrong with my mother's heart. I tried to explain this, but the voice didn't seem convinced. She checked my mother's name with me. It tallied – but they could still have taken in a different patient from the home and been given my mother's name in error by a member of staff who didn't know the residents very well. The voice went on, quietly insisting they had my mother there and I ran out of desperate excuses.

'Mrs McGlade, are you there?' I couldn't speak, couldn't move. For-tunately, at that moment, Barry let himself in and I handed him the phone and burst into tears. While he asked sensible questions I went about putting the meal on the table, like a robot.

'It's true, then?' I asked, wonderingly, as he sat down to join me at the table.

He nodded. 'I'm not sure how bad she is. You know what they're like at hospitals. They don't give much away, certainly not over the phone. We can see her a bit later. They're still working on her so there's no point in leaving for an hour or so. Come on,' he added gently, 'get some food down you. You'll need all your strength. We may be at the hospital for a long time.'

I tried a forkful, but something had happened to my taste buds. It was like trying to get cement past the lump in my throat. I thought of all the plates Mum had put in front of me in a lifetime of caring and catering, and how even when we were very poor and Bert had resented every scrap I swallowed, those plates were full and nourishing. 'I want to go now,' I said.

'You won't be able to see her yet. You'll just be in the way. Your Mum's in good hands. There's nothing you can do.'

I knew Barry was right, but the feeling persisted that I had to be close to her. Maybe she wanted me there, was asking for me, and not understanding why I wasn't with her. We went early. I wanted to get to the hospital but at the same time I dreaded what I'd find. It was the hospital where my Nan had died, where my sister aged 3 had been treated for pneumonia – and treated badly, Mum always insisted. It had painful memories for Mum. In fact she had a real phobia about the place and, later I asked one of the nurses not to tell her where she was if she came round. Ironically this is the same hospital I now attend with my arthritis and I've had the best of treatment available. Nor have I any complaints about the care Mum received, but hurrying down the long corridors that night in March, I thought of Nan coming in here never to return home and felt a chill of foreboding.

They were wheeling Mum on to the ward as we arrived and they asked us to wait while they drew the curtains around her bed and did whatever nurses do in such circumstances. I could hear Mum's voice, strangely muffled. It wasn't possible to hear what she was saying but it was clear from the tone that she was grumbling about something.

That's my girl, I thought. Don't let them push you around. I smiled at Barry and was starting to whisper, 'I think she's all right . . .' when a nurse pulled back the curtain. There she lay, propped up slightly on pillows, looking pale and fragile, but not otherwise changed in any dramatic way. She was wearing an oxygen mask, which accounted for the muffled tones, and kept trying to remove it, which explained the grumbles. Barry and I took up positions, one on each side of the bed, he with his arms around her shoulders. I took her hand. I was so pleased that despite everything her eyes were open and she was able to speak. It had to be a good sign. She turned her head and looked directly at me – and it was clear from the terrible blankness on her face that she had no idea who I was. Of all things I'd dreaded this was the one I'd left off the list and somehow it was the most horrible.

'Mum, it's me, Shirley,' I whispered in dismay and the nurse – perhaps partly to distract me – asked,

'Have you a dog called Banger?'

I shook my head. 'Snowy. Why?'

'It's just that your Mum keeps talking about this banger. We couldn't make out what or who it was. Someone suggested it might be the family pet.' Barry and I looked at each other blankly, but it wasn't long before we discovered what the nurse meant. As we sat there Mum suddenly began to talk quietly and urgently to herself, or to someone who existed only for her. If you listened carefully and knew a bit about her past, you could make sense of it.

'Did you hear that one, Violet? That was close. A real banger that was.' She was talking to her wartime friend, Violet, and the bangers were the bombs that were falling about them in this waking dream. Mum was back in the 1940s, reliving the years which, despite the dangers and the privations, had been the happiest of her life. She was looking at me again, staring me straight in the eye. 'I think it's getting closer. It's bad tonight, isn't it, Violet? What a terrible raid.'

'I'm Shirley, Mum, your daughter. I'm not Violet.' I couldn't believe she could look straight at me, with such alertness, and not know me. There had to be an explanation and suddenly it hit me. She was playing a joke on us. She'd always had a pretty weird sense of humour. I leaned closer, touching the ribbon on the front of her nightdress, giving it a playful little tug to show I'd rumbled her.

'Come on, stop teasing us. You know who I am. You're just pretending, aren't you?' Her eyes met mine again, but they weren't seeing me. She was listening but she wasn't hearing me. She was miles and decades away in the middle of an air raid.

Quite unexpectedly she slumped forward in Barry's arms. I didn't realize what had happened. I was still fiddling with the ribbon on the front of her nightdress, trying to make some contact. Barry was staring at my hand moving, then he pulled it away and watched her chest for a few seconds.

'She's not breathing,' he said. 'Shirley, your mother is dead.'

I don't know which of us shouted for help, but within seconds it seemed as if half the hospital staff were descending on the bed, issuing instructions to each other. We were ushered into a side room, out of the way, while an emergency team went into action. Barry and I sat looking at each other, totally bewildered. I'd never seen anyone die except in the movies, where it was sudden and violent or drawn out and dramatic. Surely people didn't just slump forward and die as if nodding off to sleep in an armchair. She couldn't be dead.

The answer was that she had been, but when they took us to see her in the intensive-care unit, she no longer was. Death was no longer final as it had been in Nan's day. Mum had been resuscitated and was breathing with the help of life-support equipment. But at least she was breathing. There was hope.

The atmosphere of the unit, with its high-tech machines bleeping out the signals of life, was entirely different from the ward. Here you felt you had to walk on tiptoe and whisper for fear of disturbing these people who hung, finely balanced, between life and death. But it wasn't at all like that, I discovered. If anything were to bring Mum out of her coma, it would be noise and stimulation, not silence. Nobody really knows what someone in that condition can take in, but I was told to assume she could hear and understand me. I was to talk to her as much as possible, and once I'd got over the self-consciousness of chatting to a totally unresponsive person, it became quite easy to do. Easy, deceptively easy, perhaps – to see muscles twitch and believe that she was hearing and respond-ing, too.

I told her over and over about my plans to visit my father and how much I wanted her to get better and share the pleasure with me. I spent hours by the bed, every day, talking, talking, talking. When I wasn't there, Raymond was. My half-brother was living in Exeter and he'd come straight up as soon as I contacted him.

'Our Raymond' had a special place in Mum's heart. He was her only son and she missed him badly when he left home. She was always writing to him and his Christmas visits home were the high point of her year. I sometimes think she hung on to life, or what was left of it, for Raymond. If she had died the night of her heart attack, he would never have been able to spend those last quiet hours at her bedside, and he would have felt guilty about it for the rest of his life.

Raymond and I had never been close as children, though we had enough to bring us together, not least a shared fear of his father, my stepfather. It was hard for me to feel close to him when, as I saw it, he'd come along and taken my mother's attention away from me. I resented the little so-and-so! It wasn't until I started searching for my father in earnest that we got to know each other. I found him understanding and sympathetic. Something of a loner himself – he never married and spends much of his spare time writing – he nevertheless under-stood my need to know my father and my American family.

I no longer resented Raymond taking Mum off me. I was very grateful that there would be a familiar face there if she were to open her eyes in this strange and frightening environment. Did I really believe Mum was going to recover? Where there's life there's hope, they say, and I went on hoping right up until the moment I got the phone call from her doctor on Friday lunch-time. There was no longer any chance of Mum surviving, he told me. They had done all the tests and she was brain dead. With my permission they were going to take her off the life-support machine. Now she would never hear my news, I remember thinking. I told the doctor I wanted to be with her when she went. How long would it take?

'I'd come over now if you can,' he said. I was with Barry's Mum, Edie, who was moving house next day. Barry was over at her new place, a bungalow a couple of streets away from the family house that had grown far too large now she was a widow with none of her children living at home. I got a neighbour to take us both over to Barry, left her there, and then went on to the hospital. I felt strangely calm.

Mum had been moved from intensive care to an ordinary ward. Raymond was sitting with her. I sat down beside him and waited. She was lying on her back and all the surgical tubes and other paraphernalia had been removed except for one tube in her arm. When the doctor came round I asked about that. It was a feeding tube, he explained. I was astounded.

'Why are you feeding her when she's dying?'

'Would you like me to remove it?' he asked, and when he had I asked if they would turn her on to her side. She'd never liked sleeping on her back. They did and she looked more comfortable, as if she were tucked up in bed for the night.

I'd expected the moment of death to come quickly. So, presumably had the doctor who had encouraged me to hurry round, but Mum hung on to life through the afternoon, evening and into the night. She continued to breathe very, very shallowly. 'Butterfly breathing', the doctor called it, a pretty name for such a final action. Late in the evening, virtually under doctor's orders, I left the bedside for a short break. Getting away seemed to clear my head and lift the scales from my eyes. When I went back I could look at the frail body that lay there and think, That's not my Mother; it's just a shell. Mum had died four days ago. For some reason this realization and the exhaustion made me angry and the anger turned towards Raymond, who hadn't budged from his position at her bedside.

'I don't know what you think you're doing, sitting there, the dutiful son. Why didn't you come home more than once a year? Why didn't you visit her more often when she was alive? I'm going home. It's silly sitting here.'

'I prefer to stay,' Raymond said. He looked hurt but I think he understood how confused my emotions were. He never held the outburst against me. It was ten o'clock when I left and on the way out I bumped into a nurse we'd got to know.

'Bring your mother in some pretty soap when you come tomorrow,' she said sweetly. What was the woman thinking of? Did she not know of my mother's condition? Did she think I didn't know?

'My mother's dead,' I said. 'She died on Monday night.'

At 2 a.m. the hospital rang. My mother had just died, they said. All I could think was Thank God for that – at last she was at peace. Raymond had stayed with her until the end. Barry and I were waiting up for him with tea and an apology and we sat up talking for most of the remainder of the night.

'Let's just think of the good times we had with her,' he said, and there were plenty of those to keep us occupied. Not that we'd always seen events as humorous at the time they happened. We laughed about the way Mum would make us jump off a moving bus half-way between stops to avoid having to walk a long distance. And that brought us to the occasion when she stumbled and was dragged along the street by a bus. She wasn't injured physically, but her pride was. In her embarrassment she managed to transfer the blame to Raymond, who received a sharp slap around the ear.

I told him about the time, the previous December, when she was in hospital during a very bad spell of wintry weather. Cars and buses were useless in the icy blizzard and it had taken Barry and me hours to struggle through the snow to visit her. When we got there she was lying back on pillows. 'You're late,' she said. 'Have you brought my tissues?' Totally oblivious to the weather and our chilled countenances, she chatted cheerfully and called after us as we left, 'Don't forget the tissues tomorrow night.' We came close to strangling her that night.

We laughed a lot. It helped to keep the grief at bay. It wasn't until the next day, after three hours' sleep, that it hit me. It had snowed overnight and we woke to a white world. Barry, Martin and I went over to move my mother-in-law to her new home, an arrangement made before my mother was taken ill. I could have stayed home, I suppose, but Barry thought I'd just sit around moping if I did. Better to be with people at a time like this.

Edie was only moving around the corner, but the roads were icy and the hired van refused to climb even the small hills. Some of Barry's other relatives had turned out to help too and there was a lot of pushing and cursing the vehicle, and a fair amount of laughter too. It was the laughter – other people's laughter – that got me. Suddenly I was overcome with misery. I sat inside the van, over the back wheels where I'd been placed for some technical reason, and watched all the activity and the fun as if from a long way off. I couldn't believe that life was going on as normal, that people could be engrossed in everyday things, while my mother lay dead a few miles away.

Yet life went on for everyone but me, even my husband and my son. I knew that both Martin and Barry cared for my mother and that, in their different ways, they would miss her. But I also knew that neither of them could feel the sharp pain of loss the way I did, or the great gap that opens up in your life when someone you've seen almost every day of your life for forty years is taken away. I wanted to get out of the van and run away – or shout from the roadside that this was no ordinary day. But I didn't. I sat there while life carried on around me and felt very much alone.

The cremation was on Friday the 13th, not surprisingly the only free day at a very busy time for funerals. It was a case of going ahead then or waiting another week and Raymond had to get back to work. It was a frantic week with lots of arrangements to be made and I kept going on nervous energy. I didn't give myself time to think and it was only on the morning of the funeral that I started to go to pieces. As the hearse with the coffin inside, crawled to a standstill outside, I decided I couldn't go through with it. I couldn't face this much reality, this much finality, head on. 'I'm not going,' I announced, taking off my coat. 'I'll stay here and do the sandwiches. I'll see you when you get back.'

'You are coming,' Barry said firmly, attempting to put my coat back on. 'I know you. You need to be there. As soon as the hearse moves off you'll change your mind and regret it.'

He was probably right. I could see myself hobbling after the hearse, shouting, 'Wait for me.' I sobbed all the way there and was still crying as we took our places inside the church. It was to be a short, simple service. Mum hated 'fancy' funerals, with endless hymns and flowery prose from a clergyman who hardly knew the deceased anyway. But somehow it still turned into a bit of a farce, with people standing up when they should be sitting down and vice versa.

Mum would have enjoyed it, I found myself thinking. If her spirit was floating about somewhere up there, she'd be having a good laugh at the mess we were making of her big day. I caught sight of Raymond and thought of our conversation the night she died. Remember the good times, he'd said, and I did. I cut myself off from the sights and sounds around me and cast my mind back to the funny incidents in the past. It was the only way to get through. People must have wondered why I was smiling as the coffin slid out of view. Mum would have understood.

I'd kept my father informed throughout Mum's final illness. Afterwards I didn't try to hide my sadness from him but I couldn't bring myself to tell him about the other, irrational feelings. These were the childish fears that sprang out of nowhere and threatened to engulf me once the funeral was over and the letters of sympathy had stopped arriving. But maybe the fears didn't come from nowhere but from my childhood.

As a small child, when my Nan had died, I'd believed that God had taken her away to punish me for some unspecified crime. Now I began to feel much the same thing, as if my mother's death was a kind of punishment. I'd achieved my life's ambition, to find my father, and I had the chance to meet him face to face. Now it seemed I was being told I couldn't have both parents. The price I had to pay for my father's presence was my mother's life. I never said it was rational, but it was real to me – real enough to make me doubt I should go to America. Perhaps it just wasn't meant to be.

At the same time I was grieving for my mother. Life seemed very empty without her and in an attempt to fill that aching gap in my life I turned to Barry's mother for comfort. Edie had always seemed like a second mother to me anyway. I even called her Mum – except when my own mother was around and liable to get offended. Kind-hearted Edie fell happily into the new role I allocated her. Her husband had died a year earlier, her eyesight was beginning to fade and she lived alone, so she welcomed my extra visits. We began to get very close.

But the run of bad luck was not yet over. The morning we moved Edie into her new home had been – even in my misery I could see – like a comedy show. Not only did the van break down but we lost the tenant. She was not at her old home when we got there and could not be found at the bungalow either. This produced much mirth on the lines of which packing crate Gran had been put in, but when she turned up at the bungalow the laughter stopped. She was chilled, miserable and weeping as she explained that she'd been to the doctor and had been given medicine for gastro-enteritis. A cup of tea and a warm by the fire comforted her, and once she was smiling again, nobody gave a second thought to what we assumed was a routine tummy ailment.

But the illness never went away. Some days I'd call to find her looking quite poorly, but she was always happy to put her troubles out of her mind and chat about my trip to America. Like Barry, she thought I must go. It was, she insisted, the chance of a lifetime, and I wasn't to worry about Barry. She'd look after him while I was away. With her encouragement and reassurance, I was beginning to think I could make the trip after all.

Gradually she began to get worse. The doctor changed the medication but that didn't seem to help. On the Saturday five weeks after my mother died, Barry and I called round to see her and found her in bed, really poorly. She didn't want to let us take her back to our house and nurse her, because she feared being a nuisance. We reassured her, and when that didn't work, threatened to move in and look after her there. There was no way we were leaving her alone. That did the trick. She allowed me to help her dress, and Barry half-carried her to the car. Tucking her up in bed, I vowed to keep her there till she was better.

On Sunday morning I went in and knew at once that she was going to need far more than our tender loving care. She had deteriorated greatly in the night, and there was no doubt that the old lady was seriously ill. It was like looking at my mother in the last week of her life and I found the sight chilling.

The doctor, a locum standing in for our regular GP, who responded to my call, at first treated her condition very casually. I wasn't having any of it. I'd lost my mother and was going to do everything in my power to see that history did not repeat itself. I demanded he take her blood pressure, pleaded with him to examine her more closely. This he did – and immediately called an ambulance.

The events that followed seemed to happen with horrifying speed. Edie went into hospital, then into intensive care, then into a coma. The similarities with what had happened to my mother were almost unbelievable. After a week in this state, we were told that her kidneys had completely failed and they were going to take her off the life-support machine. Edie's family gathered around her bed. She didn't put up the fight my mother had. Just six weeks after Mum died, my lovely mother-in-law slipped quickly and quietly from us.

That was in April. I was due to go to America in May. Weighed down with a double load of grief, I was now absolutely certain that I was not meant to meet my father. I had been given clear warning. If I defied it the plane would probably be plucked from the skies and dashed to the ground. The return flight was even booked for the 13th.

And then there was Barry. I knew exactly what he was going through and how much he needed my support. Here, I might not be able to give him as much help as I should, because I was still grieving for my own mother, but to take off for the other side of the world would be tantamount to deserting him in his hour of need. On the other hand, I felt guilty about letting my father down. There he was, waiting to meet me, eagerly planning for my arrival. I should be the happiest woman in the world, but instead I was confused and depressed. I felt guilty about that too.

I told Barry I was going to call the trip off and he begged me not to. It wouldn't help him, he said; it wouldn't help me to get over my loss and neither of the Mums would have wanted it. My little girl fears that I was being punished, were just that, he insisted; childish fantasies. And then, fighting like with like, he came up with an alternative theory. Had I thought, he wondered, that God might not have taken my mother away because I had found my father, but that, knowing I had to lose my mother, He had first given me my father as a consolation, something to look forward to?

I hadn't seen it that way round, but the frightened little girl in me responded immediately to the idea. Looking at the situation from a different angle, seeing my father as a gift, made all the difference in the world. I didn't even try to shake off the grief. It was right and natural, but it was eased, if only temporarily, by the need to make practical plans. Now that I had decided to make the trip there were letters to write, shopping to do for the warm California weather. I had to arrange with the hospital the best moment to have the cortisone injections that should keep me mobile at least for the three weeks in Sacramento. I refused to arrive hobbling like an old crone, though it probably wouldn't have shocked or surprised Dad too much. Rheumatoid arthritis ran in the family, I'd discovered, one legacy I could have done without.

One lot of fears were replaced by another batch. What would I wear? Would Dad recognize me? Would he like me? Would we find anything to talk about? How were Rhoda and my half-brothers going to react to this English cuckoo in the nest? What on earth would I find to say to the American film crew joining me for the second leg of the journey to film a segment for NBC television news? How would someone who'd never been further than Europe – and then only on a package holiday – cope with two long flights and changing planes in between? Should I ask for a wheelchair to transfer me from one terminal to the other? The way I was feeling, just thinking about it all, a stretcher might be more appropriate!

At odd moments in the midst of all this action and anxiety, I'd think of Mum and the tears would start. I'd let them fall and then pull myself together as I knew she'd have wanted me to. I was about to embark on the most exciting journey of my life. She couldn't be with me in body, but I knew she was with me in spirit, warning me to behave myself and not show her up as I had so often when she was alive!

11
'Remember You're Half American'

The amazing thing was that even if I'd never seen a photograph of him, I believe I'd have known him. The moment I got off the plane and looked at my father, I knew I could have picked him out of that crowd at the airport, out of the whole world, without any clues. Across the heads of the curious onlookers, around the television cameras, our eyes met and there was a sort of instant bonding; the way it is when you first look at your newborn baby. It wasn't just the obvious family resemblance; there was a surge of chemistry between us that took me completely by surprise.

I felt too shy to talk about this to my father and it wasn't until he wrote the foreword to this book that I realized he had felt the same magic at our first meeting. If either of us had any lingering doubts that a mistake had been made, they evaporated in Sacramento airport on Friday, 22 May 1987.

Not that we said anything so deep or emotive to each other as we stood there, jostled on all sides by television people. I've often wondered what it would have been like to have conducted my relationship with my father in total anonymity. I'll never know. Once I became known to the media on both sides of the Atlantic, every move I made was in the spotlight. At times I regretted it. As we stood side by side in front of the camera, my father gazing down fondly on me, the television soundman picking up every word, Dad's voice rang out loud and clear: 'Do you dye your hair?'

'Yes,' I admitted, too shocked to think of lying. Afterwards Dad apologized and explained that he hadn't thought of my privacy – he'd been too curious to know why my hair was black when the Crowleys invariably start to go grey at around 35. I've not let him forget it. I tease him about it regularly, the indignity of travelling thousands of miles to be asked if my hair is dyed! His response is that he didn't invite me to have me publicly comment on his 'sausage fingers'! Mum had always blamed my father for passing on to me inelegant, short fat fingers and I had to give words to the moment of recognition when he took my hand in his larger but identical one.

The first day in America is a blur of sights, sounds and impressions. A warm welcome from Rhoda . . . the trip back to their home in Elk Grove, on the edge of the city – and the alarming sensation of being driven on the wrong side of the road. The feeling of space around their single-storey home, with Dad's plant nursery attached. The fact that there were no internal doors except on the bedrooms. The spa or hot tub for six on the deck in the lathe house, where Dad kept his plants. (Would I ever be able to hop in and out of it in the nude, like Rhoda, when my head could be seen poking out of it by visitors to the lathe house? The answer was no. My British reserve never wavered. I always wore my swimsuit. 'Miss Modesty', Rhoda christened me.) There was the heat – 100°F some days – and the grass kept green despite it by an endless succession of twirling water sprinklers. The lack of pavements. Where did people walk? The answer was that, of course, they didn't. Everyone drove everywhere.

I met the other resident members of the family, the three dachshunds, Bonsai, Marmie and Satsuki, and we sat up talking until 10.30 p.m. – late by Dad's and Rhoda's standards. Dad had become something of an unwilling celebrity since I'd found him, a situation he'd handled with his usual politeness and good humour. Many people who had read about us or seen him on television had written congratulating him on his persistent daughter and praising him for welcoming me so warmly and openly. It was further reassurance that the American people were on our side.

Rhoda admitted to having reservations about contacting families, but Dad completely supported the work of War Babes. He felt we had every right to find our fathers, and to the help of the government in doing so, even if the fathers subsequently didn't want to take the relationship any further. He understands from experience the need that drives someone to spend years searching for a parent. His parents' marriage broke up and his father left home and disappeared out of the lives of his two sons. When he was a young man in the army, Dad decided he wanted to see him again. He tracked him down and found not only his father but a second family of half-brothers and -sisters, for Grandad had remarried.

He told me how shocked he'd been when he first heard my 'shaky little voice' announce on the phone that I was his daughter, but he'd never thought of denying it, even though he had no idea he had a child in England. It wouldn't have been part of his moral code, and he didn't think it should be part of any other decent American's either: 'You just don't deny family.'

When I say what I did during those three weeks with my father, it sounds so mundane. His life just carried on and I slotted into it. I wouldn't have wanted it any other way. The time was not spent in deep emotional exchanges in some vain attempt to make up for forty years of missed intimacy, but in chatting about the dogs and his plants, in meeting his friends and listening to stories about his childhood and youth. I talked about my mother – how could I avoid it when she was so much in my thoughts? – but not about the sadness of my lonely childhood. There had been enough said and written about that and it didn't seem the time or place.

We hardly touched on feelings, and I think this is something that happens to many war babes when they meet their fathers, and often they find it hard to take when they've invested so much emotional energy in the relationship. They want something geared to a higher pitch, a relationship that centres on them and will cure the pains of childhood for ever. It's altogether too much to expect of an elderly man set in his ways.

For me it was enough to be close to my father, to be part of his life. Right from that first meeting at the airport I had felt totally comfortable with him, as if I'd found my safe harbour. This man was my father; he would protect me from danger. A tall order for any man! We could chat with ease, but we could also be together comfortably without the need for words.

'You're so like Ted,' Dad told me, bringing into the conversation as he often did, his only brother, now dead. 'Ted was real easy to talk to. He got on well with everybody.' It made me so happy to know I was like somebody, after years of being like nobody in my English family.

I was a lot like Dad too. At least we seemed to have the same thought processes. We each knew what the other was thinking, which isn't something that necessarily happens just because you've known someone a long time – as Barry could tell you. I don't know how many times he and I have sat together in the evening and I've come out with a remark that puzzles him. 'Hey? What are you on about?' he'll enquire, with an irritated look. I'm probably referring to something mentioned briefly two hours earlier, or a topic of conversation from two days back that had been playing on my mind but obviously not on his. With Dad there was never the need to wonder what the other was talking about. We always knew, even if nobody else did. We were in the sitting room one evening, and out of the blue, he remarked, 'By the way, was there a brick fireplace a few feet up the wall?'

It was ages since there had been any mention of my Nan's old house in Long Street, but I knew exactly what he meant. I'd talked a lot to him about his time in England with my family, trying to jog his memory. Tantalizing little snippets of information would come to him and it was obvious that the experience hadn't been wiped away but was lurking somewhere at the back of his mind. I confirmed that he was right about the fire and then the subject dropped. Much later, I was struck by another thought: 'Do you remember, the coal used to be underneath?'

'Mmm,' he said. Another long pause, then, when everyone else's mind was elsewhere, 'And someone used to take the ashes out, didn't they?' Rhoda thought it was very funny. She also thought we were the most boring pair of talkers in the world.

'Gee, if someone was eavesdropping on this conversation, they'd find it electrifying!' she laughed.

I loved to hear Dad talk about his family – our family. Everything about the Crowleys sounded exotic, not least the way they arrived in America. Dad's grandfather was one of two small boys who set sail with their parents from the poverty and starvation of Ireland for life in the new world. Conditions on board ship were terrible, however, and by the time they reached the USA, the parents were dead and the two terrified children were alone. They were taken in and raised by a kindly man who was a warden at a Crow Indian reservation and because their surname was not known someone had the bright idea of christening them Crowley. Dad's grandfather grew up to marry an Indian girl and Dad is very proud of our Indian blood.

It's a magical story, but it wasn't just the distant past that fascinated me. I could listen all day to tales of Dad and Uncle Ted's childhood in the forest country, and the exploits that drove their mother to distraction. She used to hide their shoes to stop them going out and staying out for hours, but they'd go anyway, barefoot. Despite his tendency to run wild Dad was a bright little lad, who learned to read before he went to school. When I told him that I too had picked up this skill at 4 years old – to the amazement of my Mum who hadn't even attempted to teach me – he was delighted.

'You inherited the Crowley brains,' he laughed. I suspect I inherited some less bright traits from my grandfather too. Before he took off for pastures new, Grandad ran a general store and used to make deliveries to customers in a truck that had seen better days. He also liked a drink now and then. When Dad told me how his father had once tried to see if he had enough petrol by holding a lighted match right over the top of the tank, with explosive results, I couldn't stop laughing. It was straight out of a *Tom and Jerry* cartoon, and just the sort of daft thing I could see myself doing, even without a drink! Poor old Grandad, I think I'd have liked him.

During my first two full days with him, Dad held his two annual Open House events for customers of the nursery. Nothing to do with me; it was planned before he knew I was coming, so I was just an extra name on the guest list. In point of fact, I became the floorshow. Everyone wanted to hear the story of how I traced Dad. I'd repeated it so often by the end of the two days that I was hoarse. It would have saved a lot of trouble if Dad had fixed me up with a little stage and a microphone.

To start with I was bit awestruck by the size and the efficiency of the event. Rhoda, helped by two tiny pretty Vietnamese girls, did the cooking and catering, and the influx of people began at about 2 p.m. It was a bit embarrassing at first. I didn't know if Dad expected me to tell people I was his daughter or not. We had not discussed it and I kept thinking, 'He'll brief me soon on what story to tell. I'll wait till he brings it up.' Only he didn't bring it up. It had never occurred to him that I would imagine there would be any story other than the truth.

I realized this as soon as the first batch of people walked in that first day and he trotted me up to them, saying, 'This is my daughter from England. Tell them how you found me.' He just threw me in at the deep end, introducing me to so many people that my head was spinning and there was no possibility of me remembering a fraction of their names. But they were invariably friendly, welcoming and so refreshingly open in their curiosity, and it was wonderful to know Dad had no reservations about introducing me after all the years of my telling little white lies on Mum's behalf.

Apart from how I'd traced Dad, the other question on every visitor's lips was whether I knew their English relatives. They all seemed to have one or two and I only had to admit to knowing Derby or Nottingham or wherever they lived, for them to assume I'd have come across the relative. I know England is small on a global scale but not as small as most Americans seem to believe.

On Open Day two, I met my Aunt Pat and found a soulmate. Pat is Dad's younger sister from his father's second family. He has a lovely teasing, big-brother relationship with her and he must have guessed she and I would get on. She's great fun, a fiesty and irreverent lady who knows how to come out with a choice bit of colourful language just when everyone is on their best behaviour. I would happily have sat in a corner all day talking to Aunt Pat and watching the guests coming and going, but Dad soon had me on my feet again. 'This is my daughter from England . . .'

I adapted to the Elk Grove lifestyle as if born to it. Dad and Rhoda believe in early to bed and early to rise, turning it in at around 9.30 p.m. and rising with the lark at five or six in the morning. The very thought of being dragged from my slumbers at that unearthly hour in England makes me shudder, but when the California sun is already up and about you feel you might as well join it. Day starts early there and I didn't want to waste a moment.

I quickly made friends, lovely people like neighbour Phebe and her husband Norm, from Oklahoma. Norm, now, sadly no longer with us, was one of those people I hit it off with straightaway. It was our shared silly sense of humour that did it. He told me the story about the time he borrowed his son's swish, new polaroid camera to take a picture of his calf. Not a very technically minded man, he was assured this camera was foolproof; you just pointed it and shot.

This Norm did, then he waited for his photograph to develop. When it appeared, it didn't look much like any part of a calf. Perplexed, he turned it this way and that – then realized he'd taken a picture of his own nose. It was tales like this, plus his stranger-than-fiction stories of Oklahoma, that had me in stitches. Oklahoma, where they had hurricanes that could blow a cast-iron pot inside out, or a chicken into a jug with only its head poking out. Norm knew a man who had seen both happen.

Then there was Iris, originally from Manchester and still hanging on to traces of the accent after thirty years, and her husband, Ron. They took me over in the nicest possible way, driving me around the State to see all the interesting places, when Dad was otherwise engaged in his nursery. I'll never forget Folsom, a living museum of an old cowboy town, straight out of the Westerns, but with shops and restaurants. Nor Folsom prison nearby. The prison is real, no museum piece this, you can go into the grounds and visit the gift shop, staffed by prisoners and selling goods made by other prisoners.

Then there were the giant shopping malls which make our little ones look like something out of Toytown – and the equally giant meals in restaurants. For my initiation into the American way of eating out, Iris took me out to breakfast. I couldn't believe the beaming, cheerful waitresses – at 8 a.m. – and I couldn't eat the 'ordinary breakfast' which arrived in response to my order. Sausage, three rashers, double eggs, with pancakes and syrup on the same plate. English muffins with blueberries to follow, and plenty of strong coffee.

Everywhere I went people kept forcing enormous plates of food on me, which I felt compelled to try and eat out of politeness. In the end I had to admit defeat and say, 'No thank you, I'm English,' by way of explaining my bird-like appetite. No wonder there are so many larger-than-life Americans, enormous people but unlike us not a bit self-conscious about their excess weight. They dress in shorts and skimpy T-shirts and let it all hang out. Nobody gives them a second glance, except me, the eternal tourist, gawping at everything and everyone in amazement.

I enjoyed seeing these bits of America but best of all were the days when I stayed home with Dad, just the two of us. I'd read my book or sunbathe in the lathe house, where there was just enough shade to prevent tender plants, like me and the orchids, from burning up in the heat. Dad always had work to do. He may have retired from his 'real' job, but the nursery had become his life. He loves his work and I couldn't imagine him sitting with his feet up all day drifting quietly into old age.

I'd watch him working among the plants, fascinated. I didn't try to help. I may have inherited his sausage fingers but not the green quality in them. I only have to touch a plant for it to curl up and die, and I didn't want that on my conscience. So I'd wander around or sit and watch, and wonder at the miracle of it all.

'This is my Dad,' I'd remind myself. 'After all this time, I'm here with him at last. And he's real.'

I'd watch him chew his food at lunch-time. I'd look at the grey hairs on his chest and his little mole. When we came out of the airport that first day and I heard his feet crunch on the gravel, I was surprised. He was real; he was human, not some figment of my imagination. This was the man that Mum and Nan had built up into a super-hero to comfort a fatherless little girl, and I had to take him off his pedestal and let him stand or fall as an ordinary human being. It helped that he was a nice human being.

He once said that he felt guilty about springing my existence on Rhoda. 'I guess she thought she'd married a straight arrow and maybe she didn't,' he said. But he is a straight arrow, if I understand the term, as honest and open a man as you could find anywhere. I honestly believe that I would have liked him if he wasn't my father, whatever circumstances we met under – and a lot of people can't say that about their parents.

And he seemed to like me, that was the real miracle. I'd been so scared that I wouldn't live up to his expectations, but he introduced me to people with pride and affection that made all the hard work of the past years worthwhile. He isn't an openly affectionate man, my Dad, nor is he given, usually, to touching gestures, but he excelled himself one day during my visit. I'd been reading and sunbathing and he waited till I left my position briefly. When I returned, he'd left a white orchid he'd grown himself, on my chair. I found this one little flower more touching than a whole string of flowery sentences. I took it home and tried to dry and press it, but not very successfully. It's now a rather discoloured blob of uncertain genus, but it's still very precious to me.

If I want to hear a compliment I have to listen to what he says to other people about me, and sometimes I worry that he'll say too much and irritate them. This was one of my worries when I heard that my half-brothers, Gene and Peter, were going to visit, from Nevada and South California respectively. Had Dad talked too much to them about my achievements, and my devotion in spending so long searching for him, until the very mention of sister Shirley got up their noses? Were they coming out of duty, curiosity, or a genuine desire to meet me? I very much wanted to meet them, but as usual, I was nervous.

Gene, the eldest, was first to arrive, with his wife, Susan and two of his three boys. Susan's mother lived in Sacramento and the plan was for them to stay with her and visit us. He walked in and I rushed forward, ready for a brotherly hug. I didn't get one. Instead I got a polite handshake, and I stepped back, pink with embarrassment. I felt as if I'd committed a social gaffe. It was like one of those occasions when you offer your hand and the other person doesn't notice, and by the time they've spotted your intention and thrust theirs out, you've put yours behind your back.

I couldn't understand it. Maybe embracing a stranger with whom you happened to share a father wasn't done in America. I'd make sure I was very restrained when Peter arrived. I wasn't going to make a fool of myself twice. So, when Peter, accompanied by his wife, Catherine, and 4-year-old son, Jon, arrived I made sure I kept my distance. I was polite, I was welcoming, but I made it clear this lady wasn't for hugging. When we'd got to know each other better, my little brother wanted to know why I'd been so stand-offish and made him look a fool when he was about to greet me with a hug. Two brothers, two very different people. Why did I assume they'd behave like clones?

Mind you, I discovered that Gene had a reason for being a little hesitant. Inexplicably, Dad had neglected to tell him about me until two weeks before our meeting. The first he'd heard of my existence was a letter from Rhoda, saying, 'Your sister from England is coming to stay with us.' Startled, Gene had phoned Peter to enquire if he knew anything about this mysterious sister. Yes, Peter did know. Dad had told him some time ago. Poor Gene was still at the stage of trying to take in the news when we met.

Actually it hadn't been difficult for me to keep a formal distance between me and Peter. I'd been more or less rooted to the spot with shock. He walked in late on a Friday night and it was like an optical illusion. It could have been Martin standing there: a bit older, true, but the same size, colouring, same strong dark hair. Even the way he stood, talked, used his hands – all these mannerisms were my son's, yet these two had never met. I couldn't take my eyes off him.

I was itching to get to know these two men and I jumped at the chance of a day out with them and their families in Gene's minibus. Dad, as usual, was busy in the nursery and Rhoda was out at work when we set off for the flea market. It was a fantastic hotchpotch of a place, bigger than any market I'd ever seen in England, of course, and selling everything you could – plus a great deal you couldn't – find any use for. I bought several items in each category.

We tried on funny hats of the kind you might pick up in Blackpool and looked at even funnier T-shirts, and there was a general party atmosphere that relaxed everyone. Gene's son, Ian, a great lad, took it on himself to look after me, escorting me across roads with care and courtesy. Otherwise my tendency to look to the right when traffic was coming from the left, and vice versa, would have had me squashed like a hedgehog on the highway before the day was out.

We went back to Susan's mother's house for a snack, everyone in a chatty mood. I told them about my life and they told me about theirs. We swapped experiences and I admitted that I envied them their childhood with our father. They laughed and said I had no reason to. Their lives hadn't been the fairy tale I imagined. Dad might seem genial now, but when they were young he'd been a strict father, never letting them get away with anything. They'd had to weather a divorce. When Dad and their mother broke up, they had been uprooted and separated, Gene going off to live with his mother while Peter stayed with Dad. I hadn't realized this. Dad has never talked much about his first marriage and I didn't feel it was any of my business. It took the unrealistic rosy glow off my picture of Gene's and Peter's childhood, and put my own life a little more in perspective. Perhaps there's no such thing as a totally happy childhood. Gene was surprised at the way I talked to Dad. They both were, really. They intimated they wouldn't dare to be as cheeky to him as I was. He wouldn't take the teasing and the joking from them.

I hadn't thought about the way I talked to Dad. As far as I was concerned I was just being myself and he never seemed to be offended by it. If there was a difference in his reaction to us I was sure it was down to the fact that I'm female. Fathers are notorious for letting their daughters, even grown-up ones, wrap them round their little finger, aren't they? They certainly have a different attitude to their sons. We also met for the first time as adults and equals, Dad and I, so we had no history of him as the powerful person and me the dependent child. The rules for Gene's and Peter's relationships with him had been written over thirty years earlier. There were no rules for me. We started with a fresh sheet. Besides, I told them, even if I was driving Dad mad with irritation, he knew he only had to put up with me for three weeks!

We had a lot of fun that day, but it also had its serious side. It gave me a different angle on my father. It was enlightening to hear these two men who'd known Dad all their lives, discussing him; a bit like Raymond and I talking about Mum, with affectionate irreverence. It hadn't lowered him one jot in my estimation but it had helped to humanize him. The pedestal was almost redundant and I was glad. It had only been in the way. I could get closer without it.

You think you know someone from letters and phone calls, but you can't really. It takes time. You don't even know their sense of humour. I remember agonizing over a Father's Day card for Dad and finally picking one with the message, 'To a do-it-yourself enthusiast from one of your little projects'.

It made me smile in the shop but from the moment I wrote my name on it, till I next heard from him, I worried. Would he find it funny or would it offend him? Words that were quite innocent here could mean something quite different in America. Had I inadvertently said something shocking? Should I have opted for something safe and serious instead? When he wrote and said the card had made him chuckle, the amount of relief I felt was ridiculous. I felt I had learned a great deal more about my father from seeing him in his own setting, and through other people's eyes. It taught me not to envy the relationships my brothers or anyone else had with him, but to value the very special and rare relationship that existed between us.

Before I left for home both brothers had invited me to stay with their families, but there wasn't time and I had to decline. Peter tried to persuade me to add an extra week to my holiday and spend it at his place. It was wonderful to know they accepted and wanted me and I asked if they'd keep the invitations open for another time, another trip. Right now I was beginning to feel the first pangs of homesickness.

For the first two weeks I was completely absorbed in the novelty and the excitement of it, to the exclusion of everything else. It seemed like an interval out of real life, when I could forget the sad events that had so recently overwhelmed me, and not worry about the other family I'd left behind. But suddenly homesickness hit me. Sitting on the patio in the cool of the evening, with a drink in my hand, the birds singing and the scent of flowers in the air, I yearned to exchange this corner of paradise for damp, chilly Birmingham.

A sadness that was a mixture of grief for the dead, and loneliness for the living threatened to engulf me. I wanted to see Barry and Martin and the rest of them. Most of all, I wanted to see the children in the family: Ruth, Pat's daughter, who I often looked after and my gorgeous 8-month-old granddaughter, Maria. Martin and Lorraine, his partner at the time, had made me a granny and though it made me feel ancient, I took the role seriously. Babies develop so quickly. Who knows what exciting stages I'd have missed in a few weeks away?

It wasn't that I didn't want to be with Dad. I did, but I wanted it all. I wanted my two families together and I knew that could never be. In an ideal world I would have had the resources to pop over the pond once or twice a year for visits to Dad, but that was out of the question. Even if I won the pools, my health wasn't up to the jet-setting life. Already I was beginning to dread the rigours of the return trip.

Though we'd spent a lot of time together, Dad hadn't taken me to many places during my stay and Rhoda insisted he must do his duty. He said he'd fix us up a trip, something special, and I waited with excitement to see what treat was in store for me. It turned out to be a trip to the train museum, where he pointed out the finer points of old engines and insisted on buying me postcards of his favourite locomotives. I couldn't help chuckling to myself, as he gazed at this collection of machinery. Here was a man who'd brought up two sons and no daughters! Afterwards we went to Old Sacramento for a wander around the shops and he tried to buy me everything that caught my eye. I refused to let him. The last thing I wanted, he and Rhoda having bought my air ticket and been so hospitable, was for him to spend even more money on me. Afterwards I talked to Rhoda about it.

'Oh, you should have let him buy you things,' she said. 'He's just trying to make up for all the years when he couldn't give you anything.' I suppose it's hard for him to understand that he's made up for those years already by accepting me.

I left Sacramento airport with mixed feelings – sadness at parting from my father, friends and family, but pleasure at the thought of going home. And England was home. If I'd found Dad earlier, when I had my health and Martin was a child, maybe, just maybe, we would have considered moving to America. Barry has a useful trade. As an electrician he could work anywhere. But it was too late now to think of uprooting.

The last thing Dad said was, 'Remember you're half American.' He shouted it to me with a final wave and I watched him disappear into the crowd, his blue shirt and his white hair getting smaller and smaller. I felt the warmth of those words all the way to Texas. The downside of the parting didn't hit me until I'd changed planes and was airborne on the second leg of the journey home. Until then I'd still been in my father's country. He was down there somewhere, still close. But now I was leaving America, leaving him behind, and I might never see him again. It was then, half-way between my two families, that the tears started to flow.

Barry was at Gatwick to meet me though I walked past without recognizing him. Well, I was jet-lagged and he had bought a new shirt! We stopped at the first motorway service station. 'Do you wanna go to the little boys' room?' I asked, in what had become my usual tone, as we got out. Barry's horrified face loomed up on the other side of the car.

'Keep your voice down,' he hissed, 'everyone's looking. Yes, I will be going to the Gents.' I glanced around. He was right about the looks. Shocked and amused British eyes were turned in the direction of this loud-mouthed American. It took me days and a lot of shushing and hushing from Barry to drop the Americanisms I'd picked up and to stop bellowing. Everyone I'd met, with the exception of my father, talked loudly and I'd got so tired of being told to speak up that I'd joined them with a vengeance.

Instead of going straight home we went to Barry's sister, Jeanette's house for lunch. She could see how exhausted I was – it took me weeks to adjust back to British time, though it had been so easy the other way around. 'Why don't you lie down for an hour?' Jeanette suggested, and I collapsed on to her bed with relief. It was a lovely early summer's day. The birds were singing here every bit as prettily as in California, and the flowers were in bloom. Even the sky was bluer than I remembered seeing it over England for a long time. I looked and listened with pleasure. It had been a wonderful trip, but I was glad to be home where I belonged. I turned over and fell into a deep sleep.

Barry had redecorated our house while I was away. It was therapy, he said; it took his mind off other things. Jeanette had also cleaned it from top to bottom so nothing needed to be done. A great white creature with a gigantic head had loomed up when I opened the door, sniffing at me suspiciously. If Snowy, our alsatian, found me strange, I found him even stranger. He looked so big. 'Has he grown?' I demanded of Barry. Three weeks with Dad's ankle-high dachshunds had turned our old dog into a monster.

I insisted on showing Barry the things I'd bought and in no time the floor was covered with the spoils of tourism. There were T-shirts that fitted no one, musical Beatrix Potter animals, ashtrays stamped with the number of a Folsom prisoner, a hamburger doll, with a hamburger for a head and great long legs . . . and much, much more. There were presents for everybody with plenty to spare. Barry looked on with horror as yet another American novelty appeared out of the bag and ended up on the floor.

'You've been here half an hour,' he sighed, 'and you've wrecked the place. Welcome home!'

I've made a second, shorter and equally enjoyable trip to see Dad since then, but it was the first one that established the relationship. When you first find your father, there is a sort of honeymoon period when you live in a state of nervous excitement, waiting anxiously by the phone, virtually waylaying the postman to see if he's got a letter from America. It's an exhausting time, filled with anxiety and uncertainty, and eventually the relationship has to settle down.

The sort of relationship that evolves depends on both parties, but mainly, I think, on the father. There are some who, having found their son or daughter, are loath to let them out of their sight. They write and phone weekly and make a point of visiting or being visited once or twice a year minimum. Others, often to the distress of their son or daughter, are satisfied with an occasional scribbled note.

Gradually, after meeting him, my own relationship with Dad settled down into something we both find satisfying and comfortable. I know that he has his own life in California and I have mine here. He is not the be-all and end-all of my life, nor am I in his. He missed out on my growing up so we lack that common ground most parents have with their children. You cannot make up for that. Inevitably there are people closer to him than me, but no one else has a relationship with him quite like mine. It's unique and special and very important to me.

We talk on the phone, but because there's that disconcerting little gap in transatlantic calls, between what you say and the other person hearing it, I don't find it comfortable. Dad also has a hearing loss, so there are inevitable moments of confusion and I find myself thinking, We're paying all this money just to misunderstand each other. For us, letters are better.

At first I used to write back the day his letter arrived, and I never thought anything else would take priority. But gradually I relaxed about it. I stopped panicking and thinking he'd gone off me if more than a week passed without something in the post from him, and if the pressure of work for War Babes was building up, I'd put off answering his letter for a week or even two. Occasionally I've had a second letter in the interim, saying 'I haven't heard from you so thought I would write again.' And I think, Is this me, the person who was going to write to her father every single day, without fail? What an uncomfortable relationship it would be if it were that intense.

He writes lovely letters, three to eight pages long and filled with news. I give back as good as I get, with two full typed sheets at least. He hasn't shown any enthusiasm for coming back to see England, but it's a long way from the West Coast and he couldn't leave his plants for any length of time and still expect to have a business when he got back. Besides, what would I do with him if he came here? Middle England seems so dull compared to northern California.

No, it's easier for me to go there. I have friends I like to see and I am half American, after all. I haven't forgotten.

12
Reunions I: Sons' Tales

Whatever else was happening in my life, the War Babes work never stopped. It couldn't because the calls for information and help never stopped. The phone calls and letters kept coming in, reaching a terrifying peak each time there was some publicity. It was exciting and gratifying but very worrying. I'd need 48-hour days to give the time required by each of the cases piling up in my filing cabinet. I'd also need the co-operation of the American government, and from 1987 onwards I was pinning my hopes for that on the civil action we were fighting in the American courts. But more of that later. I'd done everything possible to get my responses down to a fine art. There was standard information I could hand out to people, but fortunately or unfortunately people themselves are not standardized and often needed long sessions of personal attention on the telephone.

When not being a private detective, a public informer and the scourge of the American government, I was acting as counsellor, therapist and agony aunt to callers. Even when you have found your father – perhaps especially then – there are problems to agonize over. What could A do about an American half-sister who resented her without ever meeting and was, A felt, trying to turn their father against her? How should B break the news to his father before they met that he was gay, so that he could take along his long-time partner without having to lie about his relationship?

How could C tell her newly found father that her mother couldn't bear his name to be mentioned, let alone meet him for old times' sake? Was there any way D could placate a wife growing increasingly resentful of the amount of time he was spending phoning and writing to his new American family – or E do the same with a much loved English half-sister, bitterly hurt because she felt she had been usurped by her American counterpart? How could F find the confidence to accept her father's invitation to visit when she was so terrified he would be disappointed in her?

All human life was there on the end of a telephone line, every problem under the sun. I loved this side of my work with the group, but, my goodness, it took time. In the midst of it all, somehow, fathers were being found. By October 1991, 180 'babes' and fathers (or families where the father had died) had been reunited out of a total of 1000 members. The following are some of their stories. All the people mentioned in the next two chapters have appeared in the early part of the book.

Ray We had been looking for Ray's father, Brett, for nearly three years and Sue, Ray's wife, who'd done the bulk of the letter writing and telephoning, was at the end of her tether. Government departments consistently refused to give out any information, letters were not forwarded and there seemed no way of ever beating the system. At one particular department she was told by a clerk, rather spitefully she felt, that her father-in-law's file was in front of her but the information was not available to Sue. Would she kindly stop calling them.

But Sue, a determined Lancashire lass, decided to give it one more try. She rang the same department and this time got a young man with a more understanding attitude. His sympathy was the final straw and Sue burst into tears and poured out the whole unhappy story. He told her he wished he could help her but it just wasn't possible. The Privacy Act prevented him releasing the information she needed.

That evening Sue and Ray, a coach painter in Blackpool, talked it over.

'We were about ready to give up,' Ray recalls. 'We'd been in touch with so many people and had so much frustration and we were getting nowhere. I'm not too hot at letter writing so the load had fallen on Sue and I felt she had had enough.'

Shortly afterwards one of the many letters was returned from the department Sue had been on to – a routine procedure if they want to inform you via their official stamp why they cannot grant your request. In the corner, with no explanation, was a number. It looked as if it could have been jotted down absent-mindedly by someone using the letter as a piece of scrap paper. The figures meant nothing to Sue or Ray, but, fortunately, they had the presence of mind to wonder if it meant something to other people.

I knew it was significant, a government number of some kind, so I asked one of my helpers in the State where Sue and Ray were searching if she recognized it. She did. It was a social-security number from her area of Wisconsin. She began checking with her contacts and came up with the information that it was the social-security number of Brett, Ray's father. From there it was a short step to finding an address and telephone number and I was able to telephone a delighted Sue and give her the details. Without the number Ray and Sue say they would not have found his father. What fascinates them is whether it appeared on the letter by accident or whether the man Sue had spoken to had taken pity on her and given them as big a clue as he dared. They like to believe the latter.

A lot of husbands and wives are quietly supportive of their partner's search for their father, but few enter into the spirit as wholeheartedly as Sue. She is thirteen years younger than Ray and remembers him first mentioning his father to her when she was 19 and they had just started going out together.

'I didn't think much of it at the time. But I noticed that although he's not someone who talks about his feelings much, Ray mentioned this a lot. I realized it was important to him. Later his mother told me about her and his father, only she made it sound incredibly romantic.

'Ray's Mum had always told him his father had died in the War and he accepted this, but although I never said so to her face I didn't see how she could possibly have known this. I remember saying to Ray, when our kids were very small, "When these two start school and I've got a bit of time, I'm going to find out if your father really is dead. Imagine, he might be alive! You might be able to meet him one day." I wanted to do it for him and to satisfy my own curiosity. Ray said I was daft but he didn't say don't do it.'

One day Ray picked up a newspaper belonging to a mate at work. It wasn't a paper he normally read, but inside was a piece on me and War Babes. He tore it out and when he got home Sue was waiting with the same piece to show him. She'd spotted it on a visit to her Dad's. It was Sue who wrote to me, and three years later it was she who took my call giving her the details on her father-in-law.

'I couldn't believe it,' Ray says of coming home from work to find his father's telephone number waiting for him. 'We'd gathered he was alive – not because anyone had confirmed this but Sue could tell from the attitude of people in authority when she was talking to them. I'd never quite believed we'd trace him. Sue wanted me to phone there and then, but I couldn't. We left it for a while and then one or the other of us would ring when we plucked up the courage, but the number just rang out. There was never a reply.'

Sue takes up the story: 'I rang one day when Ray was out. I was so used to getting no reply that I wasn't even nervous, but suddenly a man answered. I checked his name and whether he'd been in England during the war and then I said, "Are you rich?"

'"Oh, my God, no," he laughed.

'"Good," I said. "That makes what I have to tell you a bit easier." We were worried that if Ray's Dad turned out to have money he might think we were after it. I'd already checked if he was alone and he'd told me that he lived alone since his wife had passed away. I asked him about Margaret, Ray's Mum, and he agreed that he went out with her. I didn't know what he thought I was up to but he was taking this in very good part.

"'Well," I said, "not long after you left, Margaret had a baby. Your baby. You have a son." I don't know what I expected but not for him to burst out laughing which was what happened. Apparently he had a friend who knew people in England and he thought this man had arranged to have a practical joke played on him.

'I didn't laugh, so after a while he said: "This is a joke, isn't it?"

"'Don't be daft. I wouldn't be spending all this money to try and make you laugh," I said. I talked to him some more and asked if Ray could phone him. When I put the phone down I felt sick with shock and delayed reaction. Ray did call him and it was a strained, awful phone call but it confirmed what I'd said and a couple of weeks later we got a nice long letter and a heap of photographs. I don't think he ever doubted the truth of our story once he accepted it wasn't a joke. Only once did he get annoyed. He started demanding to know why Ray's Mum hadn't told him she was pregnant before he left England and why she'd lied to Ray about him being dead.

'I just said, "Don't get the hump with us. We're not responsible for what she did."'

For Ray, actually speaking to his father, however strained that first conversation, was beyond his wildest dreams.

'When I'd thought about finding him I'd always half-assumed that if we did he'd refuse to believe me, or not want to know me and slam the phone down. And in an odd sort of way that wouldn't have mattered at that stage. I'd have achieved what I set out to do – proved he was alive and let him know I existed. Everything we got on top of that was a bonus.'

What they got, after six months of exchanging letters, was the chance to meet Brett and his very new wife in Wisconsin. They took out a bank loan and booked air tickets for themselves and their school-age son and daughter.

'The kids were the only ones who weren't nervous,' said Ray. 'They took it all for granted and were looking forward to the holiday and to meeting their new Grandad. I was thinking, How am I going to stand three weeks with this man if I don't like him? But there was nothing to worry about. He's a nice guy, very laid back, with a slightly sarcastic sense of humour, very droll.

'At the airport he just grabbed hold of me and hugged me. It took me by surprise and broke the ice. I'd have been hanging back, very British, wondering if I should shake hands or not. Dad had retired up north of the state, to a lodge, in a place a bit like our Lake District. He'd had a long, happy marriage with four daughters and a son, and had just remarried.

'I didn't know what to expect from our relationship. I mean, I'd never had a father to show me what the relationship should be, and anyway I wasn't exactly expecting this man to greet me as a long-lost son at this stage of our lives. We didn't delve into emotions. He seemed to accept the situation casually and that was OK by me. We went fishing together and I suppose we communicated more as friends than father and son. But maybe that's the ideal way to communicate with your father as an adult anyway. He didn't seem to want to talk about my Mum, as if that stage of his life now had no interest for him.

'It was a lovely place and Dad took us on lots of trips. The kids were having a great time, but Sue missed the shops. The only problem – and it was a big one – was the family. Dad had been wary of telling his children about me and when he broke the news some of them took it badly. You can't blame them. They were just coming to terms with his marriage and then he sprang me on them. I could have been any kind of jerk.'

Sue recalls a nightmare get-together at the home of Brett's daughter, Jennie, where they'd gone to stay for a while and meet the rest of the family.

'Jennie is a lovely girl. He'd told her first, but it was still nerve-wracking for us and for Brett. At first we all sort of circled each other warily. Two of what I'd call the most hot-headed daughters had refused to come and sent their husbands along. When the husbands, who were very nice, decided we were OK after all, they rang their wives and asked them to come over.

'I couldn't stand the tension when they came, so I just walked up to one of them and started talking. I asked her where she'd been and she said she'd been shopping. I said, "Oh, next time you go would you please take me along. I haven't been inside a shop for over a week and I'm dying for a good shopping trip."

'She laughed and it was OK after that. The ice was broken and I think they realized we were ordinary people. The Americans are good about admitting they were wrong. What had happened was that their father had been very strict with them when they were young and suddenly there was Ray, proof of what he'd been up to when he was 20. They were also unhappy about him getting married again. Really they were just punishing him through us.

'It was an amazing change after that. Most of the family live in the south of the state and we spent a little time with each of them. They all wanted us and it was quite traumatic when we had to leave, everyone crying and saying their goodbyes. It was as if we'd known each other all our lives. One of the problems we are having now is that on our next trip each of Ray's sisters and his brother wants us to base ourselves with their family, but Ray says his priority is seeing his father, so that's where we'll stay.'

Even this very happy situation has had its moments of sadness. Ray lost his mother just before he went to meet his father.

'She never liked me searching for my father and it upset her particularly that Sue was so keen. It caused tension between them. She used to say, "Why are you digging up my past?" I used to have to remind her it was my past too. She insisted that he was dead and we were wasting our time. Even when we had proof he was alive, she said the authorities had told her he'd been killed. It's feasible they did. They used to go to great lengths to make sure girls didn't try to get in touch with servicemen.

'When I told Mum I'd found my Dad, she smiled very sadly and said, "I'm happy for you but not for me." We were ruining her dream, knocking down the fantasy that had sustained her all those years.

'The other thing that has happened is that in finding one family I've lost another. My English brothers and sisters – I've never thought of them as half-relatives – have taken the whole thing in a strange way. They seem to look at me differently now; as if I'm no longer one of them. It's distanced them from me.

'It's a pity and I hope things will get better between us, but finding my father and a grandfather for my children more than compensates.'

Joe What a difference a few months can make. Talking to Joe when I first began writing this book, I found an unhappy man, almost resigned to the fact that his father didn't want to know him. The man who contacted me shortly before I finished the book was on top of the world. He might have been a different person. In some way he is a different person. He's become a son with a father who cares about him, and his outlook has changed accordingly.

But first things first. This is the story of Joe's search.

Divorced, the father of one son, Joe lives in Cornwall and works both as a jeweller and part-time in an old people's home. His father was a black American naval officer, stationed in St Austell, and named Joseph, nicknamed Big Joe. After a couple of years in the care of his grandmother and aunts in Cornwall, baby Joe was sent to join his mother in London, where she had moved after his birth and later married.

He grew up with a stepfather and two half-brothers, a confused and often unhappy boy – 'The first time I saw a black man, I ran up to him and asked if he was my father.' In fact he knew very little about his father, because his mother found it distressing – and still does – to talk about him.

'She always discouraged questions and my stepfather had a hatred of this man who'd been my mother's first love. I think there was a conspiracy of silence in the family and my stepfather was given an unrealistic idea of what had happened between my mother and father. He was never told how close they were and probably saw my father as an unscrupulous character who took advantage of a young girl.

'I was treated very badly by my stepfather and I ran away from home at 15. Years later I met him and got to know him better and he told me that he had seen me growing into the image of my father, the man he hated, and had found this impossible to take.'

It wasn't until he returned to Cornwall in his late thirties that Joe 'began to build up a picture' of Big Joe, with the help of his grandmother. The 6' 6" tall sailor had been well liked by the family and had wanted to marry his mother. It was the American authorities that vetoed the plan on grounds of race and sent him back to the States. He'd left a message for his son – that if he wanted to, Joe was welcome to find him when he grew up. It was this message that encouraged Joe to think, for a long time, about searching and eventually to get down to it in earnest.

His father should not have been too difficult to trace. There were few black officers in the US navy, and his surname was unusual. But Joe didn't have a service number, which gave the authorities an easy get-out, and in the early days, he was spelling the surname wrong, the way his grandmother had given it to him.

He'd been told that his father had been educated at a private college in his home state of Texas. A letter to the seventeen colleges he could trace brought a result. Yes, he was told by one, a man of his father's name, albeit with a slightly different spelling, had graduated from there. Could this be the man he wanted? They gave Joe the address they'd had for their student, and eight years ago, with high hopes, Joe wrote off, asking the occupier to pass the letters on if possible. He never received a reply but neither were the letters returned, which led him to believe he hadn't got totally the wrong place.

More recently a register of everyone with his father's surname in the area where he had lived, produced twenty-four individuals, one of them listed at the address he had been given by the college. Joe wrote to all of these people, explaining who he was. This time he met with success – or so it seemed at first.

'A letter arrived from a man who said he was my cousin. It was a wonderful, warm letter. This person sounded delighted to hear from me. He told me I could stop looking, that I'd found the right family, I was the son of his father's cousin. He was going to get in touch with the rest of the family.

'I was over the moon. I wrote back straightaway, and waited. Nothing happened. A couple of months later I managed to find this man's phone number and rang. I got his wife and tried to find out what was going on, but all she could tell me was that her husband had been thrilled to hear from me. She said she'd tell him I'd called and get him to phone me, but again there was no reply. I couldn't understand it. I was sure the letter was not a hoax, because it mentioned information that I hadn't given the writer but which I knew to be true.'

There were further disappointments. He found information that suggested his father ran an art business with branches in several towns. He wrote to two of these branches, left messages on an answering machine, but nobody responded. This was the position when I spoke to him a few months ago. He was very despondent.

'I don't want to sound paranoid, but it seems to make there are two possible answers. Either members of my father's family are preventing me getting to him, and my cousin, after his impulsive letter, was quickly warned off. Or, alternatively, my father is aware I'm trying to make contact and doesn't want to know.' Sadly, it seemed that he was right. It's not unknown for family members to keep it from a father that his son or daughter is trying to trace him – either to protect their own interests or, as they see it, the father's. It's rare for a father to ignore an approach, but not impossible, and Joe was reluctantly coming round to believe this was happening in his case.

'I've contacted so many people that by now half of south-west Texas must know I'm trying to trace my father. Surely he must know too. But if so, why has he let it get so big when a letter from him could have nipped it in the bud? All he has to say is, "I don't want to know you," and I'll go on my way and never bother him again.'

It looked like stalemate, the end of an unsatisfactory trail, but in the summer of 1991, in one of those 'stranger-than-fiction' stories we occasionally get in War Babes, Joe received a letter from his father. Big Joe, as he signed himself, had known for some time that his son was trying to get in touch, but he could do nothing about it because of a promise he had made to his own father. Many years earlier he had been persuaded to swear that he would not make contact with Joe junior or his English family. It was, the old man believed, the best thing for both sides.

'My father said that it had broken his heart not being able to acknowledge me but he is a man of honour and could not break his word to his father. As soon as the old man died, however, he felt the promise was no longer valid and he got in touch with me.'

Since then father and son have continued to get to know each other, writing, telephoning and sending video tapes. 'My father loves to see the places he knew in Cornwall when he was stationed here,' Joe explained. 'He remembers it all as if it happened yesterday – the good and the bad. He feels very bitter about the way he was treated by his own people for the sin of wanting to marry a white girl. Threats were made on his life, he was threatened with a charge of rape, and in the end he was literally handcuffed and shipped out.'

Joe has learned things about his father that his grandmother could never have told him – that he still has on his arm a tattoo he had done when he was in England. It bears the names of baby Joe and his mother, and he has never tried to have it removed. So Joseph's wife and family have always known of his British love affair and Joe's existence.

'I thought I'd been forgotten or that I was a secret my father wanted buried,' Joe says, 'but I needn't have worried. He's never stopped thinking about me. You've no idea how much that means to me. He's also a war hero – he has medals from Vietnam – and one of the nicest things he's told me is that he now has a picture of me beside his war medals on the wall of his studio.'

Big Joe has come a long way since he was that disgraced, handcuffed sailor. Joseph is now an artist of international repute. Joe is proud of him. 'But he could as easily have turned out to be a truck driver, and if he was the person he is I'd have felt proud of him. People have asked if I don't feel awed by finding such a successful man, but how could I when he writes such sweet letters, real father-to-son stuff right from the heart? I feel a bit unworthy of him, but that's because he is plainly such a good and honourable man.'

Joe has told his mother.

'I think she's pleased for me, but she still doesn't want to be involved. It's a sore point with me that she wouldn't help in my search. There were things she could have cleared up and saved me a lot of trouble, but she wouldn't. My father doesn't know this yet. I think it would hurt him.

'He wrote dozens and dozens of letters to her when I was a baby, but the family never passed them on to her, because they believed it was in her own interests to forget about him and get on with her life. If my mother doesn't know anything about these even now, perhaps she believes he just deserted her and forgot her. It would explain her attitude. I want to talk to her about this, and I will, but I find it so hard to bring the subject up.'

On a happier note, Big Joe plans to come to England soon and meet his son and grandson, also in the navy.

'My son is a six-footer too,' Joe said, 'but I hope Big Joe won't be disappointed in me. I'm afraid I took after my mother. I'm only 5' 6".'

Len Edna, Len's mother, was one of the lucky girls who got her GI – but lost him again. How this happened is still a bit of a mystery. Frank and Edna married in Leicester in 1944, when she was expecting Len. When the war ended, Frank returned to the United States. Edna and Len were to follow with the other GI brides and children, but when the time came her father was ill and she missed the opportunity. It was then up to the couple to make their own arrangements.

This never happened. Frank sent money to support his son but then contact ceased abruptly and Edna was forced to the conclusion many other women in the same position had reached: that her husband had returned to his other life and the relationship was over.

It wasn't until Len met his father that he heard a different story. Frank told him he had written and sent money for the fare to America. The letter had gone to the home of Len's grandparents who looked after him while his mother worked 'in service'. The money had been returned with the news that Edna had died, that Len was being brought up by his grandparents and that they no longer required financial assistance.

Len's mother still finds this story hard to accept, but Len doesn't doubt the truth of it. He believes that his grandmother 'for what she saw as the best motives' intercepted the letters and passed on the piece of misinformation which changed the course of his life.

He spent his childhood first with his grandparents, then with his mother, stepfather, brother and two sisters. He even recruited his own stepfather. As a small child he wandered away from home and was found by Jim who took him to the police station – where he caused this public-spirited stranger embarrassment by claiming that he was his father. Eventually he got his wish, but though he enjoyed a good relationship with his stepfather, he says he just didn't 'blend in' with the family.

He always knew about his real father and thanks to his grandfather, a bit of a hoarder, he acquired photographs and information about him.

'He was spoken about openly and with affection. When I said I was going to write to him at about the age of 12, there was no discouragement. From then till I left school at 15, I used to send Christmas cards and the occasional short letter to the address my grandfather gave me in Wisconsin. I got no replies to my letters for the simple reason that my father no longer lived there and never received them. But as they weren't returned at the time, I didn't know if he was getting them and not bothering to answer.

'I didn't give any thought at that stage to how hearing from me might affect my father and the family he most likely had by then. Later, when I was married myself I'd wonder how Rosemary, my wife, would feel if a letter turned up from someone claiming to be the son of a previous relationship of mine and she knew nothing about it. I still wanted to find my father but I was more aware I might cause trouble.

'I'd think I'd forgotten about it, then I'd find an old photograph and the need to know would start all over again. Nobody seemed keen to help. Even the Salvation Army was not helpful when they realized that though my parents were married I had been conceived out of wedlock.'

Then one day in February 1990, Len's wife, Rosemary, came into a room and heard the last few words of a radio interview I was doing. She found a pen just in time to take down my address and persuaded Len that it was worth a last try.

Frank was not particularly hard to trace. Len had a lot of useful information. When I phoned back six weeks later to say I was pretty sure I'd found his father, Len had trouble recalling who I was. After his previous bad experiences, I don't think he had much faith in me. I gave him the address and phone number of the man I was 99 per cent sure was his father, and advised him strongly not to phone and announce himself immediately as the long-lost son. He ignored me completely!

'All those years of waiting and now I had this phone number in my hand. I had to know the truth. Rosemary and I were getting ready to go out for the evening, but I made the call. There was no reply. That outing was really wasted on me. I couldn't wait to get home again and get on the phone. Next time, a woman answered and I asked to speak to Frank G——. As soon as he came on the line I blurted it out. "This will probably be a shock to you but I have reason to believe you may be the father I'm trying to trace."

'After a short pause he came back with, "What is your full name? What is your mother's name?" A little later he told me, "I did have a son and a wife."

'I told him I would put my case in writing with the appropriate documents – birth certificate, marriage licence and the like. It was only afterwards I realized that the crafty old goat had got all the information out of me but had never confirmed whether or not he was the man I was after. Before he hung up he said: "'By the way my army serial number is——", reeling it off so fast I could hardly write it down. I sat there for a few minutes with my heart pounding, absolutely drained of energy, then I picked myself up and went to the cupboard where we keep important papers. I found my birth certificate with my father's serial number on it. It matched the one he'd given me. That was it. A soldier's serial number is like his fingerprints. I'd found my Dad.

'I sent all the stuff to him in a big envelope addressing the letter, "Dear Mr G—" not to be too presumptuous. Three weeks later, there was a reply. It was about ten lines long. Basically it told me he had examined the papers I'd sent and told me which airport to fly to when I came to see him. At the top it said, "To my son Leonard". It was short but it was very sweet after the years of waiting. When I met his family they couldn't believe he'd written. He never writes to anyone.'

Meeting your father for the first time is always a matter of urgency, but as Frank was 85, it had a particular urgency in Len's case. At the time the BBC in Birmingham was filming a documentary on War Babes and they were keen to show a meeting between father and 'child'. Len seemed to have found his father at a fortunate moment. I asked him if he'd let the BBC pay his fare in return for appearing in the film.

'I did have qualms about a camera and half a dozen people peering over my shoulder at an emotional moment,' Len said, 'but it was an offer too good to refuse and the only way I could possibly afford to go before the following year. I asked my Dad and he said, "Why not? We've got nothing to hide."'

Len's father and his 84-year old wife, Mary, live in a trailer park near the town of Jefferson. Len says he spent his fourteen-day visit 'pottering around and meeting my father's family – my family. What can I say about them? They are great, like an old-fashioned family album come to life. Mary was like a second mother to me. In fact when it got too wearing to explain all about me to everyone we met, she started introducing me as "our son from England". I felt totally accepted.'

But of course it was his father Len really made the trip for. What was he like?

'We never really sat down and had a heart-to-heart. He's not that sort of man, but we talked a lot while we did other things. I'd go fishing with him or join him out in his little workshop when he was mending tackle. He was very matter-of-fact about the way things had turned out, but he was shocked when he realized he'd been misled about my mother's death.

'That upset him. He just kept asking why, why would someone do that? I told him I couldn't give him an answer and all we could do was pick up the relationship from now. The most important thing I learned from that visit was why I am what I am. I was never like anyone in my English family. My stepbrother and youngest stepsister were like my stepfather, and my other stepsister is just like Mum. I envied them that.

'Now I know who I'm like. I am my father's son all right, and that might not be good news for my wife because he can be a cantankerous old so-and-so if someone is not pulling their weight. We went out for a meal and the salad bar didn't impress him, so he told the waiter loudly that he'd got more salad in his ice box than they had on offer. I wrote to Rosemary to warn her what to expect in a few years, and give her the chance to pull out now!

'The similarities between us are amazing. We both did the same kind of job, engineering, though I'm no longer in that line of work. We have workshops laid out almost identically. When I got home I took a picture of mine to show him.'

It was my friend and 'mole' Lynn, who helped me find Len's father, who pointed out other similarities. She met father and son when they were visiting an aunt who lives within forty-five miles of her home, and was fascinated by their co-ordinated hand movements as they talked, and the way they unconsciously settled into identical positions when they sat down.

Back home Len keeps in touch by letter and phone with his new family. 'The only thing I regret is not meeting my father sooner. But better late than never. I've gained a lot from meeting him and his family and so have my two sons. The eldest, Martin, who is 17, is already keen to go to America, and the family is so big they've assured me there will be a relative to keep an eye on him wherever he goes.'

But perhaps the nicest and most unexpected outcome is the friendship that has grown up between Edna and Mary, Frank's second wife.

'They started writing to each other and discovered they have a lot in common – me and Dad for a start! There's no bad feeling between them at all; they're like long-lost sisters and have become dedicated pen-pals.'

13
Reunions II: Daughters' Tales

I've tried to balance the sexes in the personal stories I've told and in so doing may have given a false impression. I hear from far more daughters than sons wanting to contact their fathers, and whereas the men will often embark on a search in a spirit of curiosity and be surprised by the intense feelings the experience arouses in them, women tend to be emotionally involved from the start. They expect more from their fathers too and this can sometimes make the end result more painful for them. Here are some of their experiences.

Carol Howard, Carol's father, holds the record for the father I found fastest! Carol arrived at my house one night with a piece of paper containing the only useful information she had on her father – his name and address, near Boston, at the time her mother had known him.

The obvious is always worth a try. I left her sitting in my kitchen drinking coffee – her husband Alf was outside in the car – while I phoned international directory enquiries. I gave the operator the name and address and she promptly came back with a number. Against the odds Howard was still listed at the same address. Carol nearly fell off the chair when I handed her the number. If only they were all that easy.

Carol found out she was the daughter of a GI when she read some private papers of her mother's as an inquisitive teenager. Until then she'd believed herself to be the daughter of the man who had divorced her mother when she was 7 years old. Rifling guiltily through the papers, she discovered that the divorce had been on grounds of adultery committed several years before and resulting in her birth. Her father's first name had been Howard – she could never remember his surname – and when she first contacted me, at the age of 40, that was all the information Carol had to go on.

She had never been able to broach the subject with her mother and I explained that she'd have to if she was ever to get enough information to make a search feasible. It took courage to bring the subject out in the open after years of secrecy.

'It was always one of those strange half secrets you get in families, where people know but nobody talks about it,' Carol says. 'As I was growing up I'd hear remarks about me but nobody ever told me anything. Once Mum was showing some photographs of me to someone in the family and she said, "Who does she remind you of there?" There were smiles and raised eyebrows. The message I got was that I wasn't supposed to know – so I never let on I did, except to a few close people when I was older.

'Mum says now that it was never a secret and that I'd always known, but she was certainly surprised when I asked her about my Dad in 1985. She said, "You're not going to try and find him, are you?", but when I insisted I was, she gave me a bit of paper with his name and address and told me how they met.'

The story that emerged was not untypical. A young woman, recently married, away from home in the ATS; an 18-year-old GI in the signal corps, based nearby in north London. A short love affair that ended when Howard was sent first to France, then back to the States. He knew about the baby, even chose her name. Before leaving Britain for good, he had managed to see her and have his name placed on her birth certificate. (Carol had always used a shortened version of the certificate without such details.) After the war, her mother and stepfather had been reunited. There were two more children born and they tried, unsuccessfully, to make a go of their sorely tried marriage.

From her mid-teens when she stumbled on the information about her father, Carol had longed to meet him, but believed it was not possible. Where would she look? Who exactly would she be looking for? She married, had two children and put him out of her mind.

'At least I thought I'd put him out of my mind,' she said, 'but off and on over the years I'd think about him and get very upset. It was my fortieth birthday that brought it all back. I was born on VE day 1945, and Remembrance Day 1985, with all the news reports about the war, was the most miserable of my life.

'Turning 40 is a depressing occasion anyway, but I felt here I was stepping on to the downward slope, and I'd missed out on one of the most important relationships of my life, never having a father. I couldn't get it out of my mind after that. There were people who knew, like my sister-in-law, and I'd cry on her shoulder but though she was kind, there was nobody who really understood. I didn't see how there could be because I didn't know there was anyone else in the same position.'

It was shortly after that that she heard about my search. 'Suddenly I realized that it might be possible. If other people felt they could find their fathers, why couldn't I? I was sure it would be a long search, of course, months, years, but if I found him in the end, it would be worth it.'

It took less than five minutes.

'It was too quick, really' she says. 'I didn't have time to adjust. I just kept looking at the number on the paper all the way home, trying to take it in. By the time we got home I was hysterical. I sat on the number for a couple of days because I was just too frightened to do anything with it.

'Then, on a Saturday night, I decided I was going to phone. I dialled the number and it rang out without any answer. I didn't know whether to be relieved or miserable. I forced myself to try again on Sunday, quite late, about 11.30 p.m. Alf was sitting beside me and I had a little speech I'd been rehearsing. I was going to say I was phoning for someone who had known him in England, but when a man answered it went completely out of my head. I asked if he was Howard P— and he said yes. He sounded young somehow, so I asked how old he was. He must have thought I was mad, phoning from England to enquire his age, but he told me he was 25, and I said I was sorry, he couldn't be the man I wanted.

' "You probably want my father," he said, "his name is Howard, too. Can I get him to phone you back?" '

Carol gave her number and went to bed taking the cordless phone with her. Half an hour later, it rang. This time it was the real Howard. His son, who still lived in the family home with Howard senior's ex-wife, had rung his Dad at his home a few miles away, with the news that a nervous English woman wanted him.

This time Carol kept her cool and began to explain that she was ringing on behalf of another party who she believed had known him during the war. Howard immediately asked if this other person was Carol Anne, whereupon Carol told him who she was.

'My God!' he said. 'I've thought about you a thousand times. When are you coming over to see me?' She has been visiting him twice a year ever since and Howard and his second wife, Laura, have been to England twice to stay with Carol and her family. Sitting in Carol's house in industrial Black Country, cup of tea in his hand, Howard talked about what finding his daughter meant to him.

'It was a dream come true,' he said. 'I never believed she'd find me. I didn't even know if she knew I existed, but I never stopped thinking about her.'

He is bearded and remarkably young looking. Before retirement he was a manager for a company with international connections and in the 1970s his work brought him to England.

'I tried to think of a way to find Carol while I was here,' he said, 'but it seemed impossible. I realized she was likely to have married and changed her name. I didn't know where she would be living. I do regret not keeping in touch when she was a baby but you don't always make the right decisions when you are young, and you can't go back and change the past. I just hope I can make it up to her now. Meeting her family, knowing she's happy and settled, has taken away a lot of worries I always had at the back of my mind.'

It has turned into a close father–daughter relationship. Carol has travelled thousands of miles around America with her father, seeing the sights. She has met three of his five children, and he has got to know his two English grandchildren and renewed acquaintance with Carol's mother – who, incidentally, said she would never have recognized him. One of the first things Carol asked him for when she found him was a photograph of himself as a young man. 'I wanted to see why Mum had fallen for him,' she said. 'And yes, I could understand it. Actually he looked a lot like my son.'

Laura too has met Carol's mother and the two women got on well.

'When I told my friends back home, they were shocked and said, "How could you?" But all this happened long before I met Howard. How could I feel any resentment? When Howard told me Carol was coming to stay – well, I've got five stepchildren, it was just one more! I enjoy having her and Alf, and their son and daughter when they come. And it's given us the excuse to come to England. I love it here. I know we tend to think the English people aren't friendly, but they are if you speak first. I talk to people on the bus and they always want to chat.'

Carol's first visit to Boston wasn't quite that relaxed though.

'Alf was with me,' she recalls, 'and he's terrified of flying so he was a wreck by the time we got there. What worried me most was that my father would be disappointed in me, that I wouldn't be what he'd imagined over the years. We'd talked on the phone and exchanged letters but he was still a stranger, and certainly Laura was. I remember I used to dread her answering the phone when I rang him. I didn't know how she felt about me.

'Alf and I had agreed that if it didn't work out we wouldn't stay out of politeness, but come straight back home. That first night he was so worn out he went to bed very early. It would have looked rude for me to do the same, so I sat there, looking at my Dad, wondering what to talk about and thinking, "How could Alf do this? How could he leave me here alone with these strangers?"

'After that first tense night it was really easy to fit in. Dad has always said, "This is your home: you're always welcome here," and he means it. As for Laura, who I'd dreading meeting, she took us into the kitchen and said, "Here's the kettle, here's the teapot. If you die of hunger or thirst it'll be your own fault!" We're expected to make ourselves at home and that's what we do.'

To fund their new jet-setting lifestyle, Carol has gone out to work part-time as a cleaner.

'It costs about £1000 each time we go to America,' she said, 'and I can save that. We don't drink or smoke, or eat out at expensive restaurants. Visiting Dad is our priority and we are willing to spend on it. What else could we do with out money that would be as much fun?'

The way Howard feels about having his daughter around is probably best summed up in the words of his 6-year-old grandson, who told a group of surprised adults not in on the story:

'Grandpa is very happy. He's found his little girl.'

Janet There's often an element of luck in finding fathers, but nowhere did Lady Luck play a bigger part than in Janet's case. When Janet contacted me in 1990 she had no idea where in the States her black GI father, Walter, might be living. Laura, her mother, had thrown away his letters, and was not at all keen on discussing that period of her life.

'I respected her feelings,' Janet said. 'She must have gone through hell – a married woman with a husband in the forces, having a black baby. She's never told me how she and my stepfather came to terms with the situation. In fact my stepfather was more helpful when I began searching. He offered to look around their old papers to see if there was anything that would help me, but there was nothing.'

She knew her father had come from Mississippi but he'd rejoined the army after the war and could have settled anywhere. I suggested her best bet was the American genealogy centre which would be able to give her a printout of all the men in the country with her father's surname. I warned her there might be a lot, and there were precisely 44,331. When she recovered from the shock, Janet began to write to them. On the grounds that she had to start somewhere, she began with Mississippi.

It seemed the best bet. She sent off seventy rather vague letters – 'I didn't want to upset my father's family, if they happened to see one, by saying exactly who I was.' The replies started coming back quickly, not from her father but from strangers, mostly wishing her luck. But to her horror the letters weren't coming from Mississippi but from Michigan. The names of the states on her list had been abbreviated, and 'MI', she realized belatedly, does in fact stand for the state of Michigan.

'I could have cried with disappointment and anger at my own stupidity,' she said. 'I didn't have the heart to write any more letters immediately. It was coming up to Christmas and I thought I'd leave it until afterwards. I remember thinking, "One more Christmas I won't be getting a card from my Dad."'

Two days after Christmas a card arrived from America. Inside was a cryptic message, 'Yes, I'm the one' (designed not to upset her family if they didn't know the truth). Her father had moved to Detroit, Michigan. He'd taken a couple of months to reply because he was away staying with a sick brother when Janet's letter arrived at his home.

'My daughter rang and told me there was a letter from England and I just knew who it was from,' he told me when I met him at Janet's house. 'I always knew she'd find me one day.'

'It was actually the first letter I'd written,' Janet said. 'I did wonder if someone was conning me. I got the phone number from directory enquiries ready to ring up and check it out, but found I didn't have the nerve to do it. I was scared he wouldn't be my father – and scared he would. Finally I had a couple of stiff drinks, told my husband Paul I was ready and he dialled the number and handed me the phone. It was like waiting for your execution.

'It was a very strange phone call. I kept saying, "I can't believe it" and that nice, warm voice kept repeating, "You'd better believe it. It's your Dad." He told me he had six other children and was divorced from his second wife. He didn't seem the least bit surprised to hear from me. It was quite unreal. When I put the phone down I was frightened I'd wake up and find I'd been dreaming.'

But the very real phone calls continued. Walter didn't go in for letter writing but he sent photographs and Janet discovered she had a far from conventional father. He wore his hair in a ponytail, shared a house with his ex-wife, had a host of lady friends and loved to dance the night away. He had, belatedly, broken the news of her existence to his other children. The eldest daughter, after Janet, had been a bit upset but on the whole he felt the family had taken it well.

'Why not?' he asked. 'They are adults, plenty old enough to understand about these things.'

Plans were made for Walter to come to Birmingham, but on the day after her forty-seventh birthday ('and after I'd spent a really miserable day thinking he'd forgotten') two cards arrived, both from her father. One was for the birthday she'd just celebrated, the second 'for all the birthdays I missed when you were growing up'. She was so touched by the gesture she decided she couldn't wait several months to see this man. She and Paul got out their holiday savings and booked two tickets for Detroit for May 1991.

Janet didn't recognize her father at the airport. 'He was so dark-skinned. Much darker than I expected. I thought, Who is this man hugging me? He looked nothing like the photographs he sent, which had obviously been taken years earlier. I told him this later and he looked a bit upset and said he hoped I wouldn't be ashamed to walk down the street with him when he came to England – and of course I didn't mean it like that. It was just a shock.'

Janet and Paul arrived in the afternoon, exhausted after travelling for twenty-four hours, and had to be up at 7 a.m. next morning to do a TV show. Her father had contacted the media and they became local celebrities during their sixteen-day stay.

'People would stop us in the streets and ask for autographs,' Janet recalled incredulously. 'It was predominantly a black neighbourhood we were in and the people, black and white, were lovely, but it eventually got wearing being asked to tell my story over and over again.

'If I'm honest meeting my father didn't turn out quite as I expected. It was a bit disappointing. I'd had visions of this very emotional thing between us, and though he hugged me at the airport and would give me a goodnight kiss, he is not a man who shows his feelings. He told me as much before we met, but somehow you hope it will be different with you.

'He'd already explained that his own father was a very hard man who used to beat him and that he never saw any affection between his mother and father. Probably as a result of this, he says he could never show emotion to his four sons and two daughters. He told me he'd been very strict with them as children.

'But I still went on hoping to have emotional little chats about our feelings, just the two of us together. I wanted him to cuddle me. Maybe I wanted to go back to childhood and have the time I'd missed with him. I certainly expected to have 100 per cent of his attention and I didn't get that either. This became quite a sore point. Though he's officially retired, he does a little job for a friend and he didn't take any time off work while we were there. This meant Paul and I were left in the house all day, miles from the shops or anything interesting.

'He's obviously a busy man, always doing things for people, and he's a big success with the ladies. His phone never stops ringing with women wanting to speak to him. Even when we did get him to ourselves, the silly thing was it was my husband who got all his attention. They got on incredibly well and Dad never stopped telling me how lucky I was to have such a wonderful husband. It began to get to me eventually.

'It all came to a head the night before we were due to fly home. We had a blazing row. Dad was eating his evening meal and Paul made some tea, which Dad prefers to coffee, incidentally. I admit I didn't do much housework while I was there. I felt it was my holiday. Anyway, Dad started saying how great Paul was and how he expected the poor man had to do all the work at home.

'I felt the tears start to well up. I kept telling myself, "Don't cry, don't lose control . . ." Dad was going on about how I probably sat around watching television all day, and I just lost my temper. I went absolutely mad and started screaming at him. The last thing I remember is the look of amazement on his face, then I fled upstairs crying.

'I felt like an overemotional adolescent having a row with my father but I couldn't stop. I thought, This is ridiculous – I've waited all my life to meet this man, and all he's done is make me hysterical.

'He came upstairs and apologized. He actually got down on his knees and promised he'd only been joking. But his face had looked deadly earnest to me. Afterwards Paul explained that I was getting a bit sick of hearing how wonderful he was and that I worked hard, and was a good wife and mother.

'It soured the relationship between me and my father, at least temporarily. When we got to the airport next day, I said goodbye and I didn't even look back. But once I was on the plane all the anger evaporated and I wanted to go back, kiss him goodbye and do it all properly. He rang me several times after I got home and told me that the thing that would upset him most in the world was if I didn't want to see him again.

'I think one of the problems is that we are alike in many ways. We are both hot-tempered and liable to explode. He's a very dominant man and likes to be boss in his own home and lay down the rules. One evening we were going out and I was wearing jeans. He told me to change into a dress. Well, I dress to please myself and I don't take kindly to being given orders. I wouldn't change and that caused a bit of an atmosphere.'

Janet admits she finds her own emotions confusing. She wants to be treated as a daughter but not if that means being told what to wear at the age of 47! In retrospect, she says she enjoyed her visit.

'I met some very nice people, neighbours, relatives – even an ex-wife. My father and Jane, his second wife, still share a house. She was lovely, more like a sister. She's about my age and we got on great. I'm hoping she'll come and visit us in Birmingham. Unfortunately I didn't have the chance to get close to my two half-sisters who live nearby. My father had virtually to force the older one to come round and meet me, which was very embarrassing, but when we got together she was actually very pleasant. I spoke to the younger one on the phone.

I think they are a bit irritated with Dad for going on about me, which is understandable. I had no contact at all with my brothers. I don't think my father sees a lot of them.'

The relationship between Janet and her father weathered that first stormy meeting and he came to stay with her and Paul in a suburb of Birmingham a few months later. He celebrated his seventieth birthday with them. Talking to Janet afterwards she told me, 'I worked really hard on the house the week before he arrived. Everything had to be spick and span for him. I didn't want him believing I sat around with my feet up as he'd suggested. He came in, looked around and said, "You have a lovely home here." I felt so proud, like a kid who's got a gold star from teacher!

'For some reason he always makes me feel I'm in the wrong. He likes to be able to tell you how to do things. But I suppose that's just him. I was told in America that he's like that with his family, so maybe it means he's treating me like a daughter and I should be pleased.

'I think Dad enjoyed himself. He feels very much at home in England. Paul had a week off work and we took him to see the sights and to meet the family. He loved being with his great-grandchildren, the first he's had. At night we'd go over the road to the British Legion club, where they made a fuss of him and played wartime songs. He's got an amazing amount of energy. We went to a night club and he danced all night. I had to say, "Dad, please let's sit down. I'm exhausted."'

In the midst of this whirlwind of activity, Janet managed to tie Walter down to a serious conversation.

'I told him I find it hard to share him and get jealous when someone else takes his attention. I also explained that I get depressed and lonely now the children have grown up, particularly during the winter months when it's hard to get out.

'He was very understanding and we sat up talking for hours. He told me that I am welcome to come and stay with him any time I want. I just have to say the word and he'll send an air ticket and I can stay as long as I want, if Paul doesn't mind.

'I really missed him when he went back. Paul and I went over to the club the first Saturday after he left, but it wasn't the same without him. When we got home I was crying and I said, "I want to talk to my father." I was just about to ring him when he rang me. It was lovely to talk to him and because he knows I'm low he's promised to phone me every second day, just to have a few words, till he's sure I'm OK.'

For Janet, there's been one sad outcome of the whole affair. While he was in England, she and her father were interviewed by a national newspaper. Walter talked about the wartime relationship with her mother, whose full name was not used.

'It was a very nice story,' Janet says. 'There was nothing detrimental to Mum in it. But shortly after the article appeared I got a letter from her. I opened it straightaway, while Dad was still in bed and Paul at work, and I was so shocked by what I read I had to get out of the house and take a long walk.

'In a nutshell, she was rejecting me as a daughter. She blamed me for the stuff that had appeared in the paper and said it was a pack of lies. Basically she seems to be denying that she ever had an affair with my father. Either she's convinced herself I was a virgin birth or, more likely, she's come to believe her own story, to people who didn't know us, that I was an adopted child. I think that article faced my mother with facts she has tried to put out of her mind for decades. She doesn't want to accept that she had an affair with a black American GI, and an illegitimate child. Worst of all, she signed the letter, "From someone who despises you."

'My father had been insisting that he wanted to see Mum. I'd tried to tell him that she didn't want any contact with him, but he seemed to think I was just making this up for reasons of my own. He said my mother just wasn't the sort of person I was suggesting and he was sure she'd like to meet him.

'I felt I had to show him that letter. He read it and kept shaking his head and repeating, "I can't believe it . . ."

'Paul said, "People change, Walter. Janet's Mum is no longer the woman you knew." Poor Dad, I felt sorry for him, and sorry for myself. I've found my father, but unless I can get her to see sense, it looks as though I've lost a mother.'

Kay When the information that she was illegitimate emerged in a family row, Kay went to the Register Office and asked for a copy of her birth certificate. A teenager at the time, she confronted her mother and demanded an explanation.

'I believe she was surprised how seriously I was taking it. She really seemed to think that I could just accept without question the fact that my stepfather wasn't my real father. As if I wouldn't care who had actually fathered me.

'When I confronted her I suppose she had no option but to explain. She told me the story of how she and Ronald, my father, had tried to get married after I was born, and how everything went wrong. The wedding was arranged, she was virtually at the altar when he was shipped out. Knowing about it made a big difference to how I felt. Her marriage to my stepfather wasn't very happy and by comparison her romance with my father sounded like a real, and very sad, love story.

'She told me he had written some letters for me when I was a baby and she'd let me have them one day. It was enough for me at that time. I didn't push her because I knew she didn't like talking about it, but I developed this secret longing to find my father.

'I didn't do anything about it for a long time – too busy getting on with my own life – but the longing was always there. I didn't tell anyone about it. It was my secret and, like everybody else in this position, I believed I was unique. There must be hundreds of GI babies in Scotland. Why are there so few who come out?

'My husband knew but when my kids asked about their grandfather I said he was dead. It was easier that way. When they got to their early teens, though, I made a conscious decision to be honest with them. A lot of people had been dishonest with me and I decided it wasn't fair to do the same to them. They were quite upset to find they had a grandfather alive after all and didn't know him, but once it was out in the open, there no longer seemed to be any reason for me not to try and find him.'

Kay's mother parted with the relevant information reluctantly.

'She didn't want me raking up the past and I can understand that in a way. She probably feels bitter about the way things worked out. Perhaps she thinks my father didn't try hard enough to overcome the obstacles that got in the way of the marriage – and he didn't come back, did he? I never got the letters she promised. I believe they were there but when I started asking too many questions she burned them. I don't make an issue of it any more. I've said all I'm going to say and I don't want us to fall out completely. I don't talk about my father to my mother at all now.'

When I started writing this book, Kay had been searching for her father for over six years and, although she had not stopped trying, had almost given up hope of ever finding him. 'I was just plodding on automatically, writing letters. I couldn't seem to stop.'

When I was almost at the end of the book, I heard from a contact in America that the plot had changed. There was a happy ending after all. She had found him. To get there had taken seven years of highs and lows, of false trails and shocking disappointments. At one point she was the victim of a cruel and apparently pointless hoax. A woman, approached routinely by a contact in the States, claimed to be the widow of Kay's father. Kay wrote to her at once.

'I put my cards on the table, told her the whole story. She assured me she had been married to my father and gave me highly plausible information about him. I was obviously sad that he had died but very happy to have found some of his family. I felt comfortable with this woman and with her story. I was ready to go to the States, bag half packed, when the contact discovered massive flaws in her story and realized she couldn't be telling the truth.

'It was really weird. I've no idea why someone should do that to me. Maybe she thought there would be financial gain in it or she was not mentally stable. It took me a long time to get over the shock. It took the edge off trying to find my father. That's when I began to feel it wasn't going to happen. But still I couldn't stop sending off letters, writing to government departments in every area, even those I'd written to a dozen times before. I didn't have much hope but something kept driving me. I sometimes wonder how long I'd have kept on if I hadn't found him. Till I dropped probably.'

But good things came out of the search too. Over the years Kay had made many friends in America, mostly by accident. Years ago, while writing to all the people with her father's name in the area around Dallas, where he had lived before the war, she got a letter back from a family who knew nothing of her father but offered their help and support.

'They have been wonderful to me. They are now as much part of my family as my blood relatives.' Four years ago she went to Texas to continue her search on the spot, and stayed with this family. She enjoyed the experience but got no closer to Ronald.

Early in 1991 Kay got hold of a new set of addresses of government departments and began sending off her standard letter, explaining her situation and requesting information. One letter brought a reply from a veterans' benefit office saying they had identified her father and would be willing to forward a letter from her to him.

'I didn't get too excited. I'd had promises like this many times before from other places. They came to nothing. It seemed to be a standard way of fobbing you off. If I got into a state of excitement every time I spotted a ray of hope I'd be a wreck. I wrote the letter to my father anyway and sent it off rather cynically. Then I went on holiday and forgot about it.

'When I got back at the beginning of August, there was a letter confirming that they had received my correspondence and sent the letter on to my father. This was unusual. A few days later another American-postmarked letter arrived. This one was from my father. To say I was surprised would be an understatement. It was simply unbelievable.

'He was living in East Dallas, about 200 miles from where I'd been when I was out there, which is nothing in distance in America. He said he'd searched for me until 1960 and had paid out thousands of dollars to try and have me traced. Ironically 1960 was the year I found out he was my father, so as I'd started searching he had finished. I don't know why he stopped at that point. Maybe he reasoned that I was no longer a child and he wouldn't have any say in my life. I don't know – it's one of the million questions I have to ask him when I see him.'

Kay knows very little about this man who has dominated her life for so long. She has heard from an American contact that he bitterly regretted not marrying her mother and felt this has cast a shadow over his other relationships, but she is waiting to hear the words from him before making any judgements. A visit has been arranged. She'll stay a month with him. Though she knows little about his family or what she will find, she is not nervous at the prospect of the meeting – 'just very, very happy'.

'I've done what I set out to do, found my father. It seemed like an impossible dream and I know my family and many friends believed I wouldn't do it. There were a few times when I agreed with them, but something inside me said, "Keep trying." Not easy when you're writing a dozen letters a week and most of them are falling on deaf ears.

'I very much hope my father will like me and that we'll get on well, but at the end of the day it doesn't matter. Is that hard to understand? Well, how many people can honestly say they truly like their parents, even if they love them? What is important is that this man is my father and I need to know him. I am his daughter, part of him, and I think he feels the same way about me. It's a very basic thing and it's what has kept me going.'

Sue It was Sue's son, Laurence, who spurred her into looking for her father. 'He's never been like anyone else in the family and I was fascinated with the idea that he might be like his grandfather or someone on that side. It wasn't the whole reason – I very much wanted to meet him myself – but my curiosity over my son gave me the push I needed.'

Sue contacted me in October 1986 and it was May 1987 before I was able to get back to her with her father, James's phone number. She wasn't in when I rang and I gave the number to her mother, Nancy, who lives with the family. Nancy had always been involved in what was going on, and though she had reservations at first – she didn't want to create family problems for the man she knew as Jimmy, by raking up the past – she gave Sue all the help she could. Even so she was struck speechless by the news that I'd found him.

Sue, who'd been out shopping, rang me back in a terrible tizzy, and we discussed the business of how she should make the first gentle approach to her father – though, as it happened, it wasn't Sue who made that phone call.

'I couldn't,' she said. 'I was a jabbering wreck. Michael, my husband, had to do it while I stood beside him, chewing my nails. Michael began by saying, "Er . . . are you Mr J. C—?" To which my father apparently replied, "Yup." The conversation then went, "Were you in the air force in the war, based in Surrey?"

'"Yup."

'"Can you talk now?"

'"Yup."

'"I'm married to your daughter."

'"Yup."

'He was totally laid back, didn't ask any questions at all. Michael then explained he was putting me on and handed me the phone. I didn't know what to say. I'd expected him to be doubtful or shocked or at least surprised. I asked if his family knew about me and he said they did – though I later found out that they didn't at the time. Then I asked if I wrote and sent photos of myself and the family, would he write back, and he said he would.

'Within a month I got a letter, telling me what had happened to him after the war and about his family. I hadn't mentioned Mummy because I didn't know what to say about her or how much he had told his family. When he wrote back he said, "Why didn't you say anything about your mother? Please write and tell me how she is."'

Sue, Michael and Laurence visited James and his family for the first time in September 1987.

'Our daughter, Lydia, couldn't come,' Sue said, 'and at first we weren't planning to take Laurence out of school for the trip. There didn't seem much point in getting him involved if there wasn't going to be any long-term relationship between me and my father, and at this stage I wasn't sure there would be. After all we were two total strangers. We might find we had nothing in common. But Laurence wanted to come so we took him. My letter telling Dad there would be a third party didn't arrive in time but he was thrilled to see his grandson. And yes, Laurence *is* like the American side of the family!

'I really wanted to make a good impression. I had visions of freshening up at the airport and maybe changing my clothes before I went out to meet my father. But we changed in New York and got a smaller plane on an internal flight, and when we landed he was waiting, literally at the bottom of the steps. There was no mistaking him. He's a big bear of a man, weighing 19 stone and 6' 3" tall. He grabbed me up and hugged me. It was very emotional, very exciting. I thought, What happened to the slim, quiet, shy man my mother told me she knew forty years ago? But he was lovely just the way he was.'

James had only told his second wife and three children of her existence some time after he received her first letter.

'He told Ruth, who's three years younger than me, straight away, but it had taken him a bit longer to break it to the boys. One of them is two years older than me and the other five years younger, and Dad was worried about how they'd take it. In fact they were all absolutely delighted and Ruth wrote to me almost immediately.

'The early part of that first visit was very strange for me. Michael said I was impossible to live with for the four months from the time I found my father till we went out there, and when we arrived he said I went into a catatonic state. All I could do was sit and look at my father. I found it very hard to relate to him. There he was, my dream, my salvation, the saviour I'd dreamed would come to rescue me from my unhappy life as a child . . . and I was so afraid he might not love me.

'Then one evening Michael and Laurence tactfully disappeared and left me alone with him and that's when he started to talk about the past. He told me his version of what had happened and how he'd felt. He also told me he had wanted me and never intended for me to be left, and that he'd thought about me. At one point, he'd even come to England for a reunion and wondered about trying to trace me, but he realized that after all the moves and name changes it would be impossible.

'"But I never tried to hide," he said. "I believed that you or your mother could find me if you wanted to." He told me he was sorry he hadn't been there to help me when I was growing up. It was all right after that talk. I'd just needed him to tell me that I was wanted and that I would never be rejected again.'

Since that first visit, James has been to England to see Sue and her family, including her mother.

'It was lovely to see them together,' Sue said. 'You could see there was still a lot of love between them. It was so funny to hear them reminiscing. It was just like that song, "Ah Yes, I Remember It Well", where the couple remember everything differently.'

Nancy was married but separated when she met James, himself married with a child in America. Sue's brother, Tony, a little boy at the time of the romance, came back from his home in Germany for James's visit.

'Tony has never forgotten Dad,' said Sue, 'and you could see there was a great rapport between them. Dad was also very taken with Tony's wife and he's planning to visit them in Germany. I feel he's part of our family, in the same way I'm part of his.'

She's been back to see him every year since they met.

'We have a wonderful time. We usually go off together for three or four days, visiting places, just the two of us. You couldn't do that with someone unless you had a good relationship. We've become very, very close. I regret all the years I didn't know him and I treasure every moment we can spend together now.'

14
Finding a Family

Given the age of the men we are searching for, it's sad but inevitable that sometimes we get there too late. But even when a father has died there can be other compensations, as Mick, Heather and John have found out.

<u>Mick</u> As soon as his mother died, Mick began searching for his father. He seems to have delayed it till then out of some sense of delicacy. He would have found it embarrassing to talk to his mother about her long-ago love affair.

Mick, a social worker, was one of the people who positively enjoyed the search. 'It's the thrill of the chase and the fact that you are also searching for yourself, a pretty fascinating subject to most of us!'

It looked a fairly straightforward case, as he knew where his father, George, had come from, his date of birth and his army number. I roped in my friend Lynn in the States to help, and via one of her government sources, she quickly came back with the first piece of solid information. Mick's father had died in June 1979.

Mick was unprepared for this news and it hit him hard.

'I became very depressed,' he said. 'It was like another bereavement after losing my mother. At the back of my mind I must have realized that there was the possibility my father could have died, but I hadn't let myself think about it. I don't consider myself a very emotional person. I saw my search as being more prompted by interest and curiosity than any emotional need, and I was surprised by how this bit of news affected me.'

He didn't, however, consider calling off the search. If he couldn't find his father, he could at least find people who knew him. There was no record of where George had died, but working on the assumption that he had lived out his life in his home state of Massachusetts, Mick wrote to the state for a death certificate.

He was right. Four months later the certificate arrived. His father had died at Cape Cod. Lynn took over on his behalf, contacting the *Cape Cod Times* and asking for an obituary. American obituaries are very different from ours. They come packed with biographical details and useful information, such as the names of mourning relatives and the towns where they live.

Mick learned that he had four half-sisters and one half-brother, and that his father had left a widow, Margaret. Two of his father's sisters, Mick's aunts, were also mentioned. One of these, his aunt Jean, he already knew from letters she had written to his mother when he was a baby. The letters had been among many others his mother had kept, which proved useful in his search. He knew from the obituary that Jean lived in Alabama and decided to make her his first contact as there was no doubt she knew of his existence. Possibly she was the only living relative who did. A phone number for Jean and her husband, however, proved hard to find, so Mick hit on the idea of phoning one of his half-sisters to ask for it. Linda's number in Boston was the first one he found, so he telephoned her.

'I told her I was looking for an old friend of my mother's whom I understood was her aunt,' he explained. 'I asked if she could give me the number. She seemed quite helpful, but said she didn't have the number. She could give me the phone number of her mother who would probably know.

'At this point I must have inadvertently aroused Linda's suspicions. I began to explain that I was calling from England and it would be easier if she would be kind enough to get the number from her mother and let me phone her back. Quite suddenly, she asked, "Who are you?"

'I hadn't planned on introducing myself, but guessed from the tone of her voice that she knew something. I didn't feel I could lie. "This may come as a shock . . ." I began, and she cut in with, "Are you my brother?" I said I was and she said, "Oh, we've been meaning to look for you for a long time."

'Apparently my father had told them about me when they were teenagers and they had often talked about me. Margaret, their mother, had known from early in the marriage. This was incredibly exciting and not at all what I'd visualized when I picked up the phone. I think the sisters more or less took over the situation from there. I was outnumbered.

'Linda is a very outgoing person. We talked for an hour and she told me she was going to tell the rest of the family immediately. She was as good as her word. At 8 a.m. next morning I had a call from my sister, Christine, the youngest of the family, in Hawaii. All that day there were calls coming in. Even my brother, Rick, who is an electrician at a power station in Alaska, rang. At 44, he's the closest to me in age and we seem to have a lot in common. I suppose both being male helps. I've talked to him often since that first call, though we haven't met yet. I'm hoping he'll be able to come over next year.'

Early in 1990, Mick flew to New York, to meet his only son, Derek, also a social worker, working in the US for a year, and together they drove to Washington to meet three of Mick's sisters. His sister, Anne, married to a diplomat and resident in Washington, was about to leave with her husband for Indonesia. The other two had travelled from their homes for the big get-together.

'It was a strange and rather stressful experience,' Mick says of that first meeting in the hotel where Anne and her husband were staying since their house had already been let. 'Linda has spent a holiday in Wolverhampton with my wife and me since then, and she agrees it was stressful. They were worrying about what I'd think of them, apparently, and of course I was only concerned about what they thought of me.

'It was hard to know how to greet them. They are family but they were also strangers. Should you be emotional? Should you kiss them or just shake hands? There's nothing about this sort of occasion in the etiquette manuals. I think the sisters set the pace really, and because they have different personalities they greeted me differently, with anything from a fleeting touch to a big hug and kiss.

'It is a particularly strange experience for someone who grew up as an only child to be plunged into the middle of a big family. They were including me as part of the family but I didn't have their shared experience so I was an outsider really. Because they know each other so well they talk in a kind of code and I didn't know that code.

'You are looking out for things you might have in common and for family resemblances. Everybody agreed that I'm the spitting image of our grandfather, which made me feel more a part of things. It was interesting that we had similar sorts of job. There's a social worker and a teacher among my sisters.' Mick went back to Massachusetts with his sisters Linda and Deborah to see the house where his father had lived as a young man. He also met his father's cousin, Yvonne, unofficial keeper of the family history, who could tell him more about his father's early life and introduce him to a handful of other relatives.

One thing that worried the sisters was how their mother would cope with seeing this walking evidence of her late husband's past, though she wanted to see Mick. He had arranged to meet Deborah and go with her to Margaret's Cape Cod house, but he missed his sister and arrived at the house alone.

'They needn't have worried about Margaret. We got on very well. She's a very nice lady. She could probably tell me more about the sort of man my father was than anyone else and she talked very openly about him. She said he always feared rejection and she believed the main reason he never contacted me was because he was afraid I wouldn't want him. I found that very comforting.

'Since then, Derek, who only lives about 120 miles away, has been to stay with Margaret and with other members of the family. I feel really pleased that he has benefited from having this large family around him too.

'It was a fascinating trip, a dizzying maze of impressions. I felt I'd got to know my father, and in some ways it's changed my life. Thinking about it back home, I found what has happened quite frightening. I've got into something I can't get out of, even if I wanted to. I've taken this step and there's no turning back.'

A few months after his trip to America, Linda came to stay with Mick and his wife, Sheila, in their small terraced house – the very place his mother lived when she was going out with their father.

'I think she found Wolverhampton less awful than she expected,' he laughed. 'At least she stayed ten days, twice as long as planned. It was only meant to be a short stopover on a trip to Frankfurt to visit her son, who lives there with his German wife and their child.

'It was, on the whole, a more satisfying meeting than when I was in the States. Linda and I knew each other, and there was no need to try and create an impression. The stress had gone out of the relationship. We used to sit up talking into the early hours of the morning and I understand much more about my family from these talks. She told me how she and Christine had discussed coming to England and making a systematic search for me. For some reason, they were the two my father had talked to most about me, and they always wanted to meet me. It was like fitting in the final piece of a jigsaw puzzle when I rang, she said – and that's what I felt I was looking for when I set out to find my father, that missing piece of the puzzle.

'While Linda was with us, her mother sent a tape that she and my father had made on a trip they'd taken across America to visit their children in their various homes in 1976. They'd talked about all the sights they had seen and sent copies of the tape to the family instead of letters. Hearing my father's voice for the first time was interesting, but it was the voice of a stranger to me. To Linda it was the voice of someone she loved and had lost and she sobbed throughout the tape. I felt a bit sad that I can never have that depth of feeling about my father.'

Perhaps the most poignant bit of information to emerge during Linda's stay followed a conversation she had with an old friend of their father's living in London.

Said Mick, 'At the back of all our minds was this unspoken question – why had George, obviously a caring and decent family man, never bothered to get in touch with me? Margaret partly answered it – he was afraid of rejection. But the old friend told Linda that my father had actually come to England the year before he died with the express purpose of looking me up.

'He had been on a holiday in Spain and he took a couple of days out of it to come over to London and talk over what he planned to do. They discussed how difficult it might be to find me – ironic since I was living in my mother's house. The friend pointed out that my mother had probably married – she hadn't – and I might have grown up knowing nothing about my real background. They came to the conclusion that him turning up might be a terrible shock to me. The old friend's attitude plus my father's thing about rejection must have done the trick. He decided to let sleeping dogs lie. Imagine how it might have been if he'd decided differently.'

But Mick doesn't have time to ponder over what might have been. There are already plans afoot for visits from his sister Christine and his aunt Jean, and his brother should be arriving with his family next year. For an only child from a one-parent family, life is very busy.

Heather Heather, from Leicester, arrived on my list with a very familiar story. She'd been searching for her father, Mexican-American Richard, but had come up against the brick wall of bureaucracy. She'd had the forms with the impossible questions, the story about the fire which had damaged all documents relating to certain ex-servicemen, and her husband, Dave, had persuaded her to give up.

'Dave couldn't understand why I was going to all the trouble anyway,' she said. 'He'd say, "You've got family here. You have half-sisters and half-brothers and a stepfather you get on with. Arthur's your Dad in every way that counts. Even if you managed to find this Richard bloke, he wouldn't want to know you. You'd just be an embarrassment."'

So Heather gave up, not because she was convinced but because she saw no way round the brick wall. Not, that is, till she read a newspaper story about War Babes. The first thing she said when she rang me was, 'I thought I was the only one.'

I did the best I could but initially we didn't get anywhere. Her Mum, Dolly, had agreed to help with information, but when it came down to hard facts she knew very little about Richard. It wasn't her fault that what she thought she knew turned out to be misleadingly false. He'd told her he came from San Diego. He didn't, although he'd been stationed there. He told her the pretty girl in the photograph he carried in his wallet was his sister, Anna. That was her name all right, but she was his wife and mother of his two children. Dolly had told her wartime lover a few whoppers herself – she'd even failed to mention she was married – but he'd matched them.

In January 1990, Heather got the chance to be on an American television programme, *20/20*, with myself and some other war babes. She'd begun to feel she was never going to find her father and this was something of a last chance. She tried to convince herself that somewhere in that vast country, he'd turn on his television at just the right moment, that he'd choose the right channel and think, That's my daughter. It didn't happen quite like that, but in Baton Rouge, Louisiana, a family by the same name as her father, watched with curiosity, then interest and eventually a growing realization as Heather spoke.

But I'll let Heather tell the story, as it was later related to her.

'My father's brother, Ernest, and his wife, Betty, were watching the TV show with my cousin and her boyfriend, Gary. They weren't all that interested in the subject. They didn't think it related to them in any way. When I appeared, someone mentioned that I looked like Ellen, who was, in fact, my half-sister who had died of leukaemia.

'Then I mentioned the name of my father and this made them sit up. My cousin remarked what a coincidence it was that I not only looked like a member of the family but also had the same surname as theirs. But of course there was no one in the family called Richard, she added. It was my father's brother, uncle Ernest, as I now know him, who said, "Oh yes there is. Arnold was christened Richard only nobody in the family ever called him that."'

The television station put the family in touch with me. They explained that Richard or Arnold had died fifteen years earlier, but they believed they were the family Heather was searching for and they wanted to get in touch with her. I passed the message on to a very excited Heather, along with Gary's phone number. Gary took a special interest in the story all along because his own father had never known his father, and Gary always hoped to find this missing link in the family, his grandfather.

Heather rang him immediately but as they talked she became less convinced they were the right people. There were discrepancies, in particular the fact that her mother was convinced Richard came from San Diego, and this family, though of Mexican origin, had their roots firmly in Louisiana. Gary agreed to send some photographs.

Heather says: 'When the pictures arrived, I felt even less convinced. Dave looked at them and said, "He doesn't look very Mexican," and I had to agree, though he was dark. I don't know what we expected a Mexican to look like – someone in a poncho with a big droopy moustache, I suppose.

'I rang Mum and got her to come over. Without any clues about who was supposed to be who, I handed her the photographs. The first one she looked at was a group picture of the family, taken about twenty years before. Mum glanced at it and said immediately, "Yes, that's him, the one sitting on the chair there."

'"Are you sure?" I asked.

'She got very sniffy. "Don't you think I ought to know?" So I reread the letter where they had identified everyone in the photograph and sure enough the man she'd pointed out was Arnold, alias Richard.

'Gary had begged me to get in touch as soon as I received the photographs so I rang him. It was six o'clock in the morning there and Gary just let out a cry of "Whoopee!" They were as pleased and as excited as I was.

'It was sad to think I'd missed the chance of knowing my father, but finding a family was a wonderful bonus, something I hadn't given much thought to. We started exchanging letters. I found I'd got two half-sisters, Jean and Dorothy (the middle sister, Ellen, had died just twenty days after her father), numerous cousins, and a grandmother still alive, aged 94. I found out a lot more about my Dad too. Apparently he'd been a bit of a lad with the ladies. He'd been married three times – the family I had found were from his first wife, Anna. He already had children when he was in England. After Anna he'd married a Japanese woman and had two sons. He'd divorced her, come back to the States and married for a third time, though there were no children from that relationship.

'My relatives were very keen to meet me and they asked if I'd be able to come over for my grandmother's 95th birthday party. Well, I just thought I had to go to that. Angie, my daughter, agreed to come with me. Before we went I had a phone call from my half-sister Dorothy, explaining she wouldn't be able to be there, because her husband was having a heart-transplant operation.

'We went on 29 September 1990. I was so nervous about meeting everyone. After all I was a complete stranger, and a foreigner to boot. But I needn't have worried. From the moment I arrived to stay with Uncle Ernest and Aunt Betty, I felt really comfortable. It was as though they weren't strangers but family I hadn't seen for a long time.

'There was a party to introduce me to all the relatives. It was a wonderful occasion. My daughter and her cousin, the daughter of Ellen, took to each other immediately, and she spent a lot of time with us. And of course I met my grandmother, a wonderful old lady. She said it was nice to get another granddaughter so late in life and she talked about my father and said what a pity it was that he had never seen me.

'The whole three weeks went of beautifully. When we were leaving everyone came to the airport and there were lots of tears and hugs and kisses. It was such a big, emotional group that all the bystanders wanted to know what was going on. When we told them, everybody thought it was a beautiful story. The family's last words to me were, "Come back soon and bring your husband."'

It's here that Heather's happy story takes a sad turn. In January 1991, as they were making plans for her second visit and his first, Dave died suddenly.

'He was so looking forward to the trip,' Heather said. 'He was so pleased for me that I'd found my family. He'd come to understand how much it meant to me. He was a good man, a window cleaner for twenty-nine years. Everyone liked him. They say teenage marriages don't last, but we'd been together thirty years, through good and bad times, and I was shattered by his death. Nothing, not my family in England nor my family in America, could comfort me. I didn't feel I could go on living without him.

'But Dorothy had lost her husband too – the transplant had not been a success – and she understood better than anyone what I was going through. She asked me to come over and stay with her straight away. I said no, though, at the time. I had to do my grieving here first and there were practical things to sort out. I couldn't just run away.

'I've sorted myself out in the past few months and I'm ready to go now. I'm going alone with an open ticket, for up to six months. My sister is a very determined person and a born organizer – the family think we're a lot alike – and she wants me to move to the US. She's even approached the local hospital and checked that there would be a job for me. I've told her that I can't go permanently. It's wonderful to have found this second family, but my life is here in England. My roots are here with my daughter and my two little grandchildren and the other family I grew up with.

'My English family have been quite strange about me finding my father's people. They object to me referring to Dorothy and Jean as sisters. "They are not your sisters," they said, "we are." Of course I'm equally related to both families. I've tried to point out to my family here that finding another group of people I care about doesn't mean I have to stop caring for them.

'Arthur, my stepfather, didn't like the idea of me finding my father. I think he saw Richard as the man who took his wife off him, and might now take his daughter away. The way things have turned out he's been marvellous about it. He can laugh about the past now, though it can't have been any joke at the time.

'My mother? Well, we are still not all that close, but I was surprised and touched by how badly she took the news of my father's death, and the way she cherishes the photograph of him I gave her. It showed a side of her I haven't seen much of. There have been other men in her life, but I think Richard was something special. They were two of a kind when you think about it – they both got around a bit. I can't help wondering how it would have turned out if they'd stayed together. But I don't criticize or condemn and I don't feel any bitterness towards them.'

Heather's search is not yet over. She was fascinated to hear that Richard had two sons from his Japanese marriage, two more half-brothers for her. Even her American family have not met these. Now she is trying to trace them and she has been in touch with the Japanese Embassy.

'We know the city they were born in and my father's surname can't be a common name in Japan, so I'm quite hopeful. It would be lovely to increase the family even further now I've started!'

John G

John G I always knew John G would crack it in the end, with or without my help. He was one of the doggedly determined people who was not going to give up even if it took a lifetime to trace his father.

John is a successful businessman, married and father of three grown-up children. He's also the son of a US Air Force Captain, William, and a waitress who was already married with a small child at the time of the romance. It was a serious affair. At one point, she left her daughter with relatives and followed her airman to Norwich when he was transferred. She was pregnant when he was sent back to the States. He left money to pay her medical bills and John was born in a private nursing home in August 1945. They never heard from his father again.

John's mother was persuaded to return to her husband and John grew up believing he was a child of the family. He went on believing so until he was in his thirties, when his mother, knowing he was applying for a passport and would see his birth certificate, admitted the truth.

He says he was never treated badly by his stepfather. 'But I just had no feeling for him, no love, no hate, nothing. It was mutual, I think. I was 20 when my mother left him and I left within a few weeks. There was nothing there for me.'

It wasn't until 1984 that John began searching for his father. 'I had to wait till I'd got my business on a firm footing,' he says. He also found it hard to approach his mother with questions about the past, but although she was not keen on being involved, she tried to help by giving him what small amount of information she had. Unfortunately, she had misremembered the most vital bit of information, his father's exact name. She gave him the Christian names as Leonard William and wasn't sure if there was an 's' on the end of his surname.

'That set me back two years,' he said. 'Just one letter on a surname can make a dramatic difference. Taking the two spellings into account, there are between 70,000 and 80,000 people in the USA with my father's surname.'

He says he will always regret not starting the search earlier, particularly in view of the outcome. 'From the moment I knew I had a father somewhere in America, the urge to meet him was there, and it just grew and grew until it became overwhelming, undeniable. The main problem was that I really didn't know where to start.'

For want of any better place, he started at the boarding house where his mother told him she and his father had stayed when she left home to be with him. Norfolk in the war years had become virtually one large airfield, but the landlady was able to tell him which camp his father had been based at.

'I went back to my roots,' he said. 'I went to look at the place where the camp had stood and I began talking to people locally who might be able to give me some clues. Talking to the local vicar, I heard about a man who was studying the history of the camps and had been able to buy microfilm on this from America. The vicar put me in touch with this man and I discovered how to go about it.'

The microfilm turned out to be a taped diary or log book of day-to-day camp activities. It was not always riveting stuff and there was a lot of it. As there could be twenty to thirty units at a camp over a period of three years and John had no idea which unit his father had belonged to, he ended up with fifteen films. He bought a second-hand viewer and began working his way through them in the evenings after a hard day at work.

'I suppose it would take a day or two to check each one if you had the time to work round the clock, but I only had the evenings. I was looking for any mention of my father's name, just to confirm he had been here and which unit he'd been with. Sometimes your concentration would begin to slip after an hour or two and you'd have to start again. I saw a lot of the films twice. I was getting to the end of them with no mention of him and was ready to call it a day, when, suddenly, in the last reel I found something. It was just one small entry, beginning, "Major Larson agreed to transfer Captain William L— . . ." It had taken me fifteen months to find my father's name.'

John got in touch with me after his wife had seen me on TV-AM. By that time he was already a seasoned searcher but with depressingly little to show for his efforts. I gave him names, addresses, advice and suggestions. He would ring up regularly to bounce ideas off me – 'What if I did this . . .? Has anyone tried that . . .?' He says he was half-hearted and needed guidance. I think what he needed more was moral support and encouragement. You can get very depressed when your promising leads turn into dead ends. When he'd say, 'I'm never going to find him. I've had enough' – as even dedicated searchers do from time to time – I'd say:

'Of course you will. You've done so much work you can't give up now.' Being a cheerleader is one of my jobs. When people are flagging I give them my little pep talk. It's what they want to hear. Nobody is phoning to hear me say, 'Yes, perhaps you're right. Forget the whole thing.' The problem is that they can't forget and they'll regret it if they give up too soon. But sometimes they need a little break and if I'm doing most of the researching, I'll say, 'OK, I'll carry on looking and when you feel ready come back and join in.'

When the chance to do the American *20/20* programme for ABC television came up, I thought John would be a suitable candidate. Telling his story to American viewers might bring the big breakthrough that had evaded him. Unlike Heather, there was nobody out there who recognized him as part of their family, but he did have a lot of offers of help from the public, and from private detectives and other professionals who specialized in tracing people.

I'm always very wary of these professionals. They charge high fees and are less likely to come up with the goods than my own voluntary helpers, but John went through the offers shrewdly and took on a man in New York who he found honest and useful.

He recalls: 'The first thing my New York contact did was a computer search of all the William L—s on the East Coast. It yielded nothing. Meanwhile I had written to the American Veterans' Association to try and ascertain, once and for all, if they knew whether my father was dead or alive. I'd been in touch with all the other government agencies, without getting anywhere.

'For some reason, this time I got lucky. Lucky in that I got the information I asked for; unlucky in that it was not what I wanted to hear. They told me that a man of my father's name had died in 1981, and was buried in a cemetery in Georgia. It took a while to confirm that this Captain William L— matched all the criteria, but in the end there seemed no doubt it was my father. This was very sad news and I felt my only hope now was to find some relatives.'

John's contact in New York traced the funeral parlour in which his father had been interred and came back with even worse news. His father's wife had died two years earlier and there were no known living relatives.

'I think that was the lowest moment of the search for me,' John said. 'I'd accepted that my father was dead. I knew there was always that possibility. But to be told that there was no family at all, no one I could talk to about him, that was heart-breaking.'

It would have been one of the saddest endings ever if we'd stopped there, but fortunately I put him on to one of my helpers, an amazing man with army connections who was always willing to help 'as long as you don't ask me how I get the information'. Eddie went along to the funeral parlour and ferreted out the name of a relative for John.

'Eddie phoned me with the name of my father's nephew in Newark, New Jersey,' John said. 'I took the surname down incorrectly – one letter wrong in the middle – though, of course, I didn't know this. Then I got on to the New York detective again and had him run a check on his computer to find some addresses for this name. He came back with the devastating news that there was no one of that name in the United States. I couldn't understand it. I assumed the name was German, so I went to see a German girl who lives in our village to ask if she could find any explanation. She said, yes, I was probably spelling the name wrong and gave me the correct spelling. Amazing! As simple as that. This time my man got back to me with a telephone number. I rang straight away. A man answered.

'"Are you the nephew of William L—?" I asked.

'"Yes."

'"Was he stationed in England during the war?"

'"Yes."

'"I believe I'm your cousin," I said.

'"That's great," he replied.

'What amazed me was how readily my cousin, Gerry, accepted the truth of my story without question. He turned out to be a lot older than me, 71. His children were more my age. They were delighted too. Gerry is the son of my father's sister. He'd known my father – Willie, he calls him – all his life. He wanted to know how long Willie had known my mother and was surprised that he hadn't kept in touch with her and "not done anything" about me. Made financial provision, I think he meant.'

Within three weeks of making contact, John and his wife arrived in Newark to stay with Gerry and his wife.

'We got on very well. We met Gerry's two sons, one living at home, the other married, and his daughter, also married. He took me to see my father's grave, and I talked a great deal with him and his wife about the family, including our grandfather who had been a self-employed photographer. I began to feel that I belonged.

'Gerry did talk about my father, but though he'd known him a long time, it wasn't really the sort of close relationship that provided him with the answers to all the personal questions I wanted to ask. Because they'd lived so far apart, Gerry and Willie had seen each other perhaps once a year. They'd got on well; Gerry thought him a very nice man, but apart from biographical details like the fact that he'd been married twice and had no other children, it was hard to get deeper into what made the man tick.

'The real bonus of the trip was the relationship that was built up between myself and Gerry and the two families. We took a break for a few days during the stay, really to give him a breather from having us around, and went to see Eddie. When we got back, Gerry greeted us with, "I've missed you guys" – and it was obvious that he meant it.

'My wife remarked on how alike we are in many ways despite the age gap – the same dry sense of humour, both a bit careful with our money, she said. When we parted at the airport there were tearful goodbyes. I don't mind admitting I cried. We keep in touch by phone every other week. We are going to spend Christmas over there.'

I asked John, jokingly, what on earth he'd do with all the free time now the search is over, and he replied, quite seriously, that he'll spend more time with his wife and family 'and try to become a good husband and father again. In some ways I'm glad it's over. It's been very painful work.

'But even knowing all this and how it would turn out in the end, I'd still have done it. The way I felt it was a task that had to be done. I had to know.'

There's a footnote to John G's story, a strange event that happened in September 1981, and took on a significance only after he found out about his father's death.

This is the story, as he tells it.

'I'd been ill. I'd been through a breakdown and come out of it and I just felt I had to get away. I said to my wife, "I'm going to go to New York, hire a car and just drive around for a while."

'Why I felt the urge to go to the States rather than take a break somewhere else, I don't know. You tell me. I wasn't looking for my father. He wasn't on my mind – certainly not consciously – when I left England on 18 September.

'I did just as I said, drove around, lost track of the days a bit. One night I booked into a hotel in Boston and went to bed, tired out, at about 10.30 p.m. A little later I was woken up by what felt like a nudge in my back. I could hear the tinkling of glasses and laughter. I turned over and in the corner of the room I could make out two American servicemen and two women talking and laughing. It was like watching a scene from a film. I was there but I wasn't part of it.

'I dived under the bedclothes and told myself not to be ridiculous. When I woke up next morning I was in a perfectly normal room, with no signs of intruders or any strange event taking place. I put the incident down to overtiredness and a vivid imagination, but since then I've discovered that my father died that week, on 23 September, perhaps even on that very night.'

15
War Babes versus the American Government

In 1986 the American television station, NBC, put out a programme on War Babes and among the millions of viewers was Alan Morrison of the Public Citizen Litigation Group, a group of consumer and civil-rights lawyers in Washington DC. Who says television is a waste of time? Alan's night's viewing set in motion a chain of events that was to change a part of the American legal system and will help countless thousands of people the world over.

What had come over loud and clear from the interviews with myself and other war babes was our dissatisfaction with the way the American government had treated us. We had numerous complaints on that score, including letters being ignored, searches not being carried out and a total lack of explanation by staff in various departments about what was going on. But the overall grumble, and the one that had grabbed Alan Morrison's attention, was the refusal of agencies like the National Personnel Records Centre (NPRC) under the Department of Defense to release our fathers' last known address – and to justify this by saying the information was covered by the Privacy Act.

Typically, what occurred when you wrote to the NPRC for information was that you were sent a form to fill in. I can still feel my hackles rise with rage thinking about this form, which asked questions unanswerable unless you were in close contact with your father. If you could answer these questions you wouldn't be looking for the man in the first place. The effect on most people of being faced with this officious-looking document was to give up, which was, I'm sure, what was intended.

If you filled in what you could and sent it back incomplete it was returned saying they couldn't help because you had provided insufficient information. If you were one of the lucky few who had most of the vital bits of information, such as your father's service number, you were still refused. The explanation this time being that the records could not be traced and might have been destroyed in a department fire in 1973. Should dad's records have escaped the flames, or you discovered there were alternative sources of information and pushed to have what these contained released, the government's final card was the news that information such as the addresses of ex-servicemen could not be released under the Privacy Act. You couldn't even know if your father was dead or alive.

This was what incensed Alan Morrison, a specialist in civil liberties. He believed his government was breaking its own laws, and that the information we sought was legally available to us under the Freedom of Information Act. This Act gives individuals, whether or not they are US citizens, the right of access to documents in the possession of federal agencies, and it is not overruled by the Privacy Act. There were certain exemptions to the Freedom of Information Act and the government might argue that giving out our fathers' addresses would constitute an 'unwarranted invasion of personal privacy', but Alan didn't think this would stand up in law.

He had left a message with NBC the day after the programme for me to contact him, and when I telephoned, he explained his views to me. I agreed with everything he said, including the crucial point that the authorities shouldn't be allowed to get away with it, but I didn't see what a group of ordinary people in England could do against the government of the most powerful country in the western world. Alan suggested something we could do; we could take out a lawsuit to force the government to release the addresses. His group would be willing to represent us.

I was astounded by the suggestion. It was something I'd never imagined in my wildest and most ambitious dreams. War Babes versus the Pentagon! He told me to think about it, but I didn't need to think for long. It was ridiculous. Any court case cost money, but an American case that might last years would cost sums I couldn't begin to imagine. I thanked him for his interest and explained that all of us in War Babes were ordinary people with ordinary incomes, and something like this was financially out of the question.

Alan had realized this. He explained that if, after learning more about the organization and its members, he still felt we had a good case, his group would be prepared to take us on *pro bono publico*. It was the first time I'd heard the expression. I was told it means 'for the public good'. More importantly it means free of charge. The Public Citizen Litigation Group lawyers would give their time free – all we would have to pay for were sundry office expenses, telephone bills and filing documents in court.

When the call ended I made myself a cup of coffee and sat looking around my small kitchen, pondering this new development. I didn't know whether to laugh or cheer. I had no idea what form an American lawsuit would take, how long the process would last, what I'd be expected to do, or what were our chances of winning – though, presumably, an experienced lawyer wouldn't take on a likely loser. There hadn't been time to take in the implications, but the obvious thing it would do was speed up the tracing process. And that could mean the difference between my 300 members finding their fathers dead or alive.

I talked it over with Barry who pointed out that I didn't need to take this on on my own account – I'd just found my Dad, no thanks to the official agencies.

'But I could have found him fourteen years earlier if the American government had released the information they had.'

It was a powerful argument, but two equally powerful voices – one from Barry and the other inside my head – were insisting, 'What about the cost?' The amount War Babes was expected to contribute might be a drop in the ocean compared to the total cost, but it could still leave me bankrupt and without a roof over my head, if I took it on personally. The obvious solution was to contact all the members and ask for contributions. Asking them for cash was something I hated doing and, in any case, would they be willing to co-operate? Would they see a court case as either a good thing or sheer madness and Shirley getting above herself? As it happened I didn't have to worry on the latter score. Everyone involved was totally for bringing the action and willing to help in every way, but in the end I didn't even have to get out the begging bowl.

I think what convinced me I must go along with Alan Morrison's idea was my sheer annoyance with the American government and the way it had treated everyone – our mothers, our fathers in many cases, and us war babes. They shouldn't be allowed to get away with it.

Our mothers had suffered the stigma and shame of having us, and the sheer practical problems of being unmarried mothers at a time when welfare benefits hardly existed. Yet the American military hierarchy had done everything possible to discourage our fathers from marrying them, even bribing some women with the offer of £100 payments if they signed a form promising not to try and contact the men.

Most war babes feel no bitterness towards their fathers, but the fact remains that these young men should have been encouraged to face up to their responsibilities. Instead they were hidden, protected and nannied by the state – and this was still happening. Even in 1986, when there was no possibility of financial claims on them, the government was still mollycoddling them, insisting that an approach by one of us would cause distress and embarrassment and should be prevented at all costs.

Even worse, it was clear from my records that most of these elderly men didn't want to be 'protected' from their sons and daughters. They wanted to meet them and were horrified when they realized how the government had tried to prevent it, just as during the war many had objected to being 'protected' and tried to marry their girlfriends. The 'unwarranted invasion' into their private lives and freedom was, it seems, their government's, not ours.

And what about us, the children – didn't we have any rights? We had always made it clear that we wanted nothing material from our fathers. No financial demands would be made and no requests for American citizenship. We were people in middle age with our roots firmly planted where they'd grown. All we wanted was to know, to meet, if possible, the man who had fathered us, who had made us half of what we were. Yet we'd been treated with high-handed and infuriating disregard and often dishonesty. Here's a record of my own experience from 1984 onwards.

15 JUNE 1984   Wrote to President Reagan, explaining my own and the group's situation and asking for any help possible for myself and other children of wartime GIs who'd contacted me. The letter was transferred to the National Archives and Records Administration (NARA) which controls the National Personnel Records Centre (NPRC).

DECEMBER 1984   Letter from the assistant director of NPRC to tell me that former servicemen's home addresses are 'not releasable to the public' and that 'no further action' could be taken in my case or that of other war babes.

1985   Further requests for information were met with the reply that no details could be provided as I didn't have my father's service number.

1985   Also wrote to the Veterans' Administration asking for information on my father. They couldn't locate any. After I found my father, it turned out he had been receiving a veterans' pension courtesy of that department for forty-three years. He had also been offered treatment in a Veterans' Hospital.

1985   Asked for help from fifty senators, some of whom told me that, 'The Department of Defence was correct when they stated that they could not release information regarding a veteran without the written permission of that veteran' (which seemed to close the door pretty firmly for all of us!) because of the Privacy Act.'

One senator did, however, say that an unsealed letter (so that it could be read and checked as suitable) could be passed on to my father for me. The senator asked two agencies, the Social Security Administration and the Veterans' Administration, to forward a letter each. To this day I don't know what happened to those letters, even though I was asked to put my return address in the left-hand corner of the envelopes, so that the letters could be returned to me if they could not be delivered. The agencies did not contact me further about them, they were not returned to me and my father has never received them.

1986   Submitted a request for information to the NPRC including my father's service number. A form letter (standard, photocopied letter with various statements which can be ticked) told me that the relevant records may have been destroyed in a fire in 1973. No suggestion that there were other sources which could contain at least part of the damaged records.

1986   Sent two follow-up letters requesting referral to the appropriate Veterans' Administration office which I hoped might have records of any pension being paid to my father. Two letters came back; the first telling me that all information available had already been released, the second stating that the office would need more time to process my request. How much time? They still have not come back to me.

Some of the correspondence received by War Babes would be funny if it wasn't so annoying. Mrs C, who became one of my two co-plaintiffs in the lawsuit, was in touch, with little success, with various government departments from 1980 to 1988. She was told, like so many of us, that her father's records had been destroyed in the 1973 fire, but the clerk who wrote back inserted a middle initial 'M', into her father's name, which she hadn't given them. You didn't have to be Sherlock Holmes to spot something interesting here.

When Mrs C wrote back saying that the US Embassy in London had advised her that if they were able to supply a middle initial, it appeared that they had located her father's file, back came the time-honoured response that the Privacy Act prohibited the release of information of former servicemen.

I could work up quite a head of steam when I thought about the way we'd been treated. If nothing was done, all the people who hadn't yet found their fathers – and not just children from World War II, but from the Vietnam War and from areas where GIs were stationed in peacetime – would face exactly the same problems I had. But if I was willing to put myself out, work harder, take a few risks and a step into the unknown, I had a chance of changing all that for the babes of yesterday, today and tomorrow. There was no choice. It was an offer no self-respecting war babe could refuse.

·

I will always be grateful to Alan Morrison for setting the ball rolling, and I owe him an equal debt of gratitude for introducing me to Joan Meier. Joan, a young lawyer who had just joined the group, was allocated us as her first case. She's said since that she couldn't have achieved what she did without me, and I'm sure we would never have succeeded if we'd been given a lawyer, however good, whom I didn't get on with.

Looking through my folders of correspondence from her, I see that Joan wrote introducing herself on 23 September 1986. We were addressing each other as Mrs McGlade and Ms Meier then, but it quickly became Shirley and Joan. We made a good team: me emotional and inclined to work on instinct, Joan with a cool, logical head on her shoulders. But her heart was with us too. She cared about the people and the principles involved and never lost her ability to be shocked at the way her government had behaved towards British women during the war.

'They can't have done that,' she'd gasp in horror as I revealed proof of another bit of chicanery like the £100 payment scheme, or the rapid transfer of men who had become involved with British women, leaving no forwarding address. She was shocked by the apparent attitude by which servicemen were encouraged to fraternize but discouraged from accepting the responsibility for the outcome of that fraternization. She discovered that the phenomenon of American servicemen and British women was known and hotly debated in America at the time. 'We knew even then that there were many children being born in Britain, fathered by American servicemen,' she said.

For my part I was learning a lot about American law practice, though I never totally unravelled the mystery. When we started discussing the case I had no idea what to expect. If I thought at all about the point we were moving towards, I suppose I visualized us all in court in front of judge and jury, arguing our side and calling witnesses – real Perry Mason stuff. I wasn't the only misguided soul. Whenever I spoke to British journalists, they'd ask, 'When are you going over for the court case?' In fact, the case was to spread over four years and most of the arguing and presenting of evidence was done in writing; far less exciting to a casual observer, but it was pretty nail-biting stuff if you were involved.

But all that was a long way off in 1986 when I first heard from Joan. I suspect I'd have been very despondent if I'd known then how long it would take merely to gather all the evidence and prepare the lawsuit. That it took me so long was due in part to geography; to Joan and I being so far apart. At that distance and that cost, you thought at least twice before picking up the phone, so we did a lot of work by post, which takes time and letters occasionally do go astray. Of course, we did talk on the phone too, and to be honest, much as I liked to hear from her I rather dreaded Joan's calls in case she would try to discuss some legal point with me. I didn't understand legal terminology, particularly the American variety, and I'd be desperately trying to grasp what she meant, but afraid to ask too much in case I sounded stupid.

Letters and even legal documents were easier. Barry and I would sit there with a large dictionary, checking the words we weren't certain of. When I met Joan in Washington DC in 1989, during the filming of a BBC television documentary, I was astounded how simple it was to understand the whole thing when you were sitting side by side, with the papers in front of you. Instead of rattling off clause numbers, she could point them out and I had no difficulty grasping the point. Maybe I wasn't so thick after all. I suddenly realized we'd probably have been able to put the case together in half the time if we'd been able to meet face to face occasionally. It was good too to be able to put a face to the voice – and such a youthful face, though she'll hate me for saying so!

The trip to America came courtesy of the BBC at Pebble Mill in Birmingham. The documentary they were filming (later titled: *War Babes* and shown on BBC2 in August 1991) was the result of an idea that hit me one night while I was lying awake worrying about the legal expenses we were running up. Why not persuade someone to make a documentary? I suddenly thought. If there was a fee for me in it, I could use that to pay the expenses. I approached Dennis Adams, a producer I'd met and liked when the BBC covered Lesley's meeting with her father.

'I was just thinking of contacting you,' he told me. He'd had a similar idea – though not one that involved the War Babes expenses! – and the topicality of the lawsuit was an added bonus. He was sympathetic when I explained the financial position, and thought there would be no problem over paying me a fee, though the BBC couldn't pay a legal group direct. It was an enormous load off my mind.

Like the court case the documentary took rather a long time to get off the ground, though I can't say if there was as much going on behind the scenes with the television people as there was with us. Pieces of paper were flying back and forth across the Atlantic at a great rate. There were people to be contacted, case histories to be written up, information collated that would help the case, statistics to be investigated. How many fathers had died while we had been trying to trace them? Joan was keen to highlight the ages of the men and the urgency needed in finding them. How many had welcomed their son or daughter? And, if they hadn't, what had been the reason?

Joan had asked me to find two other members of the group who would act as plaintiffs along with me. I recruited Mrs B and Mrs C, two stalwarts with loads of 'searching' experience. We also had to sort out a small group of war babes, five or six, who knew that the government agencies had their fathers' records but had refused to release information from these on grounds of the Secrecy Act. Joan would apply on their behalf for information, quoting the Freedom of Information Act. If this was refused an appeal would be made. Only if the appeal failed could the lawsuit or complaint be filed in court.

The most time-consuming task of the lot, and the one which would prove the most valuable in the long run, was organizing affidavits. There were eighteen of these sworn statements used in the lawsuit, some from fathers telling of their feelings on hearing from their sons or daughters; others from war babes, detailing their experiences. It was the statements of the fathers, simple yet powerful, that Joan and I agree won us the day.

Collecting them though was a mammoth task, as the men were scattered all over America. It was nearly as bad with their children, who lived as far apart as Scotland and Cornwall. Statements had to be taken from every one, prepared in official form by Joan, sent back to be checked and signed. If there was the tiniest mistake, the whole thing had to be redone and the process of checking repeated. It was a long-winded process, but it was essential that nobody put their name to anything that was not completely accurate.

At times I got impatient with the slowness of the process and wondered if we'd ever achieve anything concrete. Joan would calm me down pointing out the need for perfection if the government's lawyers were not to pull the case to pieces. She, meanwhile, was busy in the law library searching out precedents, examples of favourable decisions in similar cases – though, strictly speaking, I doubt there was anything very similar to our case before or since. At one point she was ready to start the ball rolling, when, one by one, three of the six people she planned to use as test cases found their fathers. It was lovely for them and a tribute to our methods of investigation, but it held up the case nevertheless.

At last the test requests for ex-servicemen's addresses were ready and were dispatched to the Veterans' Administration (VA) Central Office and the National Personnel Records Centre in the middle of 1987. As always I received a copy of the letter before it went out and it was fascinating to see the familiar arguments put into legal terms, backed up by references to previous court cases.

Joan pointed out that the men's addresses must legally be disclosed under the Freedom of Information Act, unless, under Exemption 6, they could be described as 'personnel and medical files and similar files the disclosure of which would constitute a clearly unwarranted invasion of personal privacy'. She then went on to explain why we did not believe these files fell into that category. Firstly an address is not an 'intimate detail' of a 'personal nature' – how I'd often argued that addresses were public property, available in telephone books, electoral rolls and driving-licence centres – and did not, in themselves, reveal anything that would embarrass the individual.

In previous unsuccessful court cases over the release of addresses, the requests had usually included the name of the person as well. We war babes already knew the names and the alleged personal information – that these people were, we believed, our fathers. Nor could the government agency withhold an address on the grounds that we might cause embarrassment should we try to locate our fathers. That would be setting the government up as protectors of these men and going way beyond the bounds of Exemption 6, which does not stretch to take in actions which might or might not result from the release of information. Most importantly of all, the theory that the release of addresses would result in embarrassment to the men concerned was, Joan pointed out, sheer speculation and not backed up by the experience of those people who had already found their fathers. I'd argued this one till I was blue in the face. What right had the government to make this assumption?

But Joan's legal argument followed through. Even if there was the mere possibility that the child's attempt to contact the father would not be well received and could be regarded as an invasion of privacy, it would not be 'clearly unwarranted'. The public interest here had to be weighed against the privacy interest – and public interest would be served by strengthening family ties, not by keeping parent and child apart.

Finally, she argued, at the very least the men concerned should be made aware that their adult children were trying to trace them and be given the opportunity to decide for themselves whether or not they wanted contact. Included with the letter was an affidavit from each requester and as much identifying information as possible on the men concerned, plus affidavits from myself and a very happy father and daughter who had found each other.

Did the agencies capitulate to this missive of legal and common sense? In October 1987, Joan reported by letter that 'these agencies, as expected, denied our requests. The NPRC was unable to find the files of four of the five individuals, and for the one they found, they refused to release the address. I understand from telephone conversations that the VA was unable to locate any files, and they will officially refuse to release addresses in any case.' She was about to appeal the decisions. 'Once we receive denials of our appeals, we will be ready to file suit in federal court. We will be challenging both the privacy cause and the inadequacy of the search for the records.'

But before that could happen there was almost a major disaster – at least that's how I saw it. Towards the end of the year Joan wrote to say that she was leaving the Public Citizen Litigation Group and moving to a new job with a big law firm in Washington DC. She was not sure who would be taking over our case – everyone in the office was very busy – and though she hoped to remain involved in some capacity she didn't know yet if this would be possible.

My heart sank. I couldn't bear the thought of having to start all over again, getting to know someone else, trying to immerse them, long-distance, in our feelings and fears and our philosophy. I really didn't feel like carrying on and for over a month the future of the case hung in the balance. Then just before Christmas, Santa Claus, disguised as the postman, delivered the best present I had that year. Joan wrote to say that her new firm had agreed to let her continue with our case on a *pro bono publico* basis. She was delighted – and she wasn't the only one. I said a silent prayer for Winthrop, Stimson, Putnam and Roberts, our new legal eagles.

Joan had other cases to handle, all of us had our everyday lives to lead, and for a variety of reasons the case wasn't filed in court until the end of 1988. By that time and for technical reasons, War Babes, the organization, had joined Mrs B, Mrs C and me as official plaintiffs. The defendants were the Archivist of the National Archives and Records Administration, which controls the NPRC, and the Secretary of the Department of Defense at the Pentagon. There's nothing like aiming high. I was beginning to feel like the mouse that roared.

Basically we were saying that these agencies were not complying with the Freedom of Information Act (FOIA), both by refusing to release addresses and refusing to do adequate searches for records. The second part of the official complaint, about the procedures, was in some ways as important as the first, although the judge was not asked to rule on it and agreement was reached by negotiation.

We said that the inadequacy of the procedures left people anxious, confused and frustrated, and that was probably an understatement. The typical response of government agencies to requests for information we listed as 'ignoring, rejecting, obstructing and refusing to process' them. It was explained that we were met with routine refusals to perform adequate searches for records with misinformation on what details could be released. There were unaccountably long delays and unwarranted refusals to release even information not regarded as private. We were denied information on other sources of records and never told that there was an appeal's procedure we could use.

What exactly did I want to see changed? The linchpin of the case of course was the addresses and I was asking for last-known full street addresses, though I was aware we might have to negotiate on how much of the address was released. I also wanted the release of what might seem less valuable information, such as birth dates. Believe me, if you know the date of a father's birth there are many ways of tracing him, which I won't reveal publicly, as I may have to use them again. It's between me and my American 'moles'.

I wanted staff in the departments we dealt with to be educated properly in their own laws and policy. One of life's truly amazing experiences is being told by one clerk that you are entitled to a certain piece of information, only to be refused it by another with different ideas or a different interpretation of the rules. Or maybe the disagreeable one had just got out of bed on the wrong side that morning – you never knew.

Another major irritation was the standard form letter sent out to enquirers, with little boxes ticked to indicate the reason you were being denied information. These letters explained nothing. If, for instance, the box was ticked indicating that your father's records had been destroyed in the famous fire of 1973, there was no hint that there might be an alternative source of information available. You were given no additional information whatever, just this bald, unfriendly and very final-looking statement, which might as well have had 'Give up, this is the end of the line' scrawled across it. It was demoralizing and untrue, because there were other avenues you could try. I wanted the form letter redesigned to be more user-friendly.

Then there were the letters to be forwarded. Various government departments had, for as long as I'd been involved, offered to forward a letter to your father, if you'd got them to admit they had his address in the first place. I must have known a hundred people who took up this offer, but not one whose father actually received the letter, until after the court case.

You were told that your letter had to be left unsealed so that it could be read and checked by the department. What they didn't tell you was what would render it unsuitable for delivery. Very late in the day I discovered that anything which might cause embarrassment if the letter fell into the hands of a third person came into this category. So, if you introduced yourself as the son or daughter, the letter would not be forwarded. Only they didn't tell you this. They didn't write asking you to change it, or even return the letter saying it was unsuitable. You heard nothing so you sat at home assuming it had been delivered to your father and that he had chosen to ignore it – which was heartbreaking.

I don't personally like the idea of a letter delivered by a government department as a first approach to a father, but for some people it might be the only way, so I wanted the system reorganized. The letter should remain sealed (it's not the government's business what you say to your father after forty-five years); it should be delivered by certified mail (signed for by the person to whom it is addressed), to avoid the wife or family getting a shock. If for some reason it cannot be delivered, the sender must know this and the reason why, and a photocopy of the front of the envelope, which usually bears the reason why a letter cannot be delivered, should be sent to the child.

Last, but definitely not least, I wanted a named person assigned to War Babes at the NPRC. I'd had enough of writing to faceless bureaucrats and being passed from department to department by people who took no responsibility for what was happening. I remember asking a senator I met on my visit to Washington DC where exactly the buck stopped in cases like ours. He didn't know. I wanted a person I could call when things went wrong, a person at whose desk the buck very definitely came to a halt.

We were assigned Judge Thomas Penfield Jackson by lottery, which is how they do it in the American courts. It could have been better, apparently, as he had a reputation for sympathizing with the government, but there was no point in worrying about that. It seemed to be part of his job to act as a sort of mediator between the opposite parties as well as making judgements and rulings.

At the back of my mind I'd had this irrational fear that the judge would take one look at the case, say, 'Who are these upstarts from England challenging our government?' and throw it out, but Joan assured me that the government recognized it had a case to answer. Besides, the media was getting very interested now and it has always seemed to me that although the American government likes publicity, it hates bad publicity, and the press and the people were on our side.

.

There began a series of meetings, conferences and negotiations, which lasted nearly two years, and in which I could, of course, only be involved at second hand. Joan would keep me in touch with each move by phone or letter. Sometimes she'd be in a cheerful, optimistic mood with things looking good, other times it would be gloomier news. In a letter dated 13 March 1989, she is pointing out that the Department of Defense appears to believe that releasing addresses to us would be the thin end of the wedge, leading to them being inundated with similar requests from corporations and insurance companies with financial interests.

'It's not a sure win,' she warns.

On the other hand – same letter – negotiations about working procedure were looking perkier. She was planning on talking to senior staff from the agencies and 'finding out how things work' – which would give us a better base for what was essentially telling them how to do their job better.

The wheels of justice turned slowly but they didn't stand still. Government lawyers would come up with an offer, never quite what we were asking for but a compromise – and Joan would relay it to me. It would then have to be discussed between the three of us plaintiffs and I'd come back to Joan with a decision. The decisions were often negative. Joan has admitted that although I was an undemanding client in most ways, I posed one major difficulty – I wouldn't take no for an answer. To some extent she was in the uncomfortable position of piggy-in-the-middle. When the other side made an offer she might think it promising, but she had to convince me.

'I'd try to communicate the other side's position and you'd simply argue with it,' she said. 'It made it a little bit difficult to play the role lawyers try to play, of bringing their client together with the opposition to settle a case.'

We disagreed but we never fell out. She always seemed to understand that I was volatile and would say things on the spur of the moment. She'd come back when I'd cooled down.

I realized Joan could probably see a legal way round these things and that I was making her life more difficult, but I had to stick out for what I believed was right, 'total justice', Joan called it. This was the only chance I'd ever get to right a massive wrong and I wasn't going to blow it by compromising. I was no longer fighting on my own behalf, so I had to put myself back in the position I was in before I found my father and ask, 'Would I have been satisfied with this? Would I have stood for it?' Often the answer was, 'No way! How dare they treat me like this!'

At one point, for instance, instead of releasing addresses, they wanted us to settle for the guarantee of letters being forwarded to our fathers. Quite apart from the bad record the agencies concerned had had with letters, I just don't believe that a letter, via a government department, is the ideal way to introduce yourself to your father. Some men, particularly those who don't even know they have a child in England, getting a vague letter out of the blue would probably regard it as a hoax, or think you were after the family silver.

I said we would like the option of a forwarded letter, but I wanted a base from which we could start looking ourselves and make the approach we thought best, without the government intervening. Nothing short of an address would do. So it was back to the drawing board for Joan again. I did feel guilty, but not guilty enough to give in.

The breakthrough on the addresses came in July 1990. Once all the papers had been filed and the offers and counter-offers made, Joan was required to go to court along with the attorney for the other side to put the 'verbal argument' before the judge. She recalls that: 'The judge didn't seem to want to hear very much from me. He made me sit down very quickly, but he asked the government's attorney a lot of questions and gave her a very hard time. I knew this was a good sign, almost as if he had already made up his mind, but I was still surprised at the outcome.'

The outcome was a memorandum and order in which Judge Jackson described the case as 'of unusual poignancy'. He concluded from the evidence that 'the assertion that disclosure of the records would invite an unwelcome intrusion . . . is at the moment sheer speculation'.

He agreed with us! And what's more he ordered the government to release the addresses unless they could submit, within sixty days, declarations from ten fathers stating that they saw the information as private and would not want it disclosed. Joan gave me the news by letter because she hadn't been able to get me on the phone. 'Congratulations on your first major victory in court!' she finished.

The government's claim, put forward in one of their documents, that 'Fatherhood of an illegitimate child during youth is at worst embarrassing and at a minimum highly personal' hadn't impressed the judge. Nor, I'm glad to say, had their other classic on the same theme, 'Contact by any individual, particularly a long-lost illegitimate child, is clearly intrusive, whether wanted or not.' That had made me so angry. How did they know when they didn't appear to have spoken to any fathers? What gave them the right to pluck these views from thin air and force them on the rest of us?

Now it appeared that Judge Jackson was on our wavelength, and what had put him there were the affidavits from fathers so painstakingly compiled. These are straightforward statements made by ordinary men to whom something extraordinary had happened. Within the strictures of the legal form, they write simply and affectingly about it. Each affidavit is a potted life story. Here is an extract from Henry, father of Melanie.

'There were plans for Melanie's mother to join me in the United States but Melanie's grandmother intercepted the letters I sent to England and effectively destroyed our relationship . . . Melanie's mother did send me pictures of Melanie until she was about 9 years old but since she had married an Englishman, she did not wish me to be in contact with my daughter.

'I often thought of Melanie and wished I knew where she was. However I had no way of finding her because her mother had moved. It took two years for Melanie to find me . . . I was very excited to hear from her and immediately called her. It was 3.00 a.m. British time when I called her.

'Everyone in my family is just as thrilled as I am in finding Melanie. Melanie and her family flew to the United States and we had a joyful reunion.

Since then we have visited each other several times . . . I feel it is very important for the government to release addresses to children of servicemen like myself. If Melanie could have gotten my address, then she would have found me much sooner. I do not at all consider her locating me an invasion of my privacy. To the contrary, I welcome my daughter with open arms. Not only is she a joy to me but I now have a grandchild that looks just like me.'

The following extract is from the affidavit of the now, sadly, late Alfred, whose son, Peter, died before he could find him. Peter's stepsister eventually traced him.

'I met his [Peter's] mother while I was serving overseas . . . I married her and expected that she would join me with our son in the United States. She refused to come, even though I kept sending her money and letters pleading with her to come. We eventually got divorced.

'Peter's mother refused to answer my letters and moved so that I could not locate her. I loved my son and tried to find him for ten years but neither my brother nor I could locate him. I kept a baby picture of Peter on top of the television all this time.

'My son tried to find me for most of his adult life and had no success. Tragically, he passed away before he could find me. His stepsister continued the search . . . I was very happy to hear from her and my family was delighted to receive photographs of our grandchildren in England . . .

'I would like the government to release addresses to children of servicemen. If my son could have discovered my address we could have been together which is what we both wanted very much.'

This is part of a statement by Victor, father of Karen.

'I lost contact with Karen's mother after I was transferred to France and was discouraged from carrying my address into battle . . . In 1987 Karen located me after about two years of searching. I was overjoyed . . . My wife and family think that the situation is 100 per cent OK and accept Karen as a member of the family. There have been no negative effects from our reunion.

'Karen has visited us and we are going to visit her in England for three weeks this summer. I really like my daughter and grandchild, and I've noticed that they take after me. All of us enjoy a great relationship now . . . I think the majority of men would want to know their children. I would be angry if I knew that the reason my daughter could not find me was because the government would not release my address to her.'

There is nothing unusual about what these men are saying – nineteen out of twenty of the fathers who have been traced share these feelings – but it was they and five others, including my Dad, who helped us to win our case.

The question was, after Judge Jackson's order, could the government come up with ten affidavits from fathers saying exactly the opposite to ours? I didn't believe they would do it in sixty months, let alone sixty days, but Joan, always one step ahead, was a little worried about what they might say to the men should they get in touch with them. Could the question about privacy or otherwise of addresses be phrased in a prejudicial way? She was already cogitating on ways that we could have some input into what was said to the fathers should the government manage to find them and make the first approach.

She needn't have worried. They didn't try. Instead they decided that they were ready to talk about a settlement. We were ready too. By the autumn, agreement seemed to have been reached. Joan phoned me, half-determined, half-apologetic, and broke what she thought was the bad news. The government had agreed to give out part addresses, the city or town and state of a father, but there was no way they would agree to the full street address, which I had insisted I wanted. She paused, waiting for me to object as usual and refuse to compromise.

'That's OK,' I said. 'I only ever expected to get city and state.' There was a longer pause.

'You might have told me. I'm your lawyer and I didn't even know.'

'I couldn't tell you,' I said apologetically. 'You might have settled for something even less.'

'Do you play brag?' she laughed.

'No?'

'You should. I'm sure you'd be good at it.'

We were nearly there, but there was one little hitch at the final fence. The government decided that all the concessions would apply only to World War II children, and not children of later or future wars, or those born of peacetime liaisons between servicemen and foreign women. I didn't have to argue with Joan over this. She felt as strongly as me that this should be an across-the-board agreement and people like the Amer-Asians, born during the Vietnam War, must benefit too. We fought back and the government agreed in the end. The only concession that is exclusive to us war babes is having letters forwarded to our fathers by certified mail.

By November 1990 an agreement had been drawn up. It seemed unbelievable but we had got everything we asked for, with the exception of full street addresses – and they are not so important, as they will probably have changed since the records were made. Besides, when you know the city or area you can always look up the street in the phone book. All the changes in procedure that we demanded were agreed, including the named person at the NPRC. We didn't settle out of court because we needed to. We were winning the case and would, I believe, have even got the full street addresses if we'd hung on longer. But it would have taken perhaps another couple of years, and meanwhile fathers were dying. There wasn't time to fight on.

Joan was due to file the final papers on 16 November. I waited at home, biting what was left of my nails, convinced something would go wrong. It was too good to be true that after four years victory was in sight. At around 3.00 p.m. Joan's secretary called to say Joan was sorry she couldn't speak to me herself, but she was rushing round to the court house to get the papers in on time. A vision of a speeding Joan tripping and falling flat on her face, the precious papers fluttering away on the breeze, rose before me. That was it. It was second sight. That's what would go wrong.

She rang me as soon as she got back to the office, sounding breathless and quite light-headed. I told her about my premonition and she laughed. She had indeed tripped up, but inside, in front of the assembled dignitaries. She'd lost her dignity but she'd held on to the papers, which were signed, sealed and delivered.

The worry, the waiting, the work – they were all over. Victory was ours. It was too much to take in. Joan was going out to celebrate that night and would be sipping champagne by way of celebration. I would be sipping coffee in my little shoebox of an office. She said she wished I could have been there and we could have celebrated together, and it would have been lovely, a fitting end to the partnership.

I didn't put the phone down when I had finished speaking to her. I had a lot of calls to make – to war babes, journalists who'd supported us, relatives and friends in England, friends and helpers in America, my Dad, and many, many more. It was their victory too.

It was all over bar the press conference, which Joan held in Washington DC, with me on the end of a telephone at home so that reporters could ask me questions down a very crackly line. It was, Joan said, a historic settlement, 'one which closes a chapter of a not-too-proud part of American history and reverses forty-five years of silence. Not only does the settlement begin to redress wrongs which were done to these children during World War II but will also benefit children from more recent wars, and I'm also hopeful it may represent the beginning of a more responsible attitude by our military with respect to relationships formed by our servicemen overseas.'

She went on to quote my remark on why the ex-GIs should be given the chance to make up their own minds whether or not they want to hear from their children. In my affidavit I'd said, 'I believe the war was fought so that individuals might have freedom to make such choices for themselves, without government control of their family or personal lives.'

I'd almost forgotten writing the words but I believe them implicitly. There are many reasons why I decided to fight the American government in law, but surely that is the most important one. It was a battle dedicated to freedom and to the brave men who fought the military battles and the courageous women who fought the domestic battles back home; people like my mother and my father.

My Dad is proud of what I've achieved and that counts for a lot. Jack Crowley, the man whose mysterious place in my life started this whole thing so many years ago – it's definitely his victory too. The irony of it is that if the American government had given me the information I asked for when I first started searching for him, none of this would ever have happened . . . no War Babes, no court case, no future together for thousands of children and their fathers. I was robbed of fourteen years with my father, but how can I feel bitter about it when I see what has been gained?

POSTSCRIPT

At the time of writing there has just been long enough for the new procedures agreed in the settlement to take effect. The good news is that they are working well – searches are being made, addresses released when they can be traced, and enquirers kept informed by well-trained staff. I've even heard of letters being passed on successfully to fathers by government agencies.

I have a named contact, Charles, who is ready and willing to sort out problems for the cost of a phone call. It's wonderful, but I still keep my unofficial American helpers, because there are fathers who cannot be traced even by the best-intentioned government agency and require the undercover talents of a 'mole'.

The not-so-good news is that my workload, following publicity about the court case, has doubled. War Babes now has a thousand members. I welcome each and every one of them but just wish I could find some way of doubling the hours in the day as well!

Speaking to Joan Meier a year after the end of the court case, I tried to get her impressions of the case's impact. One of the practical outcomes was that the government, as the losers in the situation, had to pay costs. So Joan's old law firm (she has since left that job and is now teaching Law) didn't have to pick up the bill after all – not that they could have known that when they kindly took us on.

As the case progressed, Joan now admits, she seriously doubted our chances of winning. She didn't doubt the strength of our case and in 1986–7 our chances looked good. But over the next four years a number of cases with similarities to ours were lost and the position shifted subtly.

'Case law was against us by 1990,' she said. 'I wasn't optimistic and I was surprised and relieved by Judge Jackson's decision in July of that year. He was obviously very impressed by the feelings of the fathers already traced.'

She is already seeing the effects of the release of addresses and the improved procedures on the Amer-Asians, children of the Vietnam War. 'They have always had a hard time tracing their fathers. Some don't even have names, which makes the task impossible, but those who do are now receiving far more useful information. I've had several grateful letters thanking me.'

She was clearly affected by the case and is considering writing a book on it and 'the way American policy issues have combined historically to lead to the sort of situation that the war babes faced, where you cannot get to know your father. You can't blame individuals for the way mothers and babies were abandoned in Britain during the war. Our military practice and policy of encouraging fraternizing and then hiding the men away when the women, often pregnant or with a baby, wanted to contact them made it almost inevitable. I hope the War Babes case ensures that nothing like that can happen again.'

The case, Joan says, has had a huge impact in America 'on the ordinary public and the legal fraternity, including the judge, who told me so. Everyone involved with it has been touched and fascinated by the stories involved. It was a unique case, the outcome of which will help a great many people.'

It would not be practicable or helpful for me to print addresses of organizations I use in tracing fathers. There are far too many to list and each requires specific instructions on the best approach to make. Also each State has different laws. It is better for War Babes to deal individually with enquiries.

However, there is available a useful book which lists such sources of information as veteran, military and patriotic organizations, military-service associations, military-unit reunions, State drivers' licence offices and motor-vehicle registration offices and explains how to trace vital records (for example, birth, death and marriage records).

The information contained in the book, *How to Locate Anyone Who Is or Has Been in the Military* (Armed Forces Location Directory), is copyright, but you can obtain a copy direct from the publishers, Military Information Enterprises, PO Box 340081, Ft Sam Houston, Texas 78234. Tel.: 0101 512 828 4045. At the time of writing, the book costs $15.00. It also features illustrations of military insignia, something that would have been very useful for me to show my mother when we were trying to work out my father's rank.

For other information please contact: War Babes, 15 Plough Avenue, South Woodgate, Birmingham B32 3TQ.